D1571953

EXPERIENCING BERLIOZ

The Listener's Companion
Gregg Akkerman, Series Editor

Titles in **The Listener's Companion** provide readers with a deeper understanding of key musical genres and the work of major artists and composers. Aimed at nonspecialists, each volume explains in clear and accessible language how to *listen* to works from particular artists, composers, and genres. Looking at both the context in which the music first appeared and has since been heard, authors explore with readers the environments in which key musical works were written and performed.

EXPERIENCING BERLIOZ

A Listener's Companion

Melinda P. O'Neal

ROWMAN & LITTLEFIELD
Lanham • Boulder • New York • London

Published by Rowman & Littlefield
An imprint of The Rowman & Littlefield Publishing Group, Inc.
4501 Forbes Boulevard, Suite 200, Lanham, Maryland 20706
www.rowman.com

Unit A, Whitacre Mews, 26-34 Stannary Street, London SE11 4AB

British Library Cataloguing in Publication Information Available

Library of Congress Cataloging-in-Publication Data

Names: O'Neal, Melinda, author.
Title: Experiencing Berlioz : a listener's companion / Melinda P. O'Neal.
Description: Lanham : Rowman & Littlefield, [2018] | Series: Listener's companion | Includes
    bibliographical references and index.
Identifiers: LCCN 2017038313 (print) | LCCN 2017039815 (ebook) | ISBN 9780810886070 (elec-
    tronic) | ISBN 9780810886063 (cloth : alk. paper)
Subjects: LCSH: Berlioz, Hector, 1803–1869—Criticism and interpretation.
Classification: LCC ML410.B5 (ebook) | LCC ML410.B5 O54 2018 (print) | DDC 780.92—dc23
    LC record available at https://lccn.loc.gov/2017038313

Printed in the United States of America

To Maureen

CONTENTS

LIST OF TABLES

LIST OF VIGNETTES

SERIES EDITOR'S FOREWORD

The goal of the Listener's Companion series is to give readers a deeper understanding of pivotal musical genres and the creative work of iconic composers and performers. This is accomplished in an inclusive manner that does not necessitate extensive music training or elitist shoulder rubbing. Authors of the series place the reader in specific listening experiences in which the music is examined in its historical context with regard to both compositional and societal parameters. By positioning the reader in the real or supposed environment of the music's creation, the author provides for a deeper enjoyment and appreciation of the art form. Series authors, often drawing on their own expertise as both performers and scholars, deliver to readers a broad understanding of major musical genres and the achievements of artists within those genres as lived listening experiences.

Gregg Akkerman

ACKNOWLEDGMENTS

Bennett Graff, Natalie Mandziuk, Gregg Akkerman, Lara Hahn, Naomi Burns, and Katie O'Brien, editors and staff members at Rowman & Littlefield.

Team Berlioz: Carole Stashwick, Joan Conlon, Karen Endicott, Nancy Serrell Coonley, Karen Suenram, and Maureen Ragan. In addition, my special thanks to Julian Rushton, Katherine Kolb, and Donna Di Grazia.

Hugh Macdonald, D. Kern Holoman, David Cairns, Donna Di Grazia, Jacques Barzun, Julian Rushton, David Charlton, Peter Bloom, Katharine Ellis, Nicholas Temperley, Stephen Rodgers, Diana Bickley, Ralph Locke, Annegret Fauser, Katherine Kolb, Alastair Aberdare, Gunther Braam, Monir Tayeb and Michel Austin, John Nelson, Marcel Couraud and the Groupe Vocal de France, and Kristopher Sandchak, upon whose inspiring scholarship and artistry I have depended.

Permissions kindly given for reproduction or adaptation of resources by David Cairns, Annegret Fauser, Hugh Macdonald, and Monir Tayeb and Michel Austin.

The Berlioz Society (UK) for outstanding conferences and publications, with special thanks to Linda and William Edmonson, Martin Price, Helen Petchey, and Shelagh Marston.

To all my Dartmouth College students current and past, with special thanks to singers in the Dartmouth College Chamber Singers and Handel Society, who performed numerous Berlioz works, and my students in conducting, music theory, and literature courses.

For perspective and support: Carl and Betsey Schmidt, Gregory Hayes, Kate Conley and Richard Stamelman, Christian Wolff and Holly Nash Wolff, Richard Giarusso, Leneida Crawford, Kirk and Karen Endicott, and Hoyt and Marianne Alverson.

Jan Harrington, my graduate advisor and mentor at the Jacobs School of Music, Indiana University; John Nelson, my orchestra conducting professor; colleagues current and past in the choral conducting department including Betsy Burleigh, Dominick DiOrio, Walter Huff, Susan Swaney, David Villaneuva, Carmen Hellena Tellez, Alan Harler, and Gerald Souza; my students in graduate choral literature seminars 2016 and 2017; and in honor of my professors and mentors Julius Herford, Fiora Contino, and Thomas Dunn *in memorium.*

Dartmouth College colleagues Michael Casey, William Cheng, Ashley Fure, Kui Dong, Theodore Levin, Sally Pinkas, Spencer Topel, Steven Swayne, Jon Appleton, William J. Summers, Charles Hamm, John Kopper, Katie Hornstein, Catherine La Touche, Samantha Candon, Robert Duff, Filippe Ciabetti, Matthew Marsit, Tony Princiotti, Charles Houmard, Marcia Cassidy, Janet Polk, Don Baldini, and Deans Michael Mastanduno, Barbara Will, Kate Conley, and Lenore Grenoble. Many thanks to Paddock Music Library staff members Patricia Fisken, Patricia Morris, David Bowden, Rachel McConnell, Joy Weale, and Memory Apata.

Michael and Patricia Frederick and the Frederick Collection of Historic Pianos, Ashburnham, Massachusetts.

To the many who have performed Berlioz's music with me during my Berlioz journey:

Invaluable collaborative pianists Beverly Gaylord, Nancy Bent, Jeanne Chambers, Steven Morris, Gregory Hayes, Victoria Dobrushina, Christopher Lundell, and Thomas Hetrick.

Singers and board members of the Handel Society of Dartmouth College (1979–2004) with special thanks to Heywood and Bea Alexander, Joan Snell, Robert and Jean Keene, Carlos and Linda Galvan, Donald Graham and Carol Barr, Laetitia Fodor, Dave and Bonnie Robinson, Margaret Robinson, Carol Magenau, Judy Pond, and Elizabeth and William Ballard.

New Hampshire Symphony and Chorus and James Bolle, conductor; Seattle Symphony and Chorale and Gerald Schwarz, conductor.

Singers and board members of Handel Choir of Baltimore
(2004–2013), especially Daryl and Sandy Sidle, Preston and
Nancy Athey, Linda and Pete Talley, John and Cath La Costa,
Leslie and Bruce Greenwald, Anne Wilson, Nancy Hannah and
Lea Billingslea, Cindy Levering, Sandra Smith, Barbara Stone,
William and Janice Barnes, and Kathy Fleming.

Sonique, Boston Vocal Artists' professional chamber ensemble, and
Steven Morris.

The Ragan family, especially John David Ragan for simultaneous
translation during a walking tour of Berlioz's Paris.

Our Berry Hollow friends and neighbors Rick and Karen Suenram,
Jennifer and Stan Braverman, David Cox, Minna Vogel and Tom Hen-
naman, Karl and Teressa Beier, Mike and Marie Murphy, Margaret
Clifton, and Irvin Katenbrink and the Graves Mountain Lodge Tuesday
catfish dinner group.

INTRODUCTION

Opening Your Imagination

The musical works of Hector Berlioz are universally recognized as among the most compelling artistic accomplishments in nineteenth-century Europe. The purpose of this book, written for the general reader, is to offer insight into how to listen to and what to listen for in his music. Getting inside the strategies is to experience their aliveness and veracity. Then perhaps the questions so often raised may be answered: why am I attracted to Berlioz; why have his works endured? To reap the most from this listener's companion, you may elect to alternate between reading and listening. When planning to attend a concert that includes Berlioz's music, chances are combining reading and listening in advance will enhance your experience.

The focus here is on a few selected works, which are contextualized within their genres. We begin, as Berlioz did, with songs. Known in France at the time as *romances* or *mélodies*, they are delightful miniatures; he wrote, performed, and revised them throughout his long career. Next, we look into his brief, individual compositions for chorus, an intriguing and overlooked body of works. His most expansive and generally better-known compositions—symphonies and overtures, extended choral-orchestral works, and operas—complete the journey.

As a storyteller, Berlioz wrote music to illuminate the ideas and narratives that moved him most. Insight into his music, I hope, will lead you to many deeply satisfying musical experiences.

PERFORMANCE QUALITY MATTERS, BERLIOZ'S TEMPOS, PERIOD OR MODERN INSTRUMENTS

One of the first steps is finding outstanding performances; a bad recording or live performance will destroy our impression of a great work. In fact, witnessing bad performances of his music compelled Berlioz to become a conductor, and by all accounts he was an exceptional one. He believed the performer's task was to deliver a composer's message as transparently and honestly as possible. When attending a live performance, consider the artistic reputation of the organization and performers, which can usually be found in an online search. If a local community organization is presenting Berlioz's music, whether amateur or a mix of amateur and professional, accolades to them! Berlioz performed his music in France and on tour in Europe with amateurs and professionals too. In every circumstance, performance quality depends primarily on the discernment and skill of the artistic leadership.

Criteria for choosing a recording or artist are according to the tastes and priorities of a reviewer or listener. For vocal music, in general the checklist starts with good intonation, absence of excessive vibrato, compelling use of colors in the voices, excellent pronunciation and clarity of text delivery, empathy with the message, and more. In partnership with singers, a pianist or orchestra cannot be a subservient, noncommittal ("vanilla") accompanist. Rather, the relationship is of two equals who move into the foreground or background depending on the logic textually and structurally. Shared interpretive stance and a subtle interplay between the two are essential. A similar checklist for fine instrumental performances—intonation, tone colors, phrasing, balance, and subtle interplay—is just as long and longer.

In general, tempos need to be close to those Berlioz specified in his latest edition of the score. A performance that is faster or slower can significantly distort the mood and message he sought to portray. At the beginning of a work there is a standard Italian instruction, such as *andante* (walking pace) and often a descriptive characterization in Italian (sometimes French), such as *malinconico e sostenuto* (melancholy and sustained) at the beginning of mvt 2 in *Roméo et Juliette*. In a final printed edition, after revisions and more performances, Berlioz usually added a metronome numeral, such as quarter note = 66. This means there are to be sixty-six quarter-note beats or pulses per minute. Think of the pulse as the heartbeat of the music; here it is slightly faster than a second (pulse = 60).

Many today prefer to hear music by Berlioz performed on period instruments—instruments in use at the time of composition—based on the excellent premise that historically informed performances reveal the sounds Berlioz likely had in his ear. Today actual instruments from the time or replicas are used for these. Throughout the nineteenth century in France, Germany, England, and Russia, many instruments were undergoing changes. Some unusual ones Berlioz wrote for, such as the ophicleide, the serpent, and the cornet à piston, are no longer included in modern orchestras (modern tuba substitutes for the ophicleide; bassoon, for the serpent; and trumpet, for the cornet à piston). But to hear them today is a real treat because their sounds are so different and flavorful. For dramatic effect Berlioz even wrote for a specific variety of standard instrument: in *Symphonie fantastique* he asked for actual church bells (imagine a dark "bong"), and in the Queen Mab Scherzo of *Roméo et Juliette* he wanted the delicate, magical tinkle of antique finger cymbals.

Overall the timbres of early nineteenth-century strings, woodwinds, and brass are less blended than their modern counterparts, articulation and playing customs are different, their dynamic ranges are more contained, and the resulting overall sonic palette is more diverse. While period performances of Berlioz's music today have been slow to catch on, similarly to other nineteenth-century composers such as Beethoven, Schubert, Mendelssohn, and Brahms, they are revelatory and increasingly encountered. With the availability of more recordings and live performances, fortunately the listener now has a choice of which or both to listen to, period or modern. Usually the promotional materials for a concert or organization will indicate whether historically informed performance principles and instruments are being used.

Attending a live performance by a reputable organization is by far the preferred way to enjoy Berlioz's music—it is a "must do, must hear" imperative whenever the opportunity arises. The best approaches to locating high-quality recordings are to purchase recommended recordings and to read reviews of those and others. "Selected Listening" at the end of this book lists recordings and internet sites for locating recent and archival reviews. To listen to a work or portions of it for the first time or to compare recordings, use an internet application such as Spotify, which is easily searchable and will have nearly every Berlioz composition available performed by multiple artists. Unfortunately, to date that site and others similar ones do not provide essential supporting materials, such as program notes, texts and translations, and artist biographies.

When listening to vocal music, it is essential to have texts and translations in hand. Due to limited space in this book, texts and translations for songs and choruses discussed in this volume may be found (a) in recording liner notes purchased by the reader and (b) at http://www.melindaoneal.net. To date three online sites may be helpful:

- http://www.ipasource.com
- http://www.lieder.net
- http://www.artsongcentral.com

Translations of opera librettos are readily available by searching online and in recording liner notes.

WAYS TO LISTEN; BERLIOZ'S GESTURES, BE OPEN TO YOUR IMAGINATION

If you are an experienced listener and know what you want to listen for, proceed to the next chapter. For those starting to explore Berlioz, take a moment to consider the following steps. Most terms generally not familiar to the average listener are defined when they are first used, and an extensive glossary is provided.

The First Pass

Listening can happen in a variety of ways. An easy first step is to determine who is playing or singing and the general mood. Are you hearing strings or winds? Is percussion involved? What is the character of the music; can you describe it? The idea is to be open to discovery, to inquire, to allow yourself to be led, and to gently immerse yourself into the sonic landscape.

Linearity and Phrase

A next tier can be to focus just on a melody, most often the highest line but not always, or only a bass line (at the bottom), and trace the contour of the pitches in that line—how they move, whether in wide leaps or small, and whether they change frequently or infrequently. Some critics at the time considered Berlioz's bass lines unorthodox, that is, they don't move like those by Mozart or Beethoven or even his Parisian contemporaries. How do these melodies, together with their bass lines, form musical thoughts—phrases? How do the phrases begin and end? Are they short or long? Are they passive or busy? Do they soar or plunge? Who is playing them? There are endless possibilities.

Harmony

Next think vertically. Listen for simultaneity of sound and consider its properties. For example, where is dissonance (grist, crunchiness, or discomfort), and where is consonance (calm, resolution, or perhaps a sweetness)? Does the composite sound change from tension to relaxation either slowly or quickly? Is there more of one than the other? Consider where intriguing dissonances or consonances happen, how often they happen, and whether they occur earlier or later in a phrase.

Meter and Rhythm, Tempo

Get a feel for the temporal relationship between strong and weak beats (also referred to throughout the book as pulses) and how they are grouped. Is it strong-weak-weak (triple meter) or strong-weak, strong-weak (duple meter)? After a pattern is established, how does the music interfere or play with that pattern? Is the rate of strong beats fast or slow?

Instrumentation (Who Is Playing), Texture (How Many Instruments Are Combined and How), Registers (High, Middle, Low), Timbre (Color)

Often Berlioz puts the spotlight on one instrument or a section of instruments. For example, at the opening of *Symphonie fantastique*, the flutes and clarinets are followed by a long section for strings alone. Listen for individual colors of solo instruments or voices (e.g., dark or rich, light or transparent), and describe their qualities, such as the mellow coolness of a clarinet in its middle and low register or the vibrant, pulling-on-the-heart-strings singing quality of a well-played violin. Allow your imagination to run free.

Continuity, Patterns, Form

A musical theme, often a melody, is like a topic sentence in a paragraph. The possibilities for breaking a theme apart and putting it back together, stretching it or shrinking it, or making it go upside down or backward are nearly infinite. Step back and listen for threads or bits of melody, which may be in short or long groupings and quite different when they return. A motif (a short group of notes derived from a theme or the germ of a theme) may be primarily melodic or just a rhythm without pitch. Follow the thread of thematic maturation and manipulation from first hearing onward through its various guises and iterations. Consider how Berlioz changed it by using different instruments, harmonies, textures, registers, and tempos.

Gesture

Listen for brief melodic-rhythmic and harmonic figures that seem to want to speak or imitate sounds in nature—a thwap, clacking, a low roar, flighty chirping, shimmer-shaking, a sustained single note, a nudge, or silence. Consider what instruments are generating them, how rhythm is involved. A musical gesture implies an idea, event, or feeling, and it will recur.

Imagination

Finally, step into the composer's workshop and psych him out: be open, be curious, and ask why. What story could Berlioz be telling, and what does he want me to feel? Why did he choose this instrument for this bit here or that harmony there? What might be the purpose of this silence, that change of register, or this isolated sustained note? Of all the attributes Berlioz hoped his listeners would have, a willingness to accept his imagination and to unleash our own is the most important.

CONTEXT, *MÉMOIRES*

Familiarity with the historical context of a work opens wonderful new avenues for enjoyment. What prompted Berlioz to write it? Were there problems in rehearsal? Was the concert space cavernous or intimate? What else was on the concert? What did Berlioz and others think of it after a performance? What did he revise, if he did, and why? What other events were happening at the time? What kind of person was Berlioz?

If ever a composer had an outsized, blockbuster personality it was Berlioz, a fact vividly born out in his *Mémoires*. He began them at age forty-five, made additions, and then upon completion he asked they be published only after his death, which was at age sixty-five. His comments about his compositions give firsthand perspective on the process of composition, rehearsals, and performances, audience and critic response, his values and views, and much more. Consequently, selected relevant passages from his *Mémoires* are provided in appendix D. Citations correspond to David Cairns's translation, which is also a treasure trove of additional information. It is available in most public libraries and is modestly priced for purchase.

> Hector Berlioz, *The Memoirs of Hector Berlioz*. Translated and edited by David Cairns. New York: Knopf, 2002.

For more on Berlioz refer to "Selected Reading and Bibliography," which includes his six books and important biographical and analytical resources by foremost music historians.

INSIDE REHEARSING AND PERFORMING, IMAGINING YOU ARE THERE, VIGNETTES

Having painfully endured unsatisfactory performances of his music conducted by others, Berlioz became an expert tactician of the rehearsal process and among the most effective and revered conductors of the nineteenth century. So the listener may gain an insider's familiarity with Berlioz's music-making, his views on rehearsing and conducting are shared throughout this book. They are documented at length in *Grande traité d'instrumentation et d'orchestration modernes* (Grand treatise on modern instrumentation and orchestration), *Mémoires*, and letters. At times his instructions in scores regarding tempos, character, dynamics, and more are discussed to gain greater insight into his thinking. I also share my perspective as a choral-orchestral conductor, having coached singers and pianists, prepared choruses, and conducted performances of much of Berlioz's choral-orchestral music.

Finally, stepping into the moment and feeling you are there in the flesh at a performance is invaluable. To build atmosphere and a basis for such experiences, certain passages in the book begin with "imagine you are . . . ." Additionally, for a little whimsy, make-believe conversations between fictional performers, entitled vignettes, appear in several chapters. Both features are based on factual information.

BEWARE: REVISIONS, REPACKAGING, AND DESCRIPTIVE TITLES

The evolution of Berlioz's compositions over time is fascinating but complicated. Simply put, he was an occasional self-borrower and frequent revisionist. He reused themes and reshaped them for new contexts; he even lifted entire sections from one genre into another. Songs were revised, several up to five or six times over many years, and new versions were made of songs and choruses for piano or orchestral accompaniment. Previously published vocal works were repackaged in newly named collections, some updated and some not.

Performance forces in his instrumental music also changed. *Grande symphonie funèbre et triomphale*, for example, was a ceremonial work composed for an open-air processional of woodwinds, brass, and percussion. But he added strings and a chorus to it for performance in a concert hall a few years later. Berlioz also transferred music from one work to another: *Le roi de Thulé*, a *romance*, first appeared in *Huit scènes de Faust* in 1828 for soprano and piano in the key of G major; it resurfaced in *La damnation de Faust* in 1846 for mezzo-soprano and orchestra, lowered to F major. In sum, Berlioz constantly improved and adapted his works, usually for new performance opportunities at home or abroad. Adding further complication to locating specific items, every instrumental work has only a descriptive name—there is no Symphony no. 2; it is *Harold en Italie*. So, when encountering a title, whether instrumental or vocal, the plethora of names and versions make it challenging for the listener to know which genre it is, whether it exists in other guises, and if it is an excerpt.

Consternation may also arise when, after reading a description of a work in this book, the listener discovers he or she is hearing a different version than anticipated. For clarity, therefore, this book proceeds by genre. Each chapter opens with an overview of the genre and a list of titles so that works may be located easily. All titles of songs (chapter 1) and individual choral works (chapter 2) are provided in either their chapter or appendixes A and B. At times the journey of a work from conception through performance and final edition is discussed.

DIGGING DEEPER: AUTHORITATIVE SCORES, CATALOGING, AND MORE

A word on music scores for those who are interested. The *Hector Berlioz: New Edition of the Complete Works* (*NBE*), edited by Hugh Macdonald and issued from 1967 to 2006 by Bärenreiter in twenty-six volumes, is the most recent and authoritative source.[1] Although Berlioz assigned his own opus numbers, which are often encountered in printed programs and recordings (e.g., *Roméo et Juliette*, op. 17), the numbers are out of order according to date of composition, and not all works are numbered. A new catalog edited by D. Kern Holoman, volume 25 of the *NBE*, assigns each work a new number (e.g., *Roméo et Juliette* H.79) sequenced by date or estimated date of composition. Every citation contains important details: versions shown in capital letters (e.g., *Chant sacré* H.44A, 44B, 44C); basic traits; printings; repackaging in new works or collections; known performances during Berlioz's lifetime; passages Berlioz borrowed for use in later works or borrowed from previous works; references to passages in his letters and *Mémoires*; and more. *The Portraits of Hector Berlioz*, volume 26 of the *NBE* by Gunther Braam, is an extensive and invaluable resource for imagery of the time. Separately, Berlioz's complete letters are available in French in nine volumes: *Correspondance générale*, Pierre Citron general editor. See "Selected Reading and Bibliography" also for English translations of selected letters and additional resources.

ABBREVIATIONS

A or C	alto or contralto, lower female voice categories
arr	arrangement
f	*forte*
H.	Holoman catalog indication (e.g., H.79) for a Berlioz work
mf	*mezzo forte*
mvt	movement of an extended work
NBE	*Hector Berlioz: New Edition of the Complete Works*, most authoritative modern edition of scores, in 26 volumes
orch	orchestra
p	*piano*
pv	piano-vocal score
rev	revised
SATB	soprano, alto, tenor, and bass voicing of a chorus or solo ensemble
SS	first soprano and second soprano, higher female voice categories
STB or SSTTBB	three-part soprano, tenor, and bass or six-part (*divisi*) soprano, tenor, and bass voicing of a chorus or solo ensemble

TTBB   first tenor, second tenor, baritone, and bass male voicing of
        a chorus or solo ensemble (high to low)

TIMELINE

Note: Beginning in 1835, Berlioz conducted most performances of his music in Paris and on tour.

1803	Born Louis-Hector Berlioz on December 11 at La Côte-St-André near the French Alps.
1816	Falls in love with Estelle Dubœuf (later Estelle Fornier).
1817	Learns to play the flute and guitar; father engages a music teacher.
1819	Composes *romances* and offers them to Paris publishers.
1821	Receives *Bachelier ès lettres* in Grenoble; leaves for Paris and medical school.
1822	Becomes a pupil of LeSueur; frequently studies scores in the Conservatoire library.
1823	First article published in the press.
1824	*Messe solennelle* and first opera *Estelle et Némorin* (lost) composed; receives *Bachelier ès sciences physiques*; abandons medicine.
1825	Successful performance of *Messe solennelle*, composes *Scène hèroïque: la révolution grecque*.
1826	Composes first opera, *Les francs-juges*; enrolls in composition and counterpoint classes at the Conservatoire.

1827	Sings in Théatre des Nouveautés opera chorus; passes preliminary round of Prix de Rome competition; sees Harriet Smithson act in Shakespeare's *Hamlet* and *Romeo and Juliet*; conducts *Messe solennelle*.
1828	Hears Beethoven's Third and Fifth symphonies at the Conservatoire; reads translation of Goethe's *Faust*.
1829	Composes *Neuf mélodies*; publishes *Huit scènes de Faust*.
1830	Composes *Symphonie fantastique*; becomes engaged to Camille Moke; arranges *La Marseillaise*; wins Prix de Rome on fifth try; first performance of *Symphonie fantastique*; meets Liszt.
1831	Travels to Rome for Prix de Rome residency with visits to Marseilles, Florence, Nice, Naples, and Pompeii; Camille Moke breaks their engagement; meets Mendelssohn in Rome.
1832	Returns to Paris after five months at home in La Côte; introduced to Harriet Smithson.
1833	Courts and marries Harriet Smithson; writes reviews and articles for *Le Rénovateur* journal.
1834	Composes *Harold en Italie* for Paganini to play the viola solo; son Louis is born; libretto of *Benvenuto Cellini* refused by Opéra-comique; becomes music critic for *Journal des débats*.
1835	Composes *Le cinq mai*; Schumann's essay on *Symphonie fantastique* (based on Liszt's piano transcription) launches Berlioz's success in Germany; takes over conducting his works.
1836	Composes *Benvenuto Cellini* using the libretto revised for production at l'Opéra.
1837	Composes *Grande messe des morts* on government commission; successful performance.
1838	*Benvenuto Cellini* fails after four performances; Paganini gives Berlioz twenty thousand francs after hearing *Harold en Italie*.

1839	Composes and performs *Roméo et Juliette*; meets Wagner.
1840	*Grande symphonie funèbre et triomphale* commissioned and played in outdoor procession for tenth anniversary of 1830 Revolution.
1841	Completes and publishes *Les nuits d'été* (piano-vocal version); begins liaison with Marie Récio.
1842	First and second international concert tours: Brussels, Frankfurt, Stuttgart.
1843	Expanded concert touring; meets Schumann; publishes *Grand traité*; composes *Le carnaval romain* based on music from *Benvenuto Cellini*.
1844	*Hymne à la France* composed for Industrial Exhibition in Paris; separates from Harriet.
1845	Concerts in Marseilles, Lyons, Vienna; composes more songs; begins *La damnation de Faust*.
1846	Concert touring to Prague, Vienna, Pest, Breslau, Brunswick; completes and performs *La damnation de Faust* in Paris.
1847	Concertizing in St. Petersburg, Moscow, Riga, Berlin; first visit to London to conduct opera season at Drury Lane Theatre.
1848	Due to February Revolution stays in London; failure of London season promoted by Louis-Antoine Jullien; begins compiling and writing *Mémoires*.
1849	Composes *Te Deum*; begins compilations of songs and choruses: *Tristia*, *Vox populi*.
1850	Launches concert series with Société philharmonique de Paris; appointed librarian of the Conservatoire; begins composing *L'enfance du Christ*.
1851	Société philharmonique closes after second season; second London visit, this time to judge instruments at the Great Exhibition; hears six thousand children sing in St. Paul's Cathedral.

1852   Third London visit to conduct New Philharmonic Society; *Benvenuto Cellini* revised and performed in Weimar thanks to Liszt.

1853   Conducts one performance of *Benvenuto Cellini* in London during fourth visit; conducts concerts in Baden-Baden, Brunswick, Hanover, Bremen, Leipzig.

1854   Death of Harriet Smithson; completes *L'enfance du Christ* and *Mémoires*; marries Marie Récio; concert touring.

1855   Continues concert touring; *Te Deum* performed at St-Eustache; jurist for Exposition universelle in Paris; fifth visit to London; *L'impériale* first performance.

1856   *Les nuits d'été* orchestration completed; begins *Les Troyens*; elected to Institut d'art; onset of chronic intestinal illness.

1860   Wagner's concerts in Paris; commissioned to compose *Béatrice et Bénédict* for Baden-Baden, which Berlioz conducts there in 1862.

1863   *Les Troyens* is dropped by l'Opéra but is accepted by Théâtre-lyrique; *Les Troyens à Carthage* (third, fourth, and fifth acts of *Les Troyens*) is performed twenty-two times; conducts *L'enfance du Christ* in Strasbourg; writes last article for the press.

1864   Begins regular correspondence with Estelle, his first love, and several visits follow.

1866   Conducts *La damnation de Faust* in Vienna at the Redoutensaal.

1867   Son Louis dies; concerts in Cologne; visits Estelle near Lyons; departs for concerts in Russia.

1868   Returns from Russia exhausted; visits Nice to recuperate.

1869   Berlioz dies in Paris on March 8.

NOTE

Adapted from "Appendix A, Calendar" in *Berlioz* by Hugh Macdonald (Oxford: Oxford University Press, 2000), 210–19. Used by permission.

I

SONGS

For Hector Berlioz, love of text and the voice was at the core of his musical being. He wrote songs, known before and during the nineteenth century as *romances* or *mélodies*, throughout his relatively long life. At age fifteen or sixteen he arranged *romances* from popular comic operas to be accompanied by guitar and compiled them into a collection; he even considered publishing them. In 1863, at the age of sixty and having composed all his symphonies, choral-orchestral works, and operas, he realized many of his solos were no longer readily available to the public. Berlioz assembled most of them and eleven choruses into a single collection with piano accompaniment entitled *Collection de 32 mélodies*.[1] All were composed between 1829 and 1846, and some had been revised or orchestrated along the way until 1863. The collection is a wonderful testament to his lifelong commitment to vocal miniatures.

Yet Berlioz did not limit his vocal writing to only brief songs and choruses: singers are featured prominently in two of his four symphonies. *Roméo et Juliette* includes soloists, a small (petite) prologue chorus, and a large double chorus. For the second version of *Grande symphonie funèbre et triomphale* (Grand symphony of mourning and triumph), Berlioz incorporated voices into the wonderful third movement entitled *L'apothéose*. Other than symphonies and overtures, he wrote only one other orchestral work, the eight-minute *Rêverie et caprice* for violin and small orchestra, and even that melody was based on an aria from his opera *Benvenuto Cellini*. Berlioz did not write any chamber music—no string quartets, piano trios, violin or flute sonatas, woodwind quintets, or piano solo music, for example. There are only songs, brief and extended choral works, symphonies, overtures, and operas. It is remarkable to discover that the preponderance of his compositions requires singers, especially since his reputation today is based mainly on his first orchestral work, *Symphonie fantastique*, several overtures, one opera, and a few instrumental excerpts from choral-orchestral works.

Regardless of his overarching reputation as an instrumental composer, singers view Berlioz as an early and important exponent of the French *romance*, the French complement to the nineteenth-century German *lied*. He transformed the pre-1830s simple strophic (verse-by-verse) song type, known for naturalness of expression, unadventurous style, and naïve sentimentalism, into a more richly conceived French art song or *mélodie*. Yet only a few of his songs are regularly performed in concert today.

To the surprise of many, in total Berlioz published thirty-eight individual songs for solo or duet voices and one trio between 1819 and 1864. Many of them exist in multiple versions, a few have an added solo instrument (cello, viola, horn, and even castanets), and several were orchestrated for performance alongside extended works in concerts. While the quantity doesn't compare with the approximately six hundred *lieder* by Schubert or the two hundred plus *lieder* by Brahms, Berlioz's *mélodies* offer a multitude of riches for home, recital hall, and concert stage.

VOICE, TEXT, AND VOICE PREFERENCES

Because the voice is made exclusively of and is surrounded entirely by human flesh and bone, it is considered by many to be the most intimate of musical instruments. The vocal folds, not unlike an oboe reed, are the primary generator of sound, yet they are invisible and cannot easily be examined or touched. Every person's voice is unique to him or her alone. Rarely are we able to masque our emotions or vulnerability when we speak or sing. And as we sing, melodies and harmonies take on a vast new range of colors as a result of not only vowels and consonants but also the way we imbue the text with meaning. No other instrument offers anything even remotely comparable.

When spoken, each language has its own "feel," and music is written to partner and magnify that particular "feel." Heavier and lighter syllables (syllable weight or stress) are usually matched to their companion heavier or lighter places in the temporal structure of the music, although intentional disruption is an effective and frequent compositional strategy. To be sure, composers will avoid putting the most alluring note of a phrase on an article (e.g., "the"). The imperative when hearing Berlioz's songs is to luxuriate in the novelty and sensual "feel" of how the language and music fit together simply as musical sound. Then to go deeper, study of a translation is essential. Most artists provide an unrhymed paraphrased translation that gives overall clarity of message. Word-for-word literal translations (yes, every word), though, are crucial for synchronously matching a word and its meaning to what's happening in the music. Then following the meaning of a word or textual phrase on its journey becomes particularly satisfying. Consequently, having both types of translations at hand, paraphrased and word for word, is invaluable for a deeper look into a song.

Berlioz wrote most of his songs for the mezzo-soprano (middle soprano), the female voice that has a wide range but does not reach extremely high (soprano) or low (alto or contralto). Songs for tenor (higher male voice) follow next in frequency. He wrote only one solo song for soprano, *Zaïde*, and one for bass, *La chasseur danois* (The Danish huntsman). His choice of voice category depended on the text and was a matter of not only range but also color—he might choose a mezzo-soprano for burnished richness or a tenor for clarion ring. Unfortunately, present-day artists occasionally transpose songs up or down according to their comfort zone. A half step probably would not be of consequence to Berlioz, but moving the key down as far as two whole steps, as baritones have done for *Élégie en prose* (composed for tenor), or more than a whole step up as some sopranos have done for five of the six *Les nuits d'été*, substantially changes color and dramatic expression of a song.

OVERVIEW, MULTIPLE VERSIONS, FORM

Berlioz readily adapted his songs to suit a specific singer or occasion and made improvements based on having heard them performed. Some songs even began life as a quartet or chorus. *La captive* (The captive), for example, exists in an astonishing seven versions spread across thirty-one years. Quite popular during his lifetime, he felt its final version was one of his two best, along with *Absence* from *Les nuits d'été*. A remarkable sixty-two versions existed of his thirty-eight songs, reflecting his ongoing interest in them well after composition and his meticulous attention to detail.[2]

From conception to last iteration, the journey of one of Berlioz's songs could include some or even all of the following stages: (a) sketch of just a few phrases with text and some harmonies filled in; (b) autograph manuscript (score handwritten by the composer) with melody, text, piano accompaniment and specifics of tempo, character (e.g., *ardamente* or "ardently"), dynamics, and where to slow or quicken (e.g., *stringendo a poco a poco* or "faster little by little");[3] (c) first printed edition based on the autograph; (d) second printed edition, perhaps with new verses, an expanded introduction or transitions, an added solo for horn or cello, and new accompaniments for later verses; (e) first orchestrated version in print, sometimes transposed to a higher or lower key to better suit the character of the music or a particular singer, as well as new performance instructions based on having conducted it, including a metronome tempo direction; and (f) a new piano reduction of the most recent orchestra version.

In terms of form, many songs are strophic: the same music accompanies each verse of text, similarly to many folk songs and most popular music heard today; often a refrain recurs between verses. Most of his early *romances* are not technically demanding in range or agility and neither are they flashy. They have lovely tunes, they tell good stories, and some may draw a tear to the eye or even inspire a listener to sing it. Examples of Berlioz *romances* with or without refrains are the early *La captive* versions, *La belle voyageuse* (The fair traveler), *Strophes: Premiers transports* from his symphony *Roméo et Juliette*, and *Le roi de Thulé* from *La damnation de Faust*. *La mort d'Ophélie* is in a quite nifty modified strophic form, and so is *La belle Isabeau*—their tunes, harmonies, and piano gestures adjust to comport with new events in each verse.

Berlioz's more overtly dramatic songs lean toward the category of opera aria. Their melodies are less simple and require broader vocal range and agility from the singer. In addition, their keyboard or orchestral accompaniments are more engaging (and, for a pianist, more difficult) because they take on much more expressive responsibility than in a simple *romance*. The last version of *La captive*, praised by David Cairns as a miniature symphonic poem in a modified strophic form, is such a work. The through-composed (music without repeats of sections) *Élégie en prose* (Elegy in prose) has new music for each verse of text, is highly "operatic," and is among the most challenging technically for singer and pianist to perform. Berlioz started to orchestrate it but unfortunately put the draft aside.

Berlioz aimed to paint a picture in song, to evoke a mood and tell a good story. Can just a few minutes of music, a tune, and one person at the piano or with a small orchestra deliver emotional gravitas similar to that of a symphony? Undoubtedly yes but in miniature. Regardless of length or complexity, his songs have a richness of invention and appeal. Not surprisingly, they were a treasure trove from which he drew ideas and themes for his symphonies, choral-orchestral works, and operas. Many are true gems.

PARIS CONCERT LIFE AND THE *PARTIE VOCALE*

What was the music scene like in Berlioz's Paris? Where were his songs performed, and who sang them, who accompanied them? How did they fit in?

Simply put, operas—not songs, choruses, or symphonies—reigned supreme in Paris well before and during the early and mid-nineteenth century. The press covered every production, and a constant "buzz" swirled around star singers and any political intrigues small or large involving the theaters. Sets, costumes, dance, acting, singing, and orchestras were joined together to constitute, what was considered by most, the consummate performance art. Multiple production houses operated with their own orchestra and roster of singers to produce different types, from *opera-comique* (comic opera) to the new French grand opera requiring immense forces and a larger stage. Those in the upper echelons of society wanted to be seen at the opera, of course, but so did many other Parisians and visitors to the city. With the emergence of the merchant classes during the industrial revolution, more were able to afford tickets.

By contrast, concerts of unstaged instrumental and vocal music in Paris were of lesser prestige and income for artists. Lengthy choral-orchestral oratorios were usually performed in churches, and a mix of instrumental and vocal music was presented in concert halls such as Salle du Conservatoire, Salle Herz, or Salle Pleyel, and occasionally the theaters. While symphonies by Mozart and Haydn were familiar to audiences, it was not until the late 1820s that Beethoven's symphonies took Paris by storm. Precedent-setting performances of them at the Conservatoire were under the direction of violinist/conductor François Habeneck.

Orchestra programs as we know them today, often in the template of "overture-concerto-intermission-symphony," did not exist until well into the latter part of the century. Rather, concerts in Berlioz's Paris of the 1830s, 1840s, and 1850s offered a tremendous variety of genres. A concert might contain only one or several movements from a symphony and a concerto, and an overture could have opened the concert or even closed the first half or the end. Invariably concerts included a *partie vocale* (vocal portion), which might include a solo *romance*, one or several solo or duet opera excerpts featuring a star singer from one of the opera houses, and an a cappella motet or madrigal by a renaissance composer sung by a small ensemble of Conservatoire students. Variety was the name of the game, probably so that concerts would compare favorably with the constantly changing sonic and visual stimuli of opera productions. That said and on the other hand, concerts offered audiences something quite different and amazing: music first and foremost.

For a professional singer, the ride to fame and fortune depended on singing in the most prestigious opera houses of Europe, not in recitals or orchestra concerts, and the same was true for composers. Berlioz worked on an extraordinary number of opera projects beginning from his earliest years in Paris,[4] and he attended numerous productions as a reviewer, sometimes several in a week. Nonetheless, throughout his career he composed songs and brief choruses for the *partie vocale*, which were heard mostly in orchestral concerts that he organized and conducted. Several were composed or revised for his mistress, Marie Récio, or for famous opera singers whose voices he particularly admired, such as mezzo-soprano Pauline Viardot, and he dedicated them to other singers, patrons, and friends.

Songs and choruses performed in the concert *partie vocale* often became hits, and upon publication, many were performed with piano in other more intimate settings. Those included home entertainment, recitals, and the salon soirée, which was an evening gathering held usually by invitation in an aristocratic or wealthy person's residence. Due to demand, the publishing industry thrived—vocal music by numerous composers appeared in weekly or monthly journals and was printed in album collections. As it turned out, Berlioz maintained his foothold in Paris primarily via performance of his concert works and his songs and choruses in the *partie vocale*, not via production of his operas in the opera house.

NEUF MÉLODIES: NINE SONGS ON IRISH POETRY

Berlioz initially published all his thirty-eight solo songs as separate titles except for the collection *Neuf mélodies* (Nine songs) *and Les nuits d'été.* Printed under one cover in 1829, *Neuf mélodies* includes five songs, a duet, and three choruses that all have solo portions. While all share the same poetry source, they were not intended to be a cycle; rather, they are available to be chosen from. No overarching narrative connects them other than depictions of Irish sensitivities, stories, and scenery. The last song is unique: a paraphrase of the speech of Irish rebel Robert Emmet just before his execution in 1803.

Neuf mélodies 1829, H.38; retitled *Irlande* in 1849

1. *Le coucher du soleil* (The setting of the sun), tenor
2. *Hélène* (Helen), duet for tenor and bass or soprano and contralto; orchestrated when later arranged for male voices
3. *Chant guerrier* (Song of war), tenor and bass solos and four-part men's chorus
4. *La belle voyageuse* (The fair traveler), voice (often sung by mezzo-soprano); orchestrated when later arranged for two soloists or two-part women's chorus
5. *Chanson à boire* (Drinking song), tenor solo and four-part men's chorus

6. *Chant sacré* (Sacred song), tenor solo and six-part mixed chorus of sopranos, tenors, and basses; orchestrated when later arranged for only chorus
7. *L'origine de la harpe* (Origin of the harp), voice (often sung by soprano)
8. *Adieu Bessy* (Goodbye Bessy), tenor
9. *Élégie en prose* (Elegy in prose), tenor

Fascinated with the Emerald Isle and ideals of chivalry and self-determination, Berlioz had fallen in love with all things Irish after seeing Irish actress Harriet Smithson perform the Shakespearean roles of Ophelia and Juliet in 1827. Irishman Thomas Moore, a contemporary of Berlioz, wrote the poetry, and except for the last song, all were translated into French verse for Berlioz by his good friend Thomas Gounet.

To provide context, Berlioz gave each solo song a descriptive term or phrase in addition to its title. In order, they are as follows: (1) *rêverie* (daydream); (2) *ballade* (narrative poem); (4) *légende irlandaise* (Irish legend); (7) *ballade*; (8) *romance* (a simple song on an amorous topic); and (9) *Élégie* (lament for the dead). By contrast, each chorus title simply names its topic: (3) *Chant guerrier* (war); (5) *Chanson à boire* (drinking); (6) *Chant sacré* (sacred). With a good recording and text and translation in hand, let's look more closely at two songs from *Neuf mélodies*.

La belle voyageuse

In a nineteenth-century advertisement for an English edition of Berlioz's score, an anonymous author provided a superb encapsulation of the story of *La belle voyageuse* (The fair traveler). Note: Brian Boru (King Brien below) was king of Ireland 1002–1014.

> The ballad is founded on the legend that, in the time of King Brien [*sic*], the people of Ireland were inspired with such a sense of honour, virtue and religion, that a young lady of great beauty, adorned with jewels and a costly dress, and with only a wand in her hand, at the top of which was a ring of great price, undertook a journey alone from one end of the kingdom to the other; and such an impression had the laws and government of this monarch made on the minds of

all the people, that no attempt was made upon her honour, nor was she robbed of her clothes or jewels.[5]

What an enticing introduction for a prospective purchaser—we are talking about the integrity of an entire nation! Upon reading the first lines of the poem's translation, beguiling details about the fair traveler come alive: "Her beauty surpasses the luster of her rubies and her whiteness eclipses the white dew of the lily." The points of view in the poem are threefold: a narrator speaks in verses 1 and 4; the *chevalier* (cavalier or courtly knight) in verse 2; and the fair traveler in verse 3.

The piano accompaniment opens with just two notes imitating a Celtic harp or the drone of bagpipes (an interval spanning five steps)— already we are out in the countryside of Ireland. The meter of two pulses, each of which has three inner pulses, has an easy loping feel. The piano fills out the texture sounding like routine travel music; a harp or guitar could easily play this folk-style accompaniment. As for tempo, marked by Berlioz as *Allegretto non troppo* (somewhat fast, not too, pulse = 76), the song should not plod as though our voyager is fearful or hesitant, for she is not. Rather, Berlioz briskly recounts her story with confidence and lightheartedness. In the final verse, we learn our traveler not only is blessed to be safe among the Irish but also, in turn, is a blessing to the Irish because she trusted their integrity.

In strophic form with no refrain, the song is simple, attractive, and easily sung by an amateur or professional. The melody of sweeping arcs is the same for all four verses. Each phrase contains two lines of text (eight lines total in four pairs), and accompaniments for each verse are the same harmonically but subtly varied texturally. The same somewhat diffident "walking" figure in the pianist's right hand persists throughout each verse up until the seventh line. Here the voice reaches its highest note simultaneously with the most poignant, strategically important words (in verse 1: *Et sa blancheur efface* [and her whiteness erases]), and the piano line smooths out to harmonize with the voice in a gentle parallel descent. In effect at this point Berlioz has suspended forward momentum so the listener has time to process the story, revel in the overall sound, and experience the feelings invited by the music. He also asks singer and pianist to *un peu retenu* (hold back the tempo a little). Then for the last line (in verse 1: *La perle au blanc de lys* [the pearl white like a lily]), the original walking accompaniment and tempo return. In the final "La la la-le-ra-la," a dreamy coda, singer and pianist share wisps of melody in dialogue, as if the traveler and wordless knights are happily confirming their companionability. The surprising bit of new dissonance near the end is a foreboding touch. It is, perhaps, a hint of sadder tales of Ireland.

Close interpretation of the text and music together is complicated by the fact that Berlioz was setting a translation from English into French. The first line of Thomas Moore's poem is, "Rich and rare were the gems she wore," while Thomas Gounet's, *Elle s'en va seulette, L'or brille à son bandeau*, is quite different: "She departs alone, The gold gleams in her headband." In Moore's poem, the words are evocative. For Gounet, her departure wearing gold headband is pedestrian by comparison. That said, as a poet and translator Gounet was obliged to capture the overall character of the poetry, not each word literally or in order, and to create his own rhymes. The best approach for the listener to enjoy the song at a closer level is to review the original poem in English and then review a word-by-word English translation of Gounet's version. Only the latter will show the direct correlation between meanings of words and expressive musical details.

Clearly *La belle voyageuse* found a willing audience: Berlioz produced five versions of it over many years and gave multiple performances. The journey is fascinating. He set it first for a solo voice, a *jeune paysan* (young peasant, likely a female), to sing with piano at a tempo pulse = 84, so the song had a youthful, innocent quality. The second version was for male quartet and orchestra, presumably a more gallant musical depiction of knightly chivalry. Only one performance of it was given in 1834, and the music is lost. Possibly Berlioz was one of the four singers. For the third version, in 1842, he returned to solo voice, this time mezzo-soprano, and retained the orchestration of the second version. The tempo is slightly slower, *Allegretto*, pulse = 76, probably to allow more time for the arcing phrases to unfurl easily. Marie Récio, Berlioz's mistress, sang, and he conducted it while on tour in Stuttgart, Hechinger, Weimar, Leipzig, and Dresden. For the fourth version, prepared for a concert in 1851, Berlioz added a second soprano part to the same orchestration; then the song could be sung by either two soloists or a two-part female chorus. He added new, more specific dynamics to shape each phrase and numerous other detailed directives in consideration of performance by a chorus. The fifth version for *chant* and piano is in the collection *32/33 mélodies* published near the end of his life, bringing *La belle voyageuse* nearly full circle. It is just like the first version, but the soloist is designated simply as *chant* (voice) rather than *jeune paysan*, which likely was still intended to be a female. Also, the slightly slower tempo of the third version was maintained.

Élégie en prose

Robert Emmet (1778–1803), in whose memory Berlioz dedicated *Élégie en prose* in its second printing, was an Irish orator, patriot, and warrior opposed to domination of Ireland by the English. He made a thrilling farewell speech to his judges, known as the "Speech from the Dock," before his conviction and execution in 1803 for rebellious activities. Berlioz used the 1823 prose translation by Louise Belloc of Thomas Moore's poetic version of the speech ("When he who adores thee") rather than a translation by Gounet.

Élégie en prose is a *cri du cœur* (cry of the heart) so intense that the relentless surging of full-out passion can be difficult to process. At first hearing, the song immediately begs to be orchestrated—constant tremolos (extremely fast repetition of at least two notes) create an agitated underpinning, and the singing is resolutely declamatory. At one point Berlioz directs the singer and pianist to be *ardemente* (with ardor). Whether it was composed in 1827, when Berlioz was experiencing his first feelings of love for Harriet Smithson, as he implied in his *Mémoires*, or in 1829 when he wrote that he was in a different emotional turmoil, clearly the speech ignited his passions. Worried that he revealed too much of his own feelings, he destroyed the draft of an orchestration, deciding that the declarations of a revolutionary nearing execution were unsuitable for the concert-going public. But it is just those aspects that spark interest in the work today.

Listening to *Élégie* requires a clear understanding of who is speaking to whom. Emmet addresses both Ireland, the country he adores, and Sarah Curren, the love of his life. Her father, a lawyer and supporter of the status quo of English rule, is implicated among the enemies. The gist of the four sections is as follows:

1. Will you (the people of Ireland) weep when they (enemies of Emmet and the judges who will hang him) disparage his fame, which he gave for his country?
2. Yes, weep (Ireland and Sarah) regardless of their condemnation of your tears; though judged guilty by my accusers, I have been too faithful to you.
3. You (both) held the dreams of my first love; my every thought of reasoning was yours; in my last prayer, your name and mine shall be mingled.
4. Blessed are your lovers and friends who will live to see your days of glory; but next to this, the dearest blessing from heaven is the pride of dying for you.

Whereas *La belle voyageuse* is strophic in four stanzas with the same melody and harmony each time, *Élégie* is through-composed with the exception of a repeated music phrase at the end of sentences 2 and 4, which are, respectively, *"Car le ciel est té moin que coupable envers eux, je ne fus que trop fidèle pour toi"* (for heaven can witness though guilty to them I have been but too faithful to you), and *"la plus chère faveur que puisée accorder le ciel c'est l'orgeuil de mourir pour toi"* (the next dearest blessing that heaven can give is the pride of thus dying for you). Otherwise the music is new, just as the unrhymed (*en prose*) speech is new. Ongoing stream of consciousness was important in this instance: Berlioz wrote, "I think I have rarely found a melody of such truth and poignancy, steeped in such a surge of sombre harmony."[6]

A small gesture and some procedures are of note.

- At the third sentence, the piano's right hand lifts off into arabesques as if in whirls of a storm. But at *dans mon humble et dernière prière* (in my humble and last prayer), the whirl stops but for a feathery tremolo that continues as if breathless.
- The bass notes in the piano, often moving in contrary motion to the direction of the voice (bass moving up while voice moving down), serve to frame and hold the texture together.
- The singer's long, sustained notes throughout the song, marked to be performed *disperato ed appossionato assai* (very desperately and passionately) in *Adagio* (pulse = 54), signify both Emmet's and Berlioz's enduring loyalty to principle, to country, and to the

loves of their lives, Sarah Curren and Harriet Smithson. Meanwhile the powerful harmonic tension emulates their extreme inner torment.

Berlioz wrote that a good pianist is required; the accompaniment is far more difficult than any of the other *Neuf mélodies*, and its aggressive character matches the singer in dramatic intensity.[7] When considering the pianos of the 1830s, the sound Berlioz had in his ear was not as rich, smooth, or loud as that of modern Steinways and Bösendorfers. Rather, an early Erard piano of Berlioz's time was quieter and more varied in tone quality from the bottom to top of its range. So, today when we hear an agitated roar of rich tremolo figurations played on a modern piano, we might choose to imagine a more transparent, ringing sound instead.

Following completion of *Élégie en prose* in December 1829, Berlioz immediately began composing *Symphonie fantastique* in January 1830. His first and most renowned symphony then premiered the following December. Through the experience of composing *Neuf mélodies*, and especially *Élégie*, as well as choral-orchestral works such as *Messe solennelle* (see chapter 4), he was ready to take the gigantic leap into an hour-long, five-movement symphony. In the symphony, by contrast, words are relegated to an accompanying program and the orchestra expresses everything else.

SONG CYCLES AND *LES NUITS D'ÉTÉ*, A COLLECTION OF SIX SONGS

In nineteenth-century Germany, composers such as Beethoven, Schubert, and Schumann set collections of poems in song cycles—a group of three or more songs (each typically two to six minutes in length) on related poetry. The songs are crafted to flow naturally in sequence, connected by narrative and a balance of different moods, musical themes, and keys. Yet any one or more may also be sung individually. When performed as a complete work, a cycle offers a wonderful overarching musical entity that will reach an emotional-dramatic climax. The cycle *Die schöne müllerin* (The beautiful miller's daughter) by Schubert is a stellar example. Comprised of twenty *lieder* (German songs) to poetry by Wilhelm Müller, it was published in 1824 when young Berlioz was still new to Paris. Although Schubert's symphonies were unknown to Parisians then, his *lieder* became quite popular, and Berlioz was familiar with them.

The span of time and sustained narrative of a song cycle is similar to that of a symphonic movement. The focus, however, is on just two individual performers, a singer and a pianist, who must hold an audience's attention for anywhere from ten to thirty-five minutes. Considering the discrete forces, success depends on all aspects being thoroughly engaging, from the quality of poetry and music to the standard of performance.

It is easy to see that *Neuf mélodies* is a collection and not a cycle, even though the songs share the same poet and source. Scholars, however, debate about the "cycle or not a cycle" status of *Les nuits d'été* (Summer nights). All six songs are among Berlioz's most revered and well known to the near exclusion of his remaining thirty-two.[8] Performers present them as a cycle, in part, because initially they were published all together for a single voice, which could be either mezzo-soprano or tenor, with the exception of (5) *Au cimetière*, which was for tenor, and piano. But Berlioz never programmed either the piano or orchestrated versions as a group, although he had ample opportunity. In his lifetime, of the six he only heard (4) *Absence* in its piano version and only (4) *Absence* and (2) *Le spectre de la rose* in their orchestral versions. Ultimately, the general scholarly consensus is *Les nuits d'été* is a collection like *Neuf mélodies*, but performing them all in sequence is quite satisfying.

Background

Berlioz composed *Les nuits d'été* in 1840–1841 to six poems by his good friend Théophile Gautier, selecting them from Gautier's collection of fifty-seven poems entitled *La comédie de la mort* (The comedy of death). Berlioz gave the group his own new title and published them in their initial piano-vocal versions all together. He first orchestrated (4) *Absence* for his mistress and second wife to be, Marie Récio, to sing in Dresden, and by 1856 completed orchestrations of all the rest, transposing two of them, (2) *Le spectre de la rose* and (3) *Sur les lagunes*, to lower keys and assigning them new voice categories. Berlioz included updated piano reductions of the orchestrated versions in *32/33 mélo-*

dies, which may be considered his final word about keys, voice categories, and piano accompaniments (see table 1.1).

Table 1.1.   Keyboard and orchestrated versions of *Les nuits d'été* by key and voice

Title	Piano-vocal, tonality	Orchestra & 32/33 mélodies, tonality
1. Villanelle	mezzo-soprano or tenor, A	mezzo-soprano or tenor, A
2. Le spectre de la rose	mezzo-soprano or tenor, D	contralto, B
3. Sur les lagunes	mezzo-soprano or tenor, g minor	baritone or contralto or mezzo, f minor
4. Absence	mezzo-soprano or tenor, F sharp	mezzo-soprano or tenor, F sharp
5. Au cimetière	tenor, D	tenor, D
6. L'île inconnue	mezzo-soprano or tenor, F	mezzo-soprano or tenor, F

If all six are performed together, one can easily envision four different singers participating rather than one. Musicologist Annegret Fauser makes a case for considering *Les nuits d'été* a cycle in the imagination, because the title implies some sort of fantastical night piece in the tradition of E. T. A. Hoffmann's writings, or perhaps a Faustian dream.[9] Julian Rushton recommends *Les nuits d'été* be performed as a whole, whether by one singer or several, given the content of the music itself: the rich set of relationships among them, significant complexities, and a reconciliation of opposites.[10] If performed as a cycle (whether with piano or orchestra) in the keys and singer options Berlioz last prescribed, a novel approach could even be to alternate the male and female singers: (1) tenor, (2) contralto, (3) baritone, (4) mezzo-soprano, (5) tenor, and (6) mezzo-soprano. The overarching expanse of individual voice colors and personalities could lend a more inclusive, universal impact. Regardless of approach, whether sung by one voice or several and with piano or orchestra, every song is a gem, and the progression from one to the next is truly exciting.

Forms and Snapshot Descriptions

Table 1.2.   *Les nuits d'été* narrative summaries and forms

Title	Narrative	Form
1. Villanelle	spring-born *joie de vivre*	strophic
2. Le spectre de la rose	loss of innocence	through-composed

Title	Narrative	Form
3. Sur les lagunes	death of a beloved	through-composed
4. Absence	a command to return	strophic (ABACA)
5. Au cimetière	obliteration of her memory	strophic (ABA)
6. L'île inconnue	beginning a new future	rondo ABACA'DA"

Adapted from Fauser, "The Songs," 119. Used by permission. The prime mark
(') and double prime mark (") indicate varied iterations of the same music.

(1) *Villanelle* (Rustic song) is in bright A major and *allegretto*; "Spring
has come, my lovely one, it is the month blessed by lovers." In the
second verse, against ebullient reiterated eighth-note chords in the
right hand, the left hand of the piano is in a chase with the singer,
imitating what the singer has just sung one measure later. The form is
modified strophic in three verses: the music of each verse is subtly
varied in melody or harmony, text distribution, and accompaniment
gestures. Most informed performers will observe the tempo Berlioz
indicated, pulse = 96, not faster as some have recommended (pulse =
120). A faster tempo results in a frenetic quality and sacrifices the
delightful playfulness of the chase.

(2) *Le spectre de la rose* (The specter of the rose) in B major is a
passionate operatic scene by virtue of its variety and intensity. While
through-composed, there are phrase reiterations. Most striking is the
intensity of *Ce léger parfum est mon âme et j'arrive du paradis* (This
fragile perfume is my soul and I come from paradise). Here Berlioz
brings the song to its highest dramatic moment through harmonic tension in the orchestra (or piano) partnered with crescendos, changes of
tempo, and use of the uppermost register of the voice. At the final four
lines of text, the accompaniment and voice are locked into a heartrending lament that forms the coda.

(3) *Sur les lagunes* (On the lagoons) in F minor is also through-
composed, but the first and third verses have similarities while the
second stands out in contrast with them. The refrain is slightly different
in each of its three iterations. The mood of lament, starkly introduced
before in the last phrases of *Le spectre de la rose*, now becomes palpable anguish: "Into the tomb she takes my soul and all my love."

(4) *Absence* (Absence) in F♯ major is a command for the loved one
to return! The singer seems to be in a trance, as though in denial, and
appears not to have even heard any of *Sur les lagunes* just before. The

surreal, almost bizarre quality to the key relationships within and between these two songs undermines reality.

(5) *Au cimetière* (*clair de lune*) (At the cemetery; moonlight) begins
with repeated D major chords like a persistent throb of pain. Berlioz
soon moves to a B♭ major sonority on *tomb* (grave or tomb) for a
gloriously radiant and calming effect. Again, as in a trance, the poet/
singer has now returned to the tomb of the departed beloved. He or she
hears the solitary and mournful song of a dove and connects with the
departed: "An awakened soul weeps beneath the earth in unison with
the song." By the final verse, the poet/singer, transformed by gradual
acceptance of the loved one's death, vows never to return to the tomb,
even though the flowers and *fantôme* (specter) call.

In (6) *L'île inconnue* (The unknown island) the pianist or orchestra
opens in confident F major with a victorious melodic cascade and exciting turbulent figurations—the singer is already at sea riding the high
waves. Trance and grief are put aside; now there is healing, release,
escape, empowerment, and hope. "Take me, says the beauty, to the
faithful shore where one loves forever!" "Where would you go?" asks an
unknown. "The breeze will blow!"

LA MORT D'OPHÉLIE

Few compositions by Berlioz are overtly autobiographical. Among
them, two stand out: *La mort d'Ophélie* (The death of Ophelia), a
romance based on the Ophelia in *Hamlet* by Shakespeare, and *Symphonie fantastique*, his nearly concert-length symphony based on a narrative he devised. Both works refer to his first wife, Irish actress Harriet
Smithson. It makes perfect sense that the youthful Berlioz, age twenty-
seven and enthralled by love, would compose an entire symphony about
his own tumultuous infatuation. Twelve years later he commemorated
the near end of their relationship by writing a song, a lament for Ophélie, a woman who tragically succumbed to madness.

The musical connection between the two works, traced by David
Cairns, is in their shared melodic contours. In the song, the interval
sung on the first word *Auprès* (beside) is an ascending major sixth (two
pitches, one on each syllable, span six steps in a scale; it is a wide and
poignant-sounding leap) and soon an ascending minor second (the clos-

est possible pitch relationship) on "li," the third of four syllables of her name "Ophélie."[11] By comparison, in *Symphonie fantastique* the major sixth and minor second (with a perfect fourth in between) are near the beginning of the *idée fixe*, the signatory melody Berlioz chose to represent his beloved and the changing states of being in love.[12] One could rightly say such a correlation between the two works and themes is obscure, the kind of code accessible only to Berlioz and Berlioz insiders. Perhaps he even wrote the opening of *La mort d'Ophélie* not realizing its similarity to the *idée fixe*. Whether it occurs overtly or unconsciously, though, their resemblance points to Harriet and his deep sadness at saying farewell.

Berlioz saw Harriet portray Shakespeare's Ophelia when she was part of an Irish acting troupe performing in Paris in 1827, and he immediately fell in love. He also saw her perform the role of Juliet in *Romeo and Juliet*, which became the subject of his third symphony, *Roméo et Juliette*. Even though the plays were in English, a language he did not speak (nor did she speak French), he read the translation in advance so he could watch and follow the actors closely. Harriet was even more effective as a mime than as a declaimer of her lines, and one can easily envision Berlioz seated in the theater entranced by her magical presence.

Berlioz and Harriet were happily married in 1833 and soon had a son, Louis. But she devolved into illness and alcohol as her acting career faded. In 1841, the year prior to composing *La mort d'Ophélie*, Berlioz began his relationship with Marie Récio, a fiery Spanish mezzo-soprano of limited professional success, and she joined him on two lengthy performance tours in 1842. He provided for Harriet until her death in 1854 while also supporting Marie.

The Drama and Form

Ophelia is a minor yet pivotal character in *Hamlet*. She is the undeclared but apparent love of the young Hamlet and, quite sadly, not an entirely innocent victim of circumstance. In the aftermath of the death of her father, who was killed unintentionally by Hamlet, she has quietly gone mad with despair and grief. She loves Hamlet to the end despite his brutality.

The four-stanza poem by Ernest Legouvé, which he described next to the title as "imitating Shakespeare," was the perfect choice for Berlioz to bid both Ophélie and Harriet farewell.[13] During the first two verses, Ophélie gathers flowers along the bank of a mountain stream. But while hanging them on some willow tree branches, she falls into the water. In verse 3 she is swept into the current, and while her dress keeps her afloat, she sings old ballads as if a naiad (water nymph). Finally, her "strange melody" disappears; her skirt has become heavy and drags her down. She is left with her melody barely begun and a life prematurely cut short; without resistance Ophélie drowns.

The poem is in four verses of seven lines each, and for each verse the rhyme scheme is ab–ab–ccb. All four verses are in the voice of the poet-narrator. While Legouvé did not write a textual refrain, Berlioz added his own musical one between each verse and at the end. For it he used only a melody sung on the vowel "ah" to depict the tragically incoherent Ophélie floating downstream. The singer's "ah" melody alternates between two falling notes and brief upward sweeps; its repetitions gradually move downward as she is carried downstream.

The musical form of *La mort d'Ophélie* is fascinating, for while the poetry's organization is fixed and predictable, the music is subtly varied throughout. Table 1.3 illustrates how five sections (introductions, verses, refrains, a transition, and codas) are the same, similar, or different in length, as shown by the number of measures in the score.

Table 1.3.   *La mort d'Ophélie* in varied strophic form

Section	I^1	V^1	R^1	C^1	I^2	V^2	R^{2*}	V^3	R^{3*}	V^4	T	R^4	C^2
Measures	2	23	17	4	2	29	8	25	3	22	2	17	4 + 2
Length		$V^1 = 46$				$V^2 = 39$		$V^3 = 28$		$V^4 = 45$			

Total length 160 measures, duration approximately eight minutes. Superscript numerals indicate the sequence of appearance and version of each section. **Key:** I = Introduction by piano alone; V = Verse; R = "Ah" refrain; * = Leads into next verse without an introduction—an acceleration of form; T = Transition; C = Coda

Different lengths are caused by the stretching or contraction of recurring melodies. By massaging the fixed form of the poem with an ever-changing, evolving musical setting, Berlioz created a beguiling work. Overall, verses 1 and 4 are very similar, like bookends, and verses 2 and 3 form a center of two almost-halves.

As you listen, keep an ear open for the following:

- Warm and sunny major tonality at the opening.
- Shimmering, quivering tremolo in keyboard right hand; perhaps sunlight sparkling on the rippling surface of the stream.
- Individual low notes in the pianist's left hand, somewhat melodic, rise leisurely, giving a sense of rocking or a swirl in the current; the bass line holds the harmonies together.
- Piano anticipates the voice's entrance by playing the phrase first, as in a chase. Their ongoing dialogue induces a feeling of swaying/ rocking as both singer (narrator) and piano (water current) inexorably move downstream.
- When heard the first time, the meandering and mournful, yet seemingly lackadaisical, "Ah" refrain is surprisingly long, and the piano again precedes the voice in close juxtaposition. The melody is comprised of a single motive that begins on a strong beat, falls by step and then struggles upward. Imminently pliable, it may be moved to any pitch level and made any length. While gradually falling, it halts and then continues down to a dark melancholic depth.
- Both codas (ending verses 1 and 4) begin in silence and then a single note is heard; they connote a sense of isolation and provide the listener time to process what has occurred.
- The piano accompaniment in verse 2 is very different from before—more vigorous, like burbling. The contrast between low burbling and a high, soaring figure in the pianist's right hand results in a new variety of rocking. A long crescendo to an abrupt halt on the word *tombe* (falls) marks the moment Ophélie loses her balance and falls into the stream.
- Verse 3 begins slightly before the foreshortened refrain is over, thereby accelerating the drama. Her dress spreads wide, swells like a sail, and carries her as she sings like a water creature. The piano accompaniment changes to an intermittent patter of high notes in octaves sounding on weak beats. A chromatic descent signals her impending demise.

- Verse 4 slips in on the coattails of the even more abbreviated third refrain, foreshadowing her life is nearing an end. Again, Berlioz uses silence, this time at the word *profond* (deep, referring to watery depths) to set up the final two lines, "Leaving as yet hardly begun her melodious song."
- The last phrase ends in a somewhat bright yet not complete major sonority. The halting refrain motive is heard twice, slightly changed the second time.
- The full-length, seventeen-measure refrain, nearly identical to the first, concludes the work as though in memory of her life, all of it. Three chords, like a benediction, bring solemn closure.

Berlioz held a special place in his heart for those subject to tragedy or cruel irony. The extraordinary musical care he gave to *Ophélie* appears in numerous other works too, including his treatment of the homeless Holy Family in *L'enfance du Christ* and for Didon, the discarded Carthaginian queen and lover of Énée in *Les Troyens*. In *Élégie en prose* we see Berlioz passionately extoll the maligned and unjustly punished Robert Emmet. Empathy and compassion are leitmotifs throughout the course of his works.

A COUPLE OF OUTLIERS

Two lesser-known songs from the 1840s stand out for their sheer quirkiness and fun.

Le trébuchet: Scherzo (The Snare: A Joke), a Charming and Clever Duet

In 1846 Berlioz unearthed a draft of *Le trébuchet* from manuscripts he had written earlier, but the second and third verses were missing so he asked his friend Emile Deschamps, librettist for *Roméo et Juliette*, to write new ones. Originally a simple strophic song, Berlioz then transformed *Le trébuchet* into a delightful through-composed narrative in three sections, each with a one-line refrain.

Snapshot of the Story

Love, in the form of a handsome young shepherd, waits for a shepherd-ess, little Liza, while hidden in a bush. She, unaware of being watched, is waiting to see a warbler. The bird flies off, and Liza, surprised by the shepherd, is caught in the "snare" and "joke" of love. "Sweet excite-ment, she is pale and trembling, there's no telling why!" In verse 2 she resists and breaks free from love's advances. But because her soul is on fire with that sweet excitement, she comes back to the same place two days later. In verse 3 she is still there, alone and in tears; meanwhile, the handsome shepherd is far away, lying in wait for yet another pretty face. Who knows if or when he will return.

The three single-line refrains, one at the end of each verse, tell almost all: *Ne sais comment, Ne sais pourquoi*, and *On ne sait quand* (Don't know how, don't know why, don't know when!)—there's no tell-ing how she got caught, why she came back all pale and trembling, or when he'll return to his faithful love. Early in his *Mémoires* Berlioz described himself as a youth hiding in his grandfather's orchard "like a wounded bird, mute, suffering."[14] That experience must have led him to empathize, however playfully in retrospect (and unconventionally for the time), with the vulnerable female shepherdess rather than the cava-lier male shepherd.

The music is light and fun. The piano flits about like a herky-jerky bird hopping around and then freezes in teasing silence. Ascending, flutelike riffs recall Papageno playing his shepherd's pipe in *The Magic Flute* by Mozart. At times the bird seems a bit demented if not plain drunk with love. As in *La mort d'Ophélie* and other songs, piano and voice are co-conspirators; in the second and third verses, the piano tantalizingly anticipates the upcoming vocal melody by playing the first few notes ahead of it. And for the phrase *minois piquant* (spicy or savory little face) near the end, the music even goes into a bit of a schmaltzy swoon!

A good performer will adhere precisely to Berlioz's sudden changes, all of which are notated clearly in the score. If performers allow a rhythmic gesture to sag or dynamic contrasts to even out, then the suspense and good-natured humor will be greatly lessened. The second verse is sometimes sung more slowly than the first, but Berlioz calls only for a change in character, *dolce* (gentle or sweet), and the poem itself does not imply a need for slowing until the next-to-last line, *pâle et tremblante* (pale and trembling). Not surprisingly, performances that remain at the tempo marked *Allegretto leggiero e scherzando* (somewhat fast, light and playful), at a pulse = 88, are very effective! The descriptive term *scherzo* in the title is a double entendre for joke and a playful, fast tempo.

Toward his last years, Berlioz attractively packaged some of his songs and choruses to market them. He published *Le trébuchet* first in 1850, in his next-to-last collection of songs entitled *Fleurs des landes* (Wildflowers, or Flowers of the heath; *landes* is literally "moors"). As the title suggests, all four songs and the one chorus are closely related to nature. Later *Le trébuchet* was reprinted in a larger collection exotically entitled *Aurora* along with songs by other composers. The title evokes any number of sumptuously provocative ideas associated with romance and the pastoral: sunrise, nature, a natural light display in the sky, or even the Roman goddess of dawn.

La belle Isabeau: Conte pendant l'orage (The Lovely Isabel: Tale during a Storm)

At first this poem seems to be a scary ghost story told to children during a storm. The topic is, not surprisingly, a young woman in love and in distress. The scene is vividly set: a black mountain, an old castle, and a young girl "who is just your age." The lovely Isabeau, imprisoned by her father to keep her from her lover, a knight, is surprised and at first fearful when she sees the knight enter her cell. They escape from the castle without seeing a chaplain, never to return. After each of the three verses, a chorus sings the same short refrain: *Enfants, voici l'orage! À genoux! Priez Dieu!* (Children, here is the storm! Fall to your knees! Pray to God!).

The varied musical setting of each verse once again displays the composer's ebullient creativity. Evolving in tandem with the unfolding story, the music by the third verse is only remotely like the first. Like *La mort d'Ophélie*, the form is modified strophic, but the real protagonist for change and emotional weight is the piano more so than the singer. In the score Berlioz even labeled the piano *principal*. He spent a great deal of time revising to get the piano part just right, as is evidenced by numerous sketches for *La belle Isabeau* that were found on *collettes* (scraps of paper with music notated on the reverse sides of other manuscript scores). Important gestures to listen for in the pianist's part include the following:

1. Fairylike flicks at the end of verse 1; they seem like a twinkle of an eye—the children should not to be *too* scared!
2. During *à genoux* (to your knees), there is a weirdly dissonant, modern tinge to the sparsely pointillist raindrops.
3. Surging chromatic scales of differing lengths and range emulate the storm.
4. Quixotic changes in tonality at the ends of phrases and sections perpetuate the sense of being unsettled.

Three more attributes to listen for are as follows:

1. In the last phrase of verse 1 (which has only six lines of text), the voice reaches its highest point thus far while describing the fetching Isabeau with her unusual combination of black hair and blue eyes. At the same point in the next and longer verse 2, the hurricane rages and the sky is on fire!
2. Eerily, in verse 2 (ten lines of text, much longer than verse 1) the pianist's right hand plays a melody that was previously sung in verse 1 on the textual phrase *Elle était de votre âge* (She was your age). The elastic modifications to the music structure begin precisely at this moment.
3. In verse 3 when Isabeau is full of fear, the music is brand new. Voice and piano are breathless, even halting, when she asks, "Where's the chaplain?" The knight promises they'll return before dawn. We are somehow disappointed to learn, however, that her father is still waiting for them.

At face value *La belle Isabeau* is a scary-for-children morality tale warning against adolescent visions of elopement. However, the burst of imposed religiosity put upon the children in the refrain does appear a bit hyped, even comical. Berlioz certainly did not embrace church doctrine (e.g., requirement of a chaplain), and he may have been poking his finger at the institution of marriage. More likely, though, he was just having fun playacting a medieval tale and giving it a melodramatic spin.

Was Isabeau a real person? Possibly. Isabeau de Clugny, also known as "La belle Isabeau," was a woman of mixed race living in Paris and the subject of a Eugène Delacroix seminude painting, *A Mulatto Woman*, dating from 1821–1824. But the young Isabeau in Berlioz's song is trapped in a cell in a medieval castle. Or there's another option. Alexandre Dumas *père* (1802–1870), author of the poem, according to Berlioz, was the internationally famous author of *The Count of Monte Cristo*, *The Three Musketeers*, and much more. In 1835, Dumas published *Isabel of Bavaria; or, the Chronicles of France for the Reign of Charles VI*, who ruled from 1380 to 1422. This Isabel is a closer fit. Interestingly, though, the poem Berlioz set to music does not appear in the bibliography of Dumas. Perhaps Berlioz, a friend and admirer of Dumas's work, asked him one evening after dinner to write a poem on an episode from Isabel's life. The chronicles may even have reminded Berlioz of the medieval knightly tales in the poetry of Thomas Moore, some of which he set in *Neuf mélodies* fourteen years before.

IN CLOSING

Romances were in the forefront of bourgeois popularity for nearly a century beginning well before Berlioz wrote his. Their nonvirtuosic melodies, simple homophonic accompaniments (chords vertically aligned, usually moving in the same or similar rhythm with the voice), and diatonic harmony (few chromatic or dissonant notes outside the key to add spice and color) had tremendous universal appeal. Initially their form was strophic and their character was naïve, sentimental, nostalgic, and elegant. Clear and uncomplicated expression of the poetry was of foremost importance. Artwork, usually in the form of lithographs, was included in publications of songs and choruses to enhance mood and spark the imagination of performers and therefore listeners alike. *Romances* were a staple of light entertainment.

When Berlioz wrote his first several *romances* for voice and guitar at age fifteen or sixteen, their formats were similarly simple. But the startling musical depths and torrents of emotion in *Élégie en prose* and the constantly evolving musical events in *La mort d'Ophélie* and *La belle Isabeau* gave the *romance* a new and much richer identity. At the same time some, like *La belle voyageuse* and *Le trébuchet*, offer pure delight. Berlioz elected to tell a story in the music as much or more as in the text, and by doing so he initiated a new era of French art song. Later composers such as Gounod, Bizet, Fauré, Duparc, Ravel, and Debussy magnificently carried Berlioz's mantle forward. They, too, matched their intensely rich imaginations with newly evolving tools of heightened musical expression.

VIGNETTE 1.1. IN SEARCH OF SINGING BERLIOZ: *LA CAPTIVE*

Mary, a mezzo-soprano, is a precocious second-year student at a university. Her voice lesson with her teacher, Ms. Duffy, has just begun.

Mary: I'd like to sing some Berlioz for my junior recital.

Ms. Duffy: Really? What made you think of him?

Mary: We've been studying his symphony *Roméo et Juliette* in my music history class, and the melody in the love scene *Scène d'amour* is so incredibly beautiful. Did you know, after Berlioz conducted that movement in Germany, he felt tugging from behind when he bowed—it was an orchestra player kissing his coattails! I wonder, do you know of any music by Berlioz that I could sing?

Ms. Duffy: That's a terrific story. The only Berlioz songs I know are the six *Les nuits d'été*. They too are incredibly beautiful, especially *Absence*, but the set may be technically a bit too advanced for you at the moment. I don't know of any others, I wonder if there are any!

Mary: Well, I must confess, I found a song described in my music history book called *La captive*. The story of how it came about is kind of fun. Berlioz was just hanging out, and a friend inadvertently knocked a book of Victor Hugo's poetry off a table. It landed on the floor open to the page of *La captive*. Berlioz picked up the book, read the poem, and when he finished told his friend that he had heard the music for it while reading! That's magical; how can that be? Berlioz wrote down the melody right there on the spot. A few days later, when he was back at a villa in Rome with a bunch of other Prix de Rome winners, he wondered if what he wrote was any good. So, he asked a singer friend to try it out while he accompanied. Since he didn't play much piano, I bet he used his guitar. Later she wrote to Berlioz, jokingly cursing him because everyone was singing snatches of *La captive* around the villa, and the song was driving her crazy! She was going to have to fire her servant and hire another one on the condition she not sing *La captive*.

Ms. Duffy: I love that story! Well, let's look at the music. I see you've already found a score.

Mary: Well, yes. And I also learned that Berlioz rewrote it multiple times. I found this one for mezzo-soprano, cello, and piano. I can ask my friend Andrew to play cello in the recital. If you approve, that is.

Ms. Duffy: Sure, let's take a listen. [*The teacher plays the piano accompaniment as Mary sings through the first verse and refrain.*] What a beautiful melody. It's so organic—each phrase seems to un-furl from one to the next. There, see where the line increases in energy and then kind of sighs? And these harmonies! Hmm, gently nuanced and so sumptuous. It's good that you've been working on some Fauré songs so your French is in good shape.

Mary: What do you think? I read Berlioz complained about opera singers screaming so that their voices would fill large halls and how they added ornaments to show off their virtuosity and get good re-views. But he preferred a singer who had empathy for the compos-er's point of view. Maybe that's me! I'd like to try.

Ms. Duffy: Yes, I think you will do *La captive* justice. Thank you so much for bringing it in; it's really lovely.

2

MUSIC FOR CHORUS

The extent and quality of Hector Berlioz's compositions for voices is unheralded. As already noted, his first compositions were songs, and vocal music continued to play a central role. Berlioz wrote twenty-four brief independent choral works of ten minutes or less with piano or orchestra; many include passages for soloists. Plus, there are six cantatas, defined here as solo or choral works of ten to thirty minutes with orchestra. While chorus and soloists are centrally featured in his extended choral-orchestral works, of course, surprisingly two of his four symphonies also include choral forces. Then there are the many choruses fulfilling multiple dramatic roles in Berlioz's three operas.

To understand Berlioz's choral music more clearly, it's important to be familiar with the singing traditions in France before and during Berlioz's career.

SINGING IN NINETEENTH-CENTURY FRANCE

Imagine you are in Paris during the French Revolution. It's June 7, 1794, the night before the Festival of the Supreme Being, one of the massive patriotic-propaganda celebrations organized by the antimonarchist Robespierre. The city is buzzing with anticipation, and instrumentalists from the Conservatoire-to-be have ventured out to teach citizens the songs of liberty that are planned for performance the next day. That day arrives, and combined forces of amateurs and professionals perform

Gossec's hymn *Père de l'univers* (Father of the universe) before a crowd at the Tuileries Palace. Hundreds of drummers signal the main events of the ceremonies with thunderous drumrolls. Then you and thousands more, including groups of cavalry, firemen, and multiple bands and choruses associated with different groups, all join and march to Champ de Mars to play and sing patriotic tunes. Performance of a great symphony for band then leads up to the event climax: at the top of your lungs, you and the entire crowd sing new verses to *La Marseillaise*. En mass singing, an important feature of most formal and informal public events in the nineteenth century, enabled *everyone* to take part in sociopolitical changes, of which there were many. Even in theaters before a play or comic opera, tempers could flare as audience members battled over which politically loaded song they would sing together before the curtain rose. Imagine the raucous atmosphere!

Training to sing in professional groups was customary in France. Prior to the revolution against Louis XVI, the church sponsored *maîtrises*, schools for cantors and choristers in church services; some of those singers went on to solo careers in the opera houses. After the revolution, Napoléon I encouraged the opening of Alexandre Choron's school founded to preserve the Catholic musical heritage of Gregorian chant and renaissance polyphony. But during the July Monarchy of Louis-Philippe (1830–1848), when Berlioz was at the height of his concert activities in Paris, Louis-Philippe revoked funding for cathedral choirs and royal bands such as the Chapelle royale and Musique du Roi, which constituted most of the officially sponsored sacred and secular professional music organizations. To Berlioz's distress, he also closed Alexandre Choron's school. Fortunately, though, opera productions and the Conservatoire continued under government sponsorship.

With free training provided by the Conservatoire and the rise of the new Orphéon music education movement in 1815, music literacy in the general populace began to flourish. Founded by Guillaume-Louis Bocquillon Wilhem, the Orphéon movement developed a new singing method based on the fundamentals of music notation and *solfège*—learning to sing pitch intervals at sight without the aid of an instrument. By the early 1830s Wilhem's approach was widely adopted for use in Parisian schools.

Wilhem also established the first official Orphéon all-male choir for former students to continue singing after they finished school. Although the evening choral classes originally included women and girls, starting in 1838 only adult men were permitted. Its purpose was to provide structured leisure activity for the working and artisan classes and to encourage "disciplined learning through art under the banner of brotherhood and in the . . . spirit of association."[1] Orphéon events catered to huge numbers of performers and were often held by necessity in the open air or in large venues. A whole middle-class generation of children and adult men were provided a solid musical education and learned to love choral singing.

By the 1850s, the Orphéon movement was a fixture in France, and various regional organizations engaged the capital's most active composers to write compositions. In 1859, the first Orphéon reunion brought together some six thousand voices representing two hundred Orphéon societies and choruses from all over France. By the early 1860s, toward the end of Berlioz's life, three thousand provincial, all-male Orphéon choirs involving about 140,000 singers were active.[2] Little acknowledged today, a revolution in amateur, all-male choral singing had occurred during Berlioz's career.

Women, excluded from singing in church choirs and the adult, male Orphéon movement, learned to read music and sing in public schools and convents or in private lessons. Meanwhile the Conservatoire provided voice lessons to women and men and required all voice students to participate in a chorus class. Students aspiring to leading roles in the Paris opera houses succeeded or settled for the opera chorus. Women in particular became a central feature of the salon entertainment culture. Almost every professional singer and many amateurs, particularly women, had some training in playing harpsichord or piano, the most important instruments found in middle- and upper-class homes along with harp and flute.

With the rise of music literacy across the general population, publishers printed an enormous number of *romances* and choruses for home enjoyment. They appeared in collections and as single works in popular weekly journals for diversionary entertainment, not unlike distribution of crossword puzzles in newspapers and magazines today. The goal was to provide a continuous, fresh supply for homes, recitals, elite salons, and club soirées. Collections of music for church services were also published.

Given burgeoning musical literacy in France, the overall male chorus tradition, and availability of professional singers trained by the church and Conservatoire, Berlioz knew there were suitable forces available for performing his choral music. Of his works for chorus, nearly one-third were written in response to or in support of political movements or events, and many were sung and played by extremely large forces. On many occasions all present were ready at the drop of a hat to join in for the refrain or, if given the text, the next verse.

OVERVIEW OF BERLIOZ'S CHORAL MUSIC, 1828–1868

Berlioz's expansive offering of choral music may be considered in five groupings as indicated at the beginning of this chapter: brief independent choruses, cantatas, extended choral-orchestral works, symphonies, and operas. This chapter addresses the first two groupings, brief independent choruses and cantatas. For more information and to locate titles of choruses, some of which also exist in song versions, refer to part 1 in appendix B, which lists titles by grouping. In part 2 of appendix B, all patriotic choruses are listed chronologically according to the five governmental regimes during which they were written and Berlioz's age at the time.

Due to Berlioz's penchant for "it can always be better" and "let's adapt this work for the next concert's performers," sorting out multiple versions of his choral works can be daunting. You may wonder, does it matter to the nonexpert listener? Yes! Imagine you will be attending a concert and you see *Sara la baigneuse* is on the program. Having decided you'll learn about the piece and listen to it in advance, you select a great recording for soprano and contralto soloists accompanied by piano. You arrive at the concert, though, and lo and behold it's performed by three choruses and orchestra. It sounds quite different! By checking appendix B, which also lists all versions of Berlioz's choral works, you would have discovered that Berlioz composed four different versions of *Sara la baigneuse*. Please refer to appendix B when choosing recordings of the works discussed in detail below.

A word about choral voicing, that is, the voice categories and number of parts in a work. Berlioz recognized, as did his French predecessors and contemporaries, that few true altos (or contraltos; the terms are often used synonymously), the lowest female voice, existed. Furthermore, most voices do not project well in their lower range. Although other European countries composed for altos, most women were actually sopranos or mezzo-sopranos (second sopranos). Accordingly, French composers wrote for sopranos only or sopranos divided into higher and lower groups, first and second sopranos. Conductors assigned their true alto and contralto singers to the second soprano part or, presumably, didn't have them sing. It is highly unlikely, for cultural reasons, that female altos would have sung with tenors as is sometimes done in choruses today.

All Berlioz's choral works for mixed voices composed before 1850 are scored for three parts, soprano-tenor-bass (STB), or divided some or all of the time into six parts (SSTTBB), both of which result in a particularly rich male sound. Consequently, his desired proportion of singers was roughly one-third women to two-thirds men as is indicated by the desired number of singers he specified in scores. Later, having concertized regularly outside of France, he adopted the soprano-alto-tenor-bass, four-part format (SATB) of Austro-Germanic and English practice for most choral works, but he continued to divide each section into multiple parts as desired (SSAATTBB). Regarding his two late operas, *Les Troyens* has a five-part chorus (SSATB) for acts 1 and 2 and four-part (SATB) for acts 3–5; again, sections are divided into two or more parts as desired. In *Béatrice et Bénédict*, generally Berlioz used a five-part voicing, dividing the women three ways (SSATB). All to say, Berlioz's choices in voicing were guided by desired musical effect and customs of time and place. A chorus divided into more parts offers a richer color.

Brief, Independent Choruses

Berlioz composed twenty-four brief, independent choruses between 1829 and circa 1860–1868. Many have roles for one or more soloists, most often tenor or mezzo-soprano. Overall, most are secular and many of those patriotic. Of his seven "sacred" titles (containing reference to a higher being), three were intended for worship: *Veni Creator* (Come Creator), *Tantum ergo sacramentum* (So great therefore a sacrament), and his arrangement of music by the French Baroque composer

François Couperin, *Invitation à louer Dieu* (Invitation to praise God). All of these were written for treble voices in Berlioz's last years at the request of Prosper Saint d'Arod (1814–1887), a French composer, choirmaster, and music critic, and published in a book of choral music, *Livre choral*, for the Catholic church. All other works in the brief independent chorus category are accompanied by either piano or orchestra with the exception of one for organ (first version of *Le temple universel*, H.137A), and three that are a cappella: *Veni Creator*, *Tantum ergo sacramentum*, and *Le temple universel* (The universal temple, second version, H.137B). *Prière du matin* (Prayer of the morning), also known as *Chœur d'enfants* (Chorus of children) and with piano, was probably intended for children to sing in concert or possibly a worship setting, either convent or church. Women and girls were generally still not allowed to sing in regular worship services during the nineteenth century.

Berlioz made a clear topical and sound palette distinction between music for only men's voices and for only women's. We see demure music for women in two and sometimes three voice parts; they sound silky, atmospheric, charming, and at times childlike. In fact, his three works for three-part treble voices referred to above and the two-part *Prière du matin* sound beguilingly pristine when sung by children. By contrast, men's choruses in two, three, or four parts radiate robust camaraderie, virtue, and heroic valor. Berlioz composed more choruses for only men than for only women. His mixed choruses have a more gender-neutral compositional approach, but still there is gender role-playing—the men are strong and virtuous and the women are sensual, delicate, naïve.

A Note about Berlioz's Cantatas

Berlioz's six cantatas with chorus were composed from 1825 to 1854. Two of his earlier ones, *La mort d'Orphée* (The death of Orpheus) and *Sardanapale* (Sardanapalus) were written for the Prix de Rome competition; he won the prize on his fifth attempt with *Sardanapale*. Apart from those, which were written according to prescribed competition rules, Berlioz's other choral cantatas are on patriotic themes. *Chant des chemins de fer* (Song of the railroads) was commissioned for outdoor performance during the July Monarchy of Louis-Philippe (1830–1848) to commemorate the burgeoning industrial revolution and construction of the new railroad line from Lille to Paris. *L'impériale*, composed during the Second Empire (1852–1870), was written to honor (that is, win favor with) then leader Napoléon III.

TWO CHORUSES FOR MEN

Two brief men's choruses with piano from Berlioz's early song collection, *Neuf mélodies*, are great fun to sing and listen to.

Chant guerrier (War Song)

Oh, to have been a tenor or bass in the streets of Paris in 1830 amidst the excitement and melee of the July Revolution. Charles X, the oppressive Bourbon monarch, was soon to be overthrown and replaced by a constitutional monarchy. Had we been there in the streets with Berlioz, we too would have sung his *Chant guerrier*, which he was startled to hear as he crossed the courtyard of the Palais Royal near where he lived. Yes, he joined in singing with the dozen or so young men! He had published *Neuf mélodies* at his own expense the prior January, so hearing a spontaneous rendition of *Chant guerrier* was not surprising—the singers were probably Orphéonists who learned it in rehearsals.

What a thrill to sing it with the composer—he even complained it was too slow! (The tempo is *Allegro non troppo* [fast but not too fast], pulse = 72). And how exciting it would have been to attend the first concert in which *Chant guerrier* was performed, December 5, 1830, in the Salle du Conservatoire. This was the same night and concert that Berlioz's signature work, *Symphonie fantastique*, was premiered. *Chant guerrier* introduced Berlioz's vocal music to a large concert audience and helped establish his place in the French choral tradition.

The poem, translated into French by Berlioz's friend Thomas Gounet from Thomas Moore's *Irish Melodies*, recalls sentiments surrounding Ireland's historic fight for freedom from English domination. Berlioz found Moore's poetry deeply compelling and ripe for composition, especially due to France's tenuous political climate and his enthrallment with Harriet Smithson and all things Irish. He wrote to his sister Nanci that Moore understood the art of music and knew its heights.

That said, at the time he was not yet able to read it in the original English.[3]

The rousing piano introduction and opening chorus refrain is a great start for a song about war: magnificent, determined piano chords open the work, followed by heroic voices in a rocket-like trajectory. But, actually, the message of the song is not a call to arms at all but rather a testament of commemoration. Tenor and basses in the refrain first tell us not to forget the field in which dust is tinged with our warriors' blood. Rather we must focus on our commonalities: remembrance and love of the land. The last phrase is sung twice for emphasis, surely to be delivered more exuberantly the second time. The tenor soloist in the first verse declares fallen men are owed our tears and a prayer, and, because of their sacrifice, freedom shines in our homes.

In verse 3, the bass soloist, a king, is thoughtful and giving. In contrast to Charles X, he recognizes the costs of conflict and wisely grants the people freedom without war. With grandeur and warmth, he sings a brand-new melody joined by a new hymnlike accompaniment: happiest are those who established their rights without having to battle against kings. Here Berlioz's advocacy for reconciliation shines through.

In another subtle touch, Berlioz gives the tenor soloist a short lead-in to each refrain (except the first) using its first phrase, *N'oublions pas* (let's not forget). Sung on a single unaccompanied note, it is like a pronouncement, and we are reminded that remembrance is a profound duty. In a fine performance, the tenor will interpret that phrase differently each time in response to the verse just sung. The styles of delivery for the soloist could be as follows: after verse 1, cheerful bravura, a call for a new world of equality that shall never end; after verse 2, solemnity of remembrance and commemoration; and after verse 3, celebration of a dream realized—imagining the transfer of power without loss of life.

Chanson à boire

Chanson à boire (Drinking song) resembles a robust English or German drinking song, and its sparkling piano accompaniment displays an effervescence often found in opera composer Rossini's party music. The text for the *Allegro frenetico* (frenetically lively, pulse = 112) opening refrain is, "Friends, our cup is foaming, its fire will revive us, good that this trial is passing, let us drown our sorrows!" Notice the stalwart, percussive "k" sounds (underlined), most of them on strong beats on the words "cup" (*coupe*), "foam" (*écume*), "who" (*que*), and then at the end of the phrase on "hearts" (*coeurs*): *Amis, la coupe écume; Que son feu, que son feu rallume Un instant nos cœurs!* The boisterous enthusiasm of the music is irresistible.

The two verses are in startling contrast to the refrain; they are slower, in triple meter rather than duple, and introspective. The tenor soloist begins unaccompanied and in a melancholic state as he descends into his lowest register: unnamed torments will not spare his soul. In a flourish of bold ascending melodic leaps, we learn his songs are echoes of his ardor and will always be heavy with tears. The voice rises and lingers on the second syllable of *toujours* (always) so that the soothing "oo" vowel feels just a bit everlasting. The sense of heaviness continues as the line unwinds while he sings *de larmes imprégnés* (tinged by tears).

In verse 1, two contrasting ideas are conveyed concurrently with the simplest of musical means, beginning with *Ce sourire qui rayonne . . .* (This smile that shines on my somber and pensive face is like the crown that decks a captive king). The pianist plays a dancing two-note pattern of neighboring half steps in the upper register; it begins ahead of the voice and persists like a hypnotic thread. In juxtaposition to it and the voice, the harmonies below slowly descend. The two distinct and interlocked layers in the accompaniment are reminiscent, respectively, of the captive king's radiant smile (two-note motif) and the tenor's destiny of torment (descending harmonies). We learn the smile is the king's crown, a totem that is both enigmatic and mournful. Likening his own smile to the king's, the tenor moves to his highest register on *couronne* (crown) but then falls into a dark color for *un roi captif* (a captive king) at the verse's end.

"There is fire in them, and tears," wrote Berlioz of *Neuf mélodies*, his early collection of *romances* and choruses.[4] Not only are *Chant guerrier* and *Chanson à boire* flashy and proud men's choruses, they are also imbued with great tenderness.

THE EXOTIC *SARA LA BAIGNEUSE* FOR THREE CHORUSES

In *Sara la baigneuse*, Berlioz set a long, suggestive, and playful poem by one of France's most revered romantic poets and his contemporary, Victor Hugo. It occupies a unique place among Berlioz's choral-orchestral compositions by virtue of its configuration for three intertwined and dialoguing choruses.

The Story

Outside Athens near the river Ilyssus, which runs south of the Acropolis, a lovely, lazy bather swings in a hammock above a pool brimming with spring water. Reeds line the banks, solemn and elegant plane trees provide shade, and flecks of sunshine refract on the water, dancing brightly. As she swings, our bather leans over to view her own lovely neck and ankle mirrored in the water's wrinkled surface. Her foot just grazes it, causing the reflection to ripple differently, and she laughs at the water's coolness. Such is the scene we encounter in the first four stanzas of *Sara la baigneuse* (Sara the bather), Berlioz's second setting of poems by Victor Hugo from *Les Orientales*.

The poet-narrator continues, to our surprise, by addressing his audience directly: if you stay hidden and wait, you'll see a vision of loveliness—a naked and shivering girl will step out from her morning bath, arms folded over her breasts, checking to see if anyone is coming. *Oh no!* With this change in point of view, we are unexpectedly drawn into a lighthearted but suggestive scene, only then to be caught ogling her! But Sara does not take her bath. She knows we are secretly watching her although we hadn't intended to. She reads our unacknowledged desires and plays a trick. Taking her time, she sings of an imagined bath: she is a sultaness in a marble pool near a throne with two griffins; she swings in a silk hammock, and her pillow gives off a perfume that arouses desire. Unhurried, confident, and alone, she can leave her clothes scattered on the flagstones. How wonderful, she will never fear being seen by "a pair of eyes aflame!" Again, oh no! Is that *us, our* eyes? We've been caught! Her friends, presumably peasants like her, walk nearby; they are going to the fields and tease her for being lazy during the harvest. We, the audience, are trapped and fooled, but we, like them, can be good-natured too.

Evolution of Versions

Berlioz crafted this lengthy poem of fourteen stanzas, six lines each, into a work of incredible originality. Scored for three choruses and orchestra, it is nearly cantata-like in length. As with many compositions, Berlioz was not satisfied with first tries. *Sara* was originally written in 1834, for men's four-part solo quartet (TTBB) and orchestra. It was premiered at the Salle du Conservatoire along with his men's quartet arrangement of *La belle voyageuse* with piano and the highlight of that evening, *Symphonie fantastique*. Was *Sara* too suggestive, too voyeuresque for men to be singing it by themselves, even in Paris? Perhaps, for in 1840 Berlioz conducted a new version with women: a soprano-tenor-tenor-bass (STTB) solo vocal quartet, mixed chorus, and orchestra. A review of it refers to charming hallucinations, voluptuous dreaminess, and the seductive combination of the quartet in dialogue with the chorus and orchestra. Sadly, both quartet versions are lost.[5]

Berlioz's third version, made in 1849 for three choruses and orchestra, was a configuration unique in his repertoire and unknown elsewhere: (1) four-part mixed chorus (STBB), (2) two-part women's chorus (SA), and (3) four-part men's chorus (TTBB). The expanded voicing of ten vocal lines involved more singers, particularly women. While the new format has more variety of texture and dialogue, it leaves unanswered which chorus is foreground and which is background at any given moment. A discerning conductor must decide and balance the sound accordingly. In many passages, the women provide a halo of a color, whereas the lush, close harmonies of men's voices draw the listener in the most. Only three performances during Berlioz's lifetime are known of the third version: two in Paris in 1850 and another in Baden-Baden in 1858, all conducted by Berlioz.

Finally, at Berlioz's request his friend Auguste Morel crafted a piano reduction of the orchestration for only two soloists, either soprano and contralto or tenor and bass, and much later Berlioz included it in his *Collection de 32/33 mélodies* collection of 1863/1864. If sung by only female soloists, was the suggestion of inappropriate male voyeurism reduced? Perhaps, but by then attitudes might have changed. More importantly, which version—solo duet with piano or triple chorus with orchestra—is Berlioz's best? Interestingly, some modern recordings use the third version's orchestration to accompany two female soloists, a conflation of his last two versions! Surely a *Sara la baigneuse* performed by three conversing choruses offers a lot more adventure and variety.

The Music

In his personal catalog, Berlioz added the description *quatuor madriga-lesque* (a madrigal-like quartet) to the title, showing he considered *Sara* to be chamber music (a madrigal is a secular vocal piece written for one voice per part) and, perhaps like numerous sixteenth-century madrigals, amorous or even sexually suggestive. But the term "madrigalism" also denotes musical illustration of a word or phrase. Here are some madrigal-like musical gestures in *Sara la baigneuse*.

- Gesture 1—Swaying hammock. The triple meter of the chorus (strong-weak-weak) is to be felt "in one" as a single pulse = 44. The short-long rhythm of the melody and harmony over this interior triple meter gives the impression of Sara swaying in a hammock and has a lovely lilt. The gesture is first played by the winds (piccolo, flute, oboe, two clarinets, three horns, and four bassoons) in the introduction, and then everyone sings it together in the same rhythm (homorhythmically). Strong text syllables match strong beats over the four-measure phrase: *Sara, belle d'indolence* (Sara, lovely and lazy). The hammock's weightiness at the beginning of the swing is followed by a delicious feeling of being suspended in the air at the top.
- Gesture 2—Flowing water. After the first phrase of text, strings play scale-like descending patterns of faster notes. They begin ahead of the swaying hammock (gesture 1) but then happen simultaneously. Gesture 2 repeats itself, but pitches are varied to add new interest and move along within the changing harmonies. It can be easily imagined as flowing water, ripples, or reflections in the pond that are constantly changing.
- Gesture 3—Breathless gaiety. Gesture 3 begins at the text *au-dessus Du bassin d'une fontaine* (over the pool of a spring) and recurs in varied iterations throughout the remainder of the work. One or more of the choruses sings fast repeated pitches on rapidly changing syllables. Although the tempo is leisurely, the syllables must be executed so quickly that they incite a flurry of trepida-

tion. The pitter-patter occurs at different pitch levels for each group of words, and phrase endings are adjusted to partner with different closing harmonic cadences. These closeouts are delicately pointillist and at times like a dancer's pirouette. Kudos to non-native speakers striving to sing so much French text so fast—there is plenty of tongue-twisting. While the overall effect is unhurried, the pitter-patter is breathless and elated.

- Gesture 4—Squiggle-wiggle of delight. Beginning at stanza 2 with the text *Et la frêle escarpolette* (And the fragile hammock), violins play four quick notes. It sounds like a squiggle or wiggle and is followed by several staccato notes. The other strings play only pizzicatos on first or second beats. Meanwhile flute, clarinet, and horn sustain chords to provide a serene backdrop. Each string part plays this squiggle-wiggle in conversation with other string sections while the three choruses sing a combination of gestures 1 and 3. *Three* gestures are happening simultaneously!

The most intriguing part of the composition begins at the fifth stanza with *Reste ici caché* (Rest hidden here) where the bassoons begin crazily bouncing up and down in octaves. Squiggle-wiggle gesture 4 is given to two flutes and heard over a long and sustained chromatic rise by vocal and instrumental bass lines. Piccolo and clarinet add pop and sparkle with chords that seemingly come out of nowhere, and strings add new pointillist quivers. These events, combined with the inexorably increasing volume, culminate at the description of Sara at her most titillating: she rises from her bath *toute nue* (all naked).

A few more of Berlioz's special touches and adjustments are important to note:

- Only men sing stanza 6, which describes her as a vision of loveliness, all wet and naked in the open air. Some women in the Paris chorus may have been uncomfortable singing the passage; in fact, women in the Baden-Baden performance complained the text was too revealing, so the objectionable phrases were replaced.
- Toward the end of stanza 6, just after *frissonne* (shivering) is sung, the strings shiver, another playful madrigalism.
- The music generates its own narrative by progressively introducing new gestures. In stanza 9, frolicking/chattering woodwinds; in

stanza 10, orchestra "pops" on weak beats as Sara romps naked beneath the sky; in stanza 12, a lovely descant on "ah" sung by tenors and sopranos in combination with gestures 1 and 2. At this moment music from the beginning returns in the same tonality, but it is not a simple repetition.

- In final stanza 14 Berlioz's treatment of *Oh, Oh, Oh, Oh* (gesture 1 and antiphonal calls and responds by the choruses) is totally tongue in cheek. Sara's friends are teasing her; they are as fun-loving as she.
- The coda, beginning with *La la la la*, is happily sung by all as the sturdy strings trudge along fading into the exotic Grecian landscape. The sustained *La la*'s end with a coquettish upward flick of a half step, again all in good fun.

VIGNETTE 2.1. *SARA LA BAIGNEUSE*: PARTBOOKS AND SECTIONALS

Janet and Thomas, members of a choral society in Washington, D.C., in 1991, are at their first rehearsal of Sara la baigneuse. *Using the newest music notation software, their chorus master has made partbooks for each voice section, sopranos, tenors, and basses, replicating the notation format Berlioz provided his singers. Janet and Thomas have been in different rooms for section rehearsals and get together at the refreshment table during break.*

Janet: What chorus are you in, 1 or 2 or 3? I can't believe we're not having a rehearsal all together before going into sectionals—this is backward. But kind of fun, I guess, too.

Thomas: I love this music! Who else but Berlioz would have thought of writing for three choruses? It's brilliant. With just my baritone line in this partbook (well, the bass is there too), I can truly focus on my notes and singing technique from the start, just like his singers! It's just us doing what we need to do, no distractions. I think sectionals are a really good use of time, and I feel so much better about my singing.

Janet: Well, singing from note to note like a flute player reading an orchestra part is certainly a new experience for me. With no piano accompaniment or other vocal parts in my score, I can't see what else is happening! I don't like this having to count rests while others sing or play—I actually have to listen *and* count at the same time! But you're right, I am concentrating better on my line. Miracle of all miracles, I might even get this memorized. Of course, opera singers do that all the time, and we should do it more.

Thomas: You know, I heard Berlioz brought string instruments into chorus rehearsals not only for teaching notes but also to role model how the vocal lines should be shaped. The idea of having a cello both demonstrate my line and play it with me is awesome. A piano's okay, but it's a percussion instrument so each note decays after it is struck. A string or wind instrument will crescendo or diminuendo a note like we're supposed to do. Our phrasing is going to have so much more lyricism, fewer uncalled-for accents, and more nuance.

Janet: Out of curiosity, I checked—our accompanist has the piano-vocal score, but it has only a soprano and alto part in it, not three choruses! How can that be? Meanwhile, the conductor has the full orchestral score with all ten parts—he's the only one who actually knows what we're singing, as well he should! Some diligent scribe needs to get busy working on making a piano-vocal score with all the choruses and accompaniment together. I say we all need to know what else is going on.

Thomas: Maybe there's just not enough room on the page for *everything* you want to see, Janet. Then you'd have to hold a big, heavy score, and the print would be so small. Let's keep it simple, save paper. By the way, I did take a sneak preview and listen to the orchestra version of *Sara*. Odd, the recording wasn't for three choruses, just two women soloists, same as the piano score you saw. But I have to tell you, after listening to that recording, I know we haven't heard half of what's going on in this piece. There are all sorts of fascinating bits of this and that in the instruments. If I knew my French better, I'd say the instruments are illustrating certain words and acting out specific emotions. The piano part doesn't sound nearly as intriguing.

Janet: Oh, that's *really* interesting. I heard when Berlioz performed this the three choruses didn't rehearse together or with the orchestra until the one and only tutti rehearsal just before the concert. That really is life of the wild side. Imagine hearing all those new colors and textures at the last minute!

Thomas: Well, I think *Sara* is going to be fabulous when we all combine. We're definitely going to be ready.

SINGING FOR FRANCE: *VIVE LA FRANCE! LA LIBERTÉ!*

Despite extreme devastation and lives lost in his wake, Napoléon I, emperor of France from 1804 to 1814, made an indelible impression, both heroic and tragic, on Berlioz. David Cairns has vividly described Berlioz's small provincial hometown, La Côte-St-André, during Napoléon's regime. For those at home, liberties were improving, agriculture was never short of laborers, and the military victories at Ulm, Austerlitz, Jena, and Wagram were celebrated. But nearly 180 men from the area had been drawn away for active service in the Grande Armée, and over time the losses took a toll. Berlioz's maternal uncle, Felix Marmion, was Berlioz's ideal soldier. A freewheeling cavalry officer in Napoléon's army, Marmion was gallant and high-spirited, an excellent singer of *opera-comique* songs, an amateur violinist, and dedicated to the roving life. To Marmion, Napoléon was the modern Alexander the Great, and his army represented a new age of discipline, martial vigor, esprit de corps, and the prospect of rapid advancement. For a time in France, the result was nearly universal personal devotion to the emperor. Berlioz too became fascinated with Napoléon. As Cairns describes, he "was under a spell so great that nothing subsequently—repugnance to war and conquest and all forms of human aggressiveness—could break it or reason it away."[6]

Having endured many defeats by January 1814, the Grande Armée was plundering its own local resources, having been backed up onto its own French soil. The empire was falling apart—taxes were burdensome, trade was declining, public morale had collapsed—and Napoléon was now despised. For safety, he traveled in disguise to the island of Elba off the Italian coast into exile. In April, Berlioz's hometown was occupied for a week by twenty thousand Austrian cavalry and infantry. Officers were billeted in the Berlioz household when Berlioz's mother was nursing his sister Adèle. He was eleven years old.

Despite witnessing France's demeaning defeat and occupation by enemy armed forces, Berlioz was a lifelong admirer of royalty and authoritarianism. He directly and indirectly expressed esteem for numerous authoritarian rulers over his lifetime, including Napoléon I and various German and Russian kings he met while on concert tours, and Napoléon III, emperor of France from 1852 to 1870. Around the time of the revolution of 1848, Berlioz even wrote statements excoriating representative forms of government. He advocated *liberté* more than *égalité*; that is, he was an elitist. The efficiencies of authoritarian, one-person rule made more sense to him than the messy process of elections and parliamentary governance. Considering that Berlioz in his music often defended the unjustly marginalized and misunderstood, his views on equality and governance are surprising. As a conductor, though, Berlioz had to be an authoritarian of sorts to rehearse and give fine performances. He also needed affirmation from whatever government was in power so he could finance and organize concerts in France.

Every ruler and government has used music to stir up civic loyalty, and protesters from the opposition inevitably march and sing to demand their rights. As an astute political observer and patriot, Berlioz wrote music for both sides. He was devoted to an idealized France, whose glory was won first in the French Revolution and again by Napoléon I in 1804–1814, according to many. During the following years of Berlioz's life, governance jolted back and forth between republican rule by equal representation and authoritarian rule by emperor or monarchy. Patriotic music composed by Berlioz during those five regimes is listed chronologically in appendix B, part 2.

Scène heroïque: la révolution grecque (Heroic scene: the Greek revolution)

Imagine Berlioz in 1824–1825. He has been in Paris just three years, having finished his *Bachelier ès sciences physiques* to please his father, and has studied composition privately for only two years. News of the Greeks' struggle for independence from the Ottomans is all over the newspapers. Their plight insults his sense of fairness and affronts his

affection for ancient Greece, which he acquired while reading the classics as a youth. As he writes the cantata *Scène heroïque: la révolution
grecque*, fresh musical ideas tumble out quickly, almost one on top of
the next. He even interrupts composition of his first completed opera,
Les francs-juges, in order to complete the task.

The first movement begins with a brass-dominated tutti, intense
digging and rustling by violins, and rumbling timpani, all of which demand our attention. What frenzy and freshness! The terrific opening
sets up a call-to-arms accompanied recitative: *Lève-toi, fils de Sparte!
Allons* (Arise, sons of Sparta, let's go!). The present-day Greeks are
accused of forgetting vengeance; instead, they are worshiping infamy
and shamefully forgoing liberty! No, get up and fight! The brass section
plays again, holding over beyond the other instruments as they did in
the beginning. Then the Greek hero (bass) sings a poignant melody, *O
mère des héros, terre chérie* (O mother of heroes, beloved soil), which is
beautifully introduced by strings playing gentle, falling patterns. Then
in succession, (1) the orchestra plays a surging rise, (2) the brass section
calls for entry of the Greek Priest as if in a glorious procession, and (3)
momentum increases as the Hero and Priest together rouse the Greeks
to arms. An inspiring, bravura men's chorus follows: *Hellènes, rassem-
blez vos tribus alarmées!* (Hellènes, unite your frightened people!). In a
tremendous call-and-response between soloists and men's chorus, Berlioz ratchets up excitement with faster and faster exchanges and unexpected harmonic twists and turns. Now all envision a victorious march
to liberty and immortality! The intensity and vigor here is mirrored in
Berlioz's other precocious youthful works, especially the overture to his
abandoned opera *Les francs-juges* and in *Messe solennelle* discussed in
chapter 4.

Le cinq mai

Also an earlier work, *Le cinq mai: chant sur la mort de l'Empereur
Napoléon* (The fifth of May: Song for the death of Emperor Napoléon)
is an unvarnished testament to Berlioz's adulation for Napoléon I. A
fifteen-minute cantata for bass soloist, chorus, and orchestra, it was
composed between 1829 and 1835 and was one of his most often performed compositions. The title is Napoléon's date of death.

Defeated by international allied forces, exiled, and imprisoned in ignominy, Napoléon Bonaparte died May 5, 1821, on the island of Sainte-Hélène. The narrator of the poem is a French soldier who has been captured by the Spanish opposition. As he approaches Sainte-Hélène by ship for his own imprisonment, he laments his helplessness to rescue his hero, and he decries the many betrayals suffered by Napoléon. When he sees the black flag of death on Sainte-Hélène, the soldier mourns, "Oh glory, how he has widowed you! All around me [even] his enemies sob."

The special potency of *Le cinq mai* comes alive in the orchestral introduction to verse 3. Four gestures in distinctly different instrumental timbres and pitch registers depict turbulence and angst. They appear additively, like component pieces of a toy or puzzle that can be fitted together in any layer, order, and space in time, and move in any direction:

- Gesture 1: Low strings play an octave leap in a piano-to-forte crescendo over just three beats; it sounds like the groan of an imaginary sea monster and is repeated in each measure.
- Gesture 2: Horns and bassoons together in the orchestra's middle register play stationary chords that, similarly to gesture 1, are rearticulated in every measure. Harmonies at first match those just heard and then change, and the long-short-long rhythm generates forward momentum.
- Gesture 3: Contrabasses enter next playing a quick four-note rising figure; it appears only in the gaps between "groans" (gesture 1) and also propels forward momentum.
- Gesture 4: A furiously played quick-note rising line in violins is added above this three-idea texture (gestures 1–3) and is repeated like the others; pitches are adjusted for unfolding harmonic progressions. The men's chorus enters for the first time in brilliant full force. They adamantly remind us of Napoléon's victories and betrayals, not once but twice, and tell us death is the crown of a victor's brow.

The refrain, *Pauvre soldat* (This poor soldier will see France again; the hand of a son will close my eyes), is the most poignant section of the cantata. The music came to Berlioz just as he was climbing out of the

Tiber River after having fallen in. In fact, the contours of the melody's four brief phrases seem a good match for pulling oneself up a river bank. Each phrase is brief, simple, and beautifully linked to the next; together they form a well-balanced pattern of fall–rise–fall–closure. Text and music are repeated, and the closing phrase is heartrendingly different. The four phrases are as follows:

1. Three-note fall in long notes; the last interval is chromatic. The effect is mournful, incomplete (*Pauvre soldat* [Poor soldier]).
2. Four-note rise on notes moving more quickly and in wider intervals; reaches just shy of the bass soloist's highest register. The last note is also chromatic and suspenseful (*je reverrai la France* [I will see France]).
3. Having arrived at the peak of the singer's register, the sequence of long-held notes and a falling pattern return. Phrase 3 balances phrase 1, but it is more of a cry of the heart (*La main d'un fils* [the hand of a son]).
4. A closing cadential turn employing faster-moving notes is similar in rhythmic configuration to phrase 2. The first time phrase 4 is sung, the cadence is deceptive—the harmony does not return to the home key. At the end of the second time, the home key is gently and forthrightly confirmed (*me fermera les yeux* [will close my eyes]).

The first performance of *Le cinq mai* in 1835 was pivotal for Berlioz on two counts. He was seated in the audience while conductor Narcisse Girard, standing with violin bow in hand and facing the audience as was the custom, started the first fast section in the wrong tempo. The swift crescendo into the *forte* entrance of woodwinds and horn, which emulates the soldier's excitement at sighting St. Hélène in the distance, was botched! The players were not prepared for such an extreme difference in tempo from what they had rehearsed, and all the notes fell out in a messy heap. Berlioz realized such incompetence could only be remedied by conducting his own music, which he subsequently did for all his compositions except *Les Troyens*.

The other problem lies with the text. Pierre-Jean de Béranger was a widely respected author of political poems sung to popular folk song melodies and, like Berlioz, was an ardent devotee of Napoléon. Although he chose Béranger's poem, Berlioz knew it was not well written. After *Le cinq mai*, he became more discriminating in his choices. Berlioz engaged a good librettist for *Roméo et Juliette* and he wrote the librettos for much of *La damnation de Faust* and all of *L'enfance du Christ* and *Les Troyens* himself.

In 1840 Napoléon's ashes were brought by ship to France and carried in a ceremonial catafalque (ornamental container on a platform) by horse-drawn cortege from the Courbevoie docks into central Paris. There on December 15, the ashes were enshrined in grandeur beneath the dome of the Invalides in the same building complex where Berlioz's *Requiem* was performed in 1837. Imagine Berlioz standing in the street that December 15, 1840, as the cortege passed by and later at the ceremony at Invalides. He had hoped to witness a splendid national event with cannonades of five hundred rounds and majestic funeral marches by grand ensembles. But the day was placid, and only disparate snatches of music could be heard as bands marched by. The performance of Mozart's *Requiem* in the church seemed anything but Napoleonic; it was unsuited to the immense scale of the catafalque and the processional, let alone the magnitude of the Napoléon myth. Berlioz wrote in his *Mémoires* that he wept for "our sublime emperor" and felt his tears freeze—not from the cold but from shame.[7]

Hymne à la France

Imagine you are in Paris in 1844 and you've heard that the Exhibition of French Industry will be held near the Champs-Elysées. Berlioz and his co-organizer, Isaac Strauss ("maestro of fashionable balls" as Berlioz described him),[8] have decided to stage a mass choral-orchestral performance in the Palais de L'Exposition, the temporary structure being erected especially for the event. No one has forgotten the grand *style énorme* (enormous style) music used in large outdoor festivals and processionals in years past, but several tiers of government ministers must be persuaded to issue permits and fund the idea. This is not an easy task since no music ceremonies occurred in past exhibitions, only displays of music instruments. Recently Britain, Germany, and cities in northern France had put on grand music festivals similar to what Berlioz and Strauss have in mind, so the ministers agree.

Berlioz designs the entire program. The music will be by well-known French and German composers Spontini, Auber, Beethoven, Rossini, Weber, Mendelssohn, Halévy, and Meyerbeer, and he will premiere his own six-minute *Hymne à la France* (Hymn to France). Ever the entrepreneur and patriot, Berlioz elevates public art and his country's image at home and abroad by assembling a massive chorus and orchestra. David Charlton relates that the handbill distributed before the event advertised 140 sopranos, 130 tenors, and 130 basses for the chorus, and an orchestra of 364 including 238 strings, for a total of 764 performers.[9] Berlioz has recruited paid musicians from multiple cities, and numerous volunteers from Paris and beyond are also playing and singing, including children who will sing the soprano part. Because the chorus is so enormous, the choral parts were printed rather than hand-copied, as was customary for a premiere. To save paper, singers share partbooks, probably three singers per copy. Imagine the crowding onstage, the expectations, excitement, and the spectacle!

How did Berlioz pull off this extraordinary extravaganza? Each performer had only two rehearsals, but Berlioz led a total of ten. First, he held a separate section rehearsal for each instrument or vocal group: violins, violas and cellos, string basses, woodwinds, brass, harps, and percussion, plus one for the women and children of the chorus (more than 140 singers) and one for men (260 singers). Berlioz led a marathon of nine sectionals. During the second rehearsal for performers, which was the only one for everyone together before the concert, reports came back from the audience seats that the orchestra could not be heard. Most if not all the players were positioned behind the chorus, as was usual at the time, but its sound was blocked because the chorus platforms were too high. Consequently, the entire stage had to be rebuilt at once, causing an unfortunate delay.

What sort of music would you or I choose for these forces on this occasion and for such a large space? A six-minute work of four verses and a refrain sounds right. It definitely must not be a quickstep march in the style of *Hymne des Marseillaise*. Rather, the music must be slow, dignified, and not too subtle or complicated but also not plain. And it must be easy to learn in the limited rehearsal time it is sharing with the five other choral works on the concert.

Berlioz's refrain, marked *andante maestoso* (walking pace, majestic; pulse = 48) in 4/4 meter, sounds resplendent and reminds us of a royal procession. *We* are France! *We* are royalty! The verses, by contrast, are tender yet still grand. They move more quickly and are in a different meter: *moderato* (moderate, slightly faster than *andante*; pulse = 76) in 3/4 meter.

Each vocal section has its own verse in which to showcase the fine art of singing a great melody. Balancing ingenuity with practicality, Berlioz made the melody of the verse in a comfortable range so that everyone could sound terrific regardless of his or her voice category. At the same time, their different vocal colors caused each verse to sound unique. Verse 1, for all tenors, speaks of France as a noble child of heaven, a country unparalleled on earth whose name is sweeter than honey. The long, memorable tune is in seven phrases equal in length; phrases 5 and 6 are the most intriguing because of harmonic wanderings and increasing intensity.

Sopranos and children are next for verse 2: the face of France is more beautiful than the whitest lily; she possesses grace, her eyes shine with intelligence, and she wears a divine headband as a crown. All 130 basses take the melody in verse 3, and in it the sopranos and tenors respond and join in phrase by phrase: bloody wars of the past are vividly remembered, not only for the wrath displayed but also for the readiness to forgive. In verse 4, all sing in unison nearly all the time. God is addressed directly: you who hold the fate of the universe in your hand, deign to shed a loving glance on our mother, France, and make sure she advances tall among the great nations.

Meticulous in all aspects of this precedent-setting venture, two months earlier Berlioz promoted the event by distributing the text of *Hymne à la France* in printed handbills. They even indicated which voice part was to sing each verse. If audience members happened to bring the handbill to the concert, or if more were distributed there, surely by the second or third verse everyone could be singing along! Undoubtedly the men who were reported standing and waving their hats and calling for the repeat of the final verse and refrain were singing at the top of their voices, too: *Dieu protége la France!* (May God protect France!). *Hymne à la France* was received ecstatically by an audience of about eight thousand despite the dry acoustics (little if any ring or reverberation) in the gargantuan space.

Over Berlioz's lifetime six more performances of *Hymne à la France* were given in Paris, Marseilles, and Lyons. For these Berlioz improved the original, straightforward orchestral accompaniment by adjusting textures and gestures to generate ever-mounting excitement from verse to verse. All performances were under his direction and with smaller forces except for the last. At the huge Paris Universal Exhibition of 1867, roughly 1,200 performed it, according to the stated number printed in the full score—a chorus of five hundred and orchestra of seven hundred. The audience was 14,500.

The 1848 Revolution against Louis-Philippe and Three Choruses with Piano

- *Hymne des Marseillais* for tenor, mixed chorus, and piano
- *La menace des Francs: marche et chœur*, for men's four-part solos or small chorus, mixed chorus, and piano
- *L'apothéose*, for solo voice, mixed chorus, and piano

From the glorious premiere of *Hymne à la France* in 1844 and relative political calm politically, jump four years forward to a period of tumult. It is February 1848, and Berlioz is now in London for the first of his five residencies there. News of the revolution in Paris has reached London. King Louis-Philippe, for whom Berlioz holds little affection or allegiance, has escaped amidst upheaval and rioting. Although Berlioz has no more scheduled engagements in London, it is unwise to return to Paris while the chaos persists. There is also no clear sign of potential employment for him there, and unpaid bills are due. As it is, he is barely managing to support both his mistress, Marie Récio, and his wife, Harriet Smithson.

During the extended stay in London, Berlioz rearranged *Hymne des Marseillais* for tenor, chorus, and piano,[10] and newly composed *L'apothéose* (derived from *Grande symphonie funèbre et triomphal*, mvt 3) to be an independent chorus for solo voice, chorus, and piano. Now both works could be sung almost any time anywhere! In addition, he composed *La menace des Francs* for tenor and bass soloists or small ensemble, chorus, and piano. All three were readied for immediate publication in London. Sensing his own personal vulnerability along with that of his country, Berlioz began compiling his *Mémoires*; he was only forty-five.

If anyone could reach *le peuple* (the people) through music, capture their ardor, and stir them to claim their rightful freedoms back home in France, it was Berlioz. He chose vivid, thrilling texts, some of which today are considered over the top:

- *La menace des Francs*: Armed with iron and flames, the entire people will march against the king.
- *Hymne des Marseillais*: Do you not hear the savage roar of the enemy soldiers coming right into our arms to cut your throats? All citizens, to arms! March on! Let impure blood water our furrows.
- *L'apothéose*: Glory and triumph to these heroes, glory and respect for their tombs. Come, chosen ones from the next life! May the blood-soaked flags of these valiant soldiers hang resplendent at the fore of the heavens!

All three choruses are in strophic form, have thrilling tunes and harmonies, and are intended for *everyone* to sing. The refrains in particular are easily learned and meant to be sung while marching in the streets and plazas, in theaters or homes, with or without accompaniment, and in unison or harmonized. *L'apothéose* is an especially fine but overlooked example of French celebratory indoor/outdoor music at its most accessible and enjoyable. Thinking of his homeland's predicament, Berlioz felt sure *L'apothéose* would quickly catch on in Paris if only it could be published there, too.

A CONDUCTOR'S JOURNEY AND A LISTENER'S PLAYLIST

As a young choral-orchestral conductor, I came under Berlioz's spell while preparing two extended choral-orchestral works for performance, *L'enfance du Christ* and *Grande messe des morts*. Having experienced them firsthand from inside out, I wanted my musicians and audiences to enjoy more of his music. What else is out there? Are there any shorter choral works with piano? What about songs?

In a stroke of incredible good luck, I came across *Collection de 33 mélodies pour chant et piano à une ou plusieurs voix et chœur* (33 melodies for voice and piano, for one or more voices and chorus) published in 1864.[11] It contains not only songs, some of which I knew, but also eleven works for chorus as well. Seemingly everything I was looking for was here under one cover, and Berlioz put it all together himself!

Collection de 32/33 mélodies [12] is comprised of previously published songs and choruses composed between 1829 and 1863. It is a treasure trove of his brief vocal works, not all but most. At the time of publication, he was age sixty to sixty-one, had been a librarian at the Conservatoire for many years, and recently had become a member of the prestigious Institut de France. He believed the moment to properly gather together his *mélodies* (songs and choruses) for reintroduction to the public had arrived. The collection shines a light on his enduring belief in the importance of his vocal miniatures.

I discovered, however, that Berlioz did not include some of his most wonderful vocal works. His fabulous *Le roi de Thulé* from *La damnation de Faust* and *Premiers transports* from *Roméo et Juliette*, two of his greatest songs, are missing. While some patriotic choruses are there, his arrangement of *Hymne des Marseillais* and his own *L'apothéose* are not. In effect, he gathered together almost all his songs and choruses that are not in extended works, and he excluded youthful works and arrangements.

Throughout his life, Berlioz was meticulous about the published presentation of his music. He personally oversaw and proofread all his music for errors—how the notation looked on the page, accuracy of notes, text, performance directions, and articulations—everything. Unfortunately, some scores prepared after Berlioz's death contain hidden edits, such as changing a dynamic mark over one note to apply to a group of notes, altering instrumentation, rewriting piano accompaniments, and more. To have a first print of *32/33 mélodies* prepared under Berlioz's supervision was golden. No editors had intervened to make undocumented changes, and most of his vocal works are there in one volume. So, I thought, why not put together a Berlioz soirée—an evening's entertainment of solos, duets, small ensembles, and choruses? For a listener's companion, how about a soirée playlist?

There is no surefire method or recipe for putting together a program or, for that matter, a playlist. Assembling a coherent, engaging concert requires similar skills to composing: establish overall mood and narrative, recognize and maximize textual and musical threads, follow ideas, and take risks. For a sample listener's playlist accompanied only by piano, let's include a few overlooked songs and choruses by Berlioz, most of which are referred to or discussed in chapters 1 and 2. These are all gems. Voicings are indicated to assist in listening for different registers and number of parts singing and for enjoying their colors and moods. Use the "Selected Listening" list and appendixes A and B to locate a good recording of the version you'd like to hear, and gather together texts and translations from liner notes and internet resources. Imagine yourself as one of the singers, or the conductor, the pianist, the poet, or the composer—or even a chef—it's a musical banquet!

A Sample Playlist of Songs and Choruses: *Vive Berlioz!*

I. Bravura and Contemplation; mixed chorus

- *L'apothéose** (recomposed 1848 for piano from mvt 3 of *Grande symphonie funèbre et triomphale*), mixed six-part chorus
- *Méditation religieuse* (1831, reduction by Matteman 1849), mixed six-part chorus, violin, and cello
- *L'adieu des bergers** from *L'enfance du Christ* (1850), mixed four-part chorus

II. Loss; women's chorus

- *La mort d'Ophélie* (1842 in B♭, rev for orchestra 1848 in A♭, reduced for piano 1863 in A♭), two-part women's chorus

III. Valor and Remembrance; men's chorus

- *Chanson à boire* (1829), men's four-part chorus, tenor solo
- *Chant guerrier* (1829), men's four-part chorus, tenor and bass solos

IV. Love Songs and Good Stories (choose four or five); solo, trio, or duet

- *Amitié, reprends ton empire** (1819–1821, rev 1823), trio for soprano, mezzo-soprano, and bass soloists
- *Le trébuchet* (1846), duet for soprano and mezzo-soprano
- *La belle voyageuse* (1829), mezzo-soprano

- *La belle Isabeau* (before 1843), mezzo-soprano with five-part mixed chorus in a brief refrain
- *Premiers transports*° from *Roméo et Juliette* (1839), mezzo-soprano, brief choral refrain, and cello
- *La captive*° (February 1832, rev December 1832), mezzo-soprano and cello[13]
- *Le chasseur Danois* (1844, reduced for piano in 1845), bass
- *Zaïde* (1845, orchestra version reduced for piano later in 1845), soprano and castanets
- *Élégie en prose*, tenor (1829)

V. *Vive la France!* for mixed chorus

- *Hymne à la France* (1844; pv reduction 1850), mixed six-part chorus (Berlioz performed it with children added to sopranos)
- *La menace des Francs* (1848), four-part male soloists or small men's ensemble, mixed six-part chorus
- *Hymne des Marseillais*° (1830) for double chorus of three-part men and six-part mixed chorus and orchestra (Berlioz performed it with children added to the soprano line); arr 1848 for tenor solo, six-part mixed chorus, and piano.[14]

Note: All titles are in piano-vocal versions published by Berlioz; most are also in orchestral-vocal versions. Works not in *32/33 mélodies* are indicated by an asterisk.

3

ORCHESTRAL MUSIC

Having started from a deep love of literature and a modest early grounding in flute, guitar, and singing, Hector Berlioz's vivid imagination soared while writing symphonies and overtures. The orchestra became Berlioz's expressive vehicle—his "instrument," his "voice"—and he conducted orchestral, choral-orchestral, and opera music in countless performances. As is evident in two of his books, *Treatise on Instrumentation and Orchestration* and *Evenings with the Orchestra*, Berlioz studied instruments as a biologist would an organism, and he analyzed behaviors of players as a psychologist would a patient.

SYMPHONIES OVERVIEW

Berlioz's four symphonies are listed by date of composition and publication. As seen elsewhere, he usually delayed publication until he had performed a work multiple times and could revise and proof it. *Symphonie fantastique* and *Roméo et Juliette* are discussed in this chapter.

1. *Symphonie fantastique: épisode de la vie d'un artiste* (1830, published 1845 in full score) to be followed in concert by its lesser-known sequel, *Le retour à la vie: mélologue en six parties*, later called *Lélio, ou le retour à la vie* (1831, mvts 1, 3, and 4 published in vocal score in 1833; published in full score 1855).[1]

2. *Harold en Italie: symphonie,* with viola solo (1834, published 1848).
3. *Roméo et Juliette: symphonie dramatique* (1839, published 1847) with alto, tenor, and bass soloists; petite chorus of alto, tenor, and bass; and mixed double chorus.
4. *Grande symphonie funèbre et triomphale,* for military band (1840, published 1843); strings and mixed chorus singing the first version of *L'apothéose* text and music were added *ad libitum* in 1842 for concert performance.

Berlioz wrote his symphonies over ten years, 1830–1840, completing them well before the halfway mark of his thirty-eight years of composing major works.[2] His first, *Symphonie fantastique,* is the most popular today followed by *Harold en Italie, Roméo et Juliette,* and *Grande symphonie funèbre et triomphale.* Interestingly, their order of popularity (high to lower) parallels their order of composition (early to later).

Based on the success of his first two symphonies, Berlioz became renowned early in his career as an important, if unconventional, composer and a native son of whom France could be proud. His most notable choral work to date, *Grande messe des morts* of 1837, complemented those successes, but the failure of his first opera, *Benvenuto Cellini,* in January 1839 broke the spell. Notably, his last two symphonies include voices, an uncommon but not surprising bending of expectations at the time.[3] Subsequent to *Grande symphonie funèbre et triomphale,* almost all of Berlioz's compositions were for voices and instruments. Whereas the orchestra was his "voice," the ineffable partnership of instruments with singing was his predominant expressive vehicle.

Rather than numbering his symphonies, as earlier and later composers often have done, Berlioz named them and their movements within. At the time, naming was customary for overtures associated with plays or operas but not yet for symphonies.[4] His first symphony, based on a narrative he devised, was derived in part from a mixture of contemporary literary influences; the next two were based on an epic poem and a play, respectively. The last was commissioned for a ceremony to commemorate lives lost in the July Revolution of 1830 and was played in a procession through the streets of Paris.

OVERTURES OVERVIEW

Berlioz's eight overtures are listed by date of composition and publication.[5] Two were published posthumously and therefore not proofed by the composer. Two are discussed with their associated opera, *Benvenuto Cellini*, in chapter 5: *Benvenuto Cellini: ouverture* and *Le carnaval romain*.

1. *Les francs-juges: ouverture* (opera composed 1826, revised 1829; overture published 1836; opera never completed)
2. *Waverley: grande ouverture* (1826–1828, published 1839)
3. *Le roi Lear: grande ouverture* (1831, published 1839)
4. *Intrata di Rob-Roy Macgregor* (1831, published 1900)
5. *Benvenuto Cellini: ouverture* (opera composed 1836–1838, overture and selections published 1838)
6. *Le carnaval romain: ouverture caractéristique* (1843, published 1844), based on material from the opera *Benvenuto Cellini*
7. *Le corsair: ouverture* (1844, published 1852)
8. *Béatrice et Bénédict: ouverture* (opera composed 1860–1862, overture published separately 1892; opera published 1907)

Berlioz composed his eight overtures either to open an opera or as single concert pieces. They are short, ranging from eight to sixteen minutes, and are all upbeat. Many are audience favorites, appreciated as much for showcasing the composer's creative panache as for the feats of technical and sonic brilliance required of the orchestra. He wrote them continuously throughout his career, similarly to his songs and choral works. Like the symphonies, they all relate to a narrative and are titled. Literary sources include Sir Walter Scott novels—for *Waverley* and *Intrata di Rob-Roy Macgregor*; a James Fenimore Cooper novel— for *Le corsair*; and the autobiography of a sixteenth-century goldsmith and sculptor—for *Benvenuto Cellini* and *Le carnaval romain*. Two are based on Shakespeare plays— *King Lear* for *Le roi Lear* and *Much Ado About Nothing* for *Béatrice et Bénédict*. Three overtures were written to open operas: *Les francs-juges*, of which only the overture and fragments survive;[6] *Benvenuto Cellini*; and *Béatrice et Bénédict*. The remaining five are stand-alone concert pieces, including *Le carnaval romain*, which is based on music in *Benvenuto Cellini*.

Today the custom is to perform overtures at the beginning of a concert, but in the nineteenth century they were placed at the end or beginning, or just before intermission. Often two overtures were performed in one evening.

SYMPHONIE FANTASTIQUE: ÉPISODE DE LA VIE D'UN ARTISTE (FANTASTIC SYMPHONY: EPISODE IN THE LIFE OF AN ARTIST)

> I was just about to begin my grand symphony [*Épisode de la vie d'un artiste*], where I am going to portray my infernal passion. It's all in my head, but I can't write anything. We'll wait.
> —Letter to Humbert Ferrand, Berlioz's friend and librettist on other projects; Paris, February 6, 1830.[7]

So began, or almost began, composition of the symphony that would lift Berlioz to international stature. Of all his works, it is the one most often performed today.

How the Music First Captures Us

When listening to the first two measures of the opening *Largo* (very slow), we may wonder if this could have been the passage that broke his writer's block disclosed in the passage above. Soft, delicately dancing notes played by woodwinds begin on one pitch and then lean into a sustained minor chord, an arrival point. This fleeting opening "bouquet" of lightness and tenderness sends a clear message: it comes from an as yet undisclosed place of fragility and naïveté, a place of longing and hope. By resting on that minor sonority, Berlioz gives us time to absorb, savor, and wonder at the possibilities such an arresting soundworld may hold. Already we are captured, transfixed, and made vulnerable. Having been caught in this strange web, we can hardly wait for the story to unfold.

From that soft, sustained, and minor woodwind chord, violins alone emerge to play the same single pitch from the opening. The melody that follows is plaintive, hesitant, and searching; it is given exclusively to violins and accompanied by the rest of the strings. We would probably never guess it came from one of Berlioz's earliest *romances* composed when he was about sixteen and still awash in his first feelings of love for Estelle Duboeuf (later Estelle Fornier). The melody, still in his head at age twenty-seven, was perfect to use here in the introduction. And so, from that brief, simple sonic "bouquet" and a melody from his child-hood, the symphony begins.

His youthful infatuation with Estelle was likely not the "infernal passion" he wrote of in his letter to Ferrand. By then he had recently encountered Harriet Smithson, the Irish Shakespearean actress re-nowned for her talent as a mime. When he saw her in *Hamlet* and *Roméo et Juliette* in 1827, his life was turned completely inside out. The *idée fixe* theme in the following *Allegro agitato* of mvt 1 emblemizes his intense infatuation with her and, undeniably, the imperative to find a voice for it. The only remedy was composition. But Harriet initially spurned his approaches, and Berlioz composed most of the symphony while involved with someone else, the pianist Camille Moke, to whom he was briefly engaged. Surely *Symphonie fantastique* would never have materialized had Harriet not turned Berlioz away.

The Journey

Symphonie fantastique was among only several works that Berlioz pre-served from his tumult of creativity during 1824 through 1830. Salient contributing forces to its composition include works of literature he newly encountered since moving to Paris; the "Estelle melody" from an early *romance* mentioned above; a new intensity of expression he found when writing a later *romance*, *Élégie en prose*; a theme he composed in 1828 for a cantata that became the famous *idée fixe*; and the influence of the three women with whom he had fallen in love.

A voracious reader, Berlioz discovered the latest works at the fore-front of progressive and romantic thought in Paris: *Faust* by Johann Wolfgang von Goethe (translated by Gérard de Nerval, 1828), *Contes fantastiques* (Fantastic tales) by E. T. A. Hoffmann (Paris, 1829), *Confessions d'un anglais mangeur d'opium* (Confessions of an English user of opium) by Thomas de Quincey (translated by Alfred de Musset, 1829), *René* by François-René de Chateaubriand (1802); and *Cromwell*, a play by Victor Hugo as well as his collection of poems, *Odes et ballades* (1826). These and the plays of Shakespeare ignited Berlioz's highly susceptible imagination and influenced his choice of subjects and narratives.

Two previously composed *romances* are cornerstones for the symphony, one thematic and the other expressive. The first is the "Estelle melody" heard immediately after the brief sonic "bouquet" of the opening *Largo*. In his *Mémoires* Berlioz tells of his adolescent love for Estelle, who was six years older than him, and the *romance* that he wrote with her in mind, *Je vais donc quitter pour jamais* (I will therefore leave forever). At the time, he also secretly read and reread a pastoral play, *Estelle et Némorin* by Jean-Pierre Claris de Florian (1755–1794), which he found in his father's library. When the "Estelle melody" came back to him in 1830, he later stated, "It seemed to me exactly right for expressing the overpowering sadness of a young heart first caught in the toils of a hopeless love."[8] For its reincarnation in the symphony, Berlioz added new intensity by setting it higher, and he placed it in a far more expressive texture than the simple quasi-guitar accompaniment of the original song.[9]

His pent-up passions also found their way into *Symphonie fantastique* via composing another *romance, Élégie en prose* (Elegy in prose), the last in his 1829 *Neuf mélodies* collection.[10] Of all Berlioz's early individual songs, *Élégie* is the outlier—the piano part has roaring tremolandos, arabesques, swells, and abrupt changes, and virtuosic singing by the tenor is requisite. Clearly the song is more suited for the climax of an opera scene than a *romance*, and Berlioz knew the story of *Symphonie fantastique*—passionate love and the disastrous consequences of rejection—demanded a breadth of expression that only an orchestra could provide. So, he set himself to match his musical resources to the subject at hand.

Surprising as it may be to many, the famous *idée fixe* (fixed or constant idea) first heard in the subsequent *Allegro* section was not composed originally for the symphony. Berlioz borrowed it from the opening instrumental passage of his 1828 Prix de Rome cantata *Herminie*. After all, there was no reason for him to relegate a good theme into obscurity simply because the cantata had not won the award! But more importantly, the melody was his best effort to date, and it spoke to him deeply. In its first appearance in the symphony, the theme represents the elegant, noble character of his ideal beloved. It also embodies his yearning and emotional vulnerability, the *vague des passions* (vague, confused feelings of passion) he had read about and already experienced. Then throughout the symphony the theme is transformed.

Finally, three women, Estelle, Harriet, and Camille, are eternally enshrined in *Symphonie fantastique*. Although Estelle turned away Berlioz's attentions when he was twelve, they became gentle friends as widow and widower in the final chapter of his life. The second, Harriet Smithson, is the acknowledged *cause célèbre*. Harriet's rejection of him influenced the later episodes in *Symphonie fantastique* during which the artist-hero-lover dreams he has killed his beloved. She, an image of Harriet, morphs into a horrible witch and joins in an orgiastic dance, and he dies by guillotine.

The third female influence on *Symphonie fantastique* was Camille Moke. Having been rejected by Harriet, Berlioz fell in love with Camille during the months he was completing the symphony. A piano teacher at the girls' school where he taught guitar, Camille likely spread malicious gossip surrounding Harriet and her manager, helping Berlioz steer away from his fixation on Harriet. Following the first performance of *Symphonie fantastique* on December 5, 1830, Camille and Berlioz became engaged. But she left him for a wealthy businessman, soon becoming Camille Pleyel, part of the prominent Parisian family that manufactured pianos and managed a small Paris concert hall.

Two years later, upon his return from his required residency in Rome, having finally won the coveted prize, mutual friends arranged a meeting between Harriet and Berlioz after a *Symphonie fantastique* performance. While seated in the audience, Harriet gradually realized the music was about her. Despite the language disparity, they married a year later, in 1833, and had a son, Louis. Sadly, their union was happy for only a few years, yet those were among his most productive years of composing. Berlioz and Harriet became estranged in about 1841, when he took on a mistress whom he later married. Harriet died in 1854.

The Program and *Idée Fixe*

Berlioz provided audiences with a printed narrative program starting with the first performance in 1830. Over the years, however, he realized the sensational aspects of the story captured more attention than the music itself. As a result, in his preface to the second printing of the full score, in 1855, he noted, "If the symphony is performed on its own as a concert piece [that is, without *Lélio*, during which the artist-hero-lover is reawakened], one may even dispense with distributing the program and keep only the titles of the five movements. The author hopes that the symphony provides on its own sufficient musical interest independently of any dramatic intention."[11] Consequently, rather than dictating how the listener "should hear" the music, Berlioz hoped the music itself would inspire the listener's own imagination, which he believed would be far more compelling than anything provided in a program.

The *idée fixe* is a theme, a manifestation in music of the artist-hero-lover's "beloved," Harriet, and his feelings toward her. Initially she is an ideal—perfect and alluring beyond his wildest imagination. His love is noble, shy, and made utterly transparent to us, and a feeling of infatuation pursues him incessantly. The *idée fixe* is "fixed" in intervallic pitch relationships and rhythmic proportions so that it is the same but different and recognizable despite having been altered. As the story unfolds and her character and his feelings for her change, so too does the *idée fixe* and its surroundings. Of course countless other musical ideas and strategies populate the symphony—Berlioz did not write five movements using one theme. But to satisfy natural curiosity, its appearances are identified in the movement-by-movement discussion below. All transformations reflect his evolving relationship to his "beloved" and progressive states of being in and out of love.

One way to open your imagination is to first listen to a movement, read the passage about it below, listen again, and then read Berlioz's program in appendix C.

Mvt I: *Rêveries—Passions* (Reveries—Passions)

Largo (pulse = 60) in 4/4 meter; *Allegro agitato e appassionato assai* (pulse = 132) in 4/4 meter; 14 minutes

After Berlioz's breathless "bouquet" (described above) opens the symphony, first violins present the Estelle theme. It proceeds plaintively, pausing at times as though to capture a new unspoken thought of the artist-hero-lover or to allow us time to process what has just been heard. It is a singable melody, long but in short phrases, and a falling interval occurs at the end of nearly every phrase. The slow, inexorable rise to the highest pitch exudes yearning; the same feeling continues into the next two phrases with perhaps shyness and uncertainty mixed in. Violins play in a comfortable medium-high register, which ensures a solid, confident tone and nuanced expressiveness. The rest of the strings respond to the theme in dialogue and support, as if in conversation with it.

Berlioz doesn't bring closure to the Estelle theme. Instead he shifts into an exuberant interlude hinting at frenzied thoughts and emotions. Horn and clarinet play a loping tune in a totally new timbre and richer texture; they are accompanied by other winds pulsing in the background and by strings in harp-like upward sweeps. The Estelle theme returns in the violins, but now the flute and clarinet enliven it with delightful arabesque patterns; later the woodwinds play what seem to be heart palpitations. This entire second statement of the Estelle melody is more noble, urgent, and full of portent. As the texture clears, we hear a solo horn, as if announcing a new event or state of being.

The *idée fixe* at the beginning of the *Allegro* is also singable, despite its genesis as an instrumental theme from *Herminie*. The theme became so popular, in fact, that Berlioz heard it sung in the streets of Prague when he was there on a concert tour in the 1840s. It is long, too, but moves quickly, furtively. After the quick flick of an anticipatory note and two widely spaced rising intervals, the pitches lengthen and move mostly conjunctly and downward. The theme's phrase structure and length in measures (see table 3.1) is refreshingly imbalanced, although it doesn't seem so when listening to it. It is forty measures in length.

Table 3.1.   *Idée fixe* phrase structure in *Symphonie fantastique*

Phrase	Measures	Description
a	8	anticipation note; two widely spaced rising intervals; notes lengthen and move mostly conjunctly and downward
a'	7	similar to phrase *a* but beginning at a lower pitch level
b	17	four subphrases (4 + 4 + 4 + 5) similar to each other; each climbs higher than the previous
c	9	starts high and works its way downward with widely spaced falling intervals, stopping at a fermata and ending with triplet rhythms

The *idée fixe* appears four times in mvt 1:

1. At the beginning of the *Allegro*, violins and flute play the *idée fixe* accompanied by lower strings in a syncopated heartbeat-like

rhythm. Listen to it several times to consider how Berlioz varies its surrounding accompaniment, which starts out quite sparingly and then is enriched by new ideas, patterns, and more instruments. Singing and memorizing the *idée fixe* will help you recognize it in future guises.

2. Long passages of development and transition include fragments of the *idée fixe* in call-and-respond juxtaposition. A contrasting and quite brief second theme is played three times by strings, each time separated by fragments of the *idée fixe*. Starting high, it quickly works downward in an exuberant convulsion of joy; by the third time, most of the orchestra has joined in. The next full statement of the *idée fixe* is played by flute, clarinet, and bassoon and accompanied by palpitating broken chords (notes of chords played separately rather than simultaneously) in strings.

3. The *idée fixe* now is a robust, snappy march played by brass, woodwinds, and violas. At full force, the orchestra declares the artist-hero-lover's delirium. His vulnerability at the opening has been transformed into sheer joy and confidence.

4. The dense texture clears out to reveal only solo woodwinds, and the tempo loosens. Part of the first phrase of the *idée fixe* is played softly and in swift succession by clarinet, then oboe, and then bassoon—the process of thematic fragmentation has begun. Their entries are accompanied by intermittent double bass heartbeats. After another intense flurry of activity, violins alone play the *idée fixe* first phrase, and the movement closes with solemn chords of portent.

Mvt 2: *Un bal* (A ball)

Valse allegro non troppo (pulse = 60) in 3/8 meter; 6 minutes

In a bright waltz meter, strings and four harps set the stage for a glittering, magical evening. All musical gestures sweep upward, swirling into a surprise pop-up bouquet reminiscent of the opening of mvt 1. Our artist-hero-lover finds himself at a ball where he spies his beloved. The sheer frothiness of the waltz theme, presented after the long introduction, is pure joy, and agile violins are particularly well suited to play it. Constructed in four long phrases, the tune slows at the end of the third phrase as though hinting there can be no assumptions about what lies ahead, dire or otherwise. Easily recognizable, the *idée fixe* appears later in the middle of the movement; it is played by flute and oboe together, and then by flute and clarinet with strings accompanying. In a stroke of genius, Berlioz follows by simultaneously combining the waltz theme with the *idée fixe*, a contrapuntal masterstroke and Berlioz hallmark (thematic combination occurs again in mvt 5). The *idée fixe* appears again, near the end of the movement in an extended coda, played softly by the clarinet while a single horn and harps delicately accompany.

Mvt 3: *Scène aux champs* (Scene in the Country)

Adagio (pulse = 84) in 6/8 meter; 16 minutes

To escape the city's hubbub and sort out his overcharged emotions, our artist-hero-lover has taken himself to the country, yet he cannot shake off thoughts of his beloved. The movement opens with the famous dialogue between an English horn onstage and an offstage oboe, as if two shepherd lovers are calling to one another across a valley. Berlioz grew up in the foothills of the French Alps, so he undoubtedly knew the ethereal effect of wistful horns and pipes ricocheting across open mountainous terrain. The leisurely, deliberate figure in the English horn begins in a major key but, upon repetition and with the change of just one note, moves into a disconsolate minor. The movement ends with what at first seems to be a repeat, but the offstage oboe—the beloved—inexplicably and disturbingly does not respond.

Following the opening English horn and oboe dialogue, a new theme is presented, which is the basis for the theme and variation form of the movement. Whereas a meter in the previous passage had been impossible to pin down due to long, unmeasured silences and phrase fragments, here the music settles into an elegant six pulses, 3 + 3 per group, a pattern often used to evoke the pastoral. Flute and violin play the new theme in unison, as they did for the first presentation of the *idée fixe* in mvt 1. Overall it has similar traits to both the Estelle theme and *idée fixe*: phrases climb in pitch to an ecstatic height to create an unmistakable sense of striving and yearning, and singing it is easy, although the high pitches after the first phrase may be discouraging. That said, having heard it multiple times, you may find singing it irresistible.

Well into the middle of the movement, the *idée fixe* is preceded and interrupted by an instrumental recitative—a passage in which instruments appear to be speaking. Precise meaning of the implied words is left to the imagination, of course, but mood and feelings are strongly implied. The intermingling of the *idée fixe* with a recitative seems to create uncertainty. Progressively the *idée fixe* becomes more strident and assertive, as if in a struggle, and it is subsumed by its sonic surroundings.

One of Berlioz's most remarkable special effects occurs near the end of the movement. Together four timpanists each play a different note, similarly to how a four-note chord is played in the low register of a piano. But the entrances and exits of the four timpani are deliberately staggered, and their dynamics are varied individually from loud to soft by use of continuous tremolo. With subsequent changes of individual pitches, spacing, and subtle volume surges and dissipations, certain pitches emerge to the foreground at different times. The effect is entirely consistent with natural events—distant thunder never sounds the same way twice.

At the end, a solitary and low French horn note, barely audible, is heard fitting gently into a sustained string sonority. The strings fall to another pitch, then twice play a complete harmony separated by rests, while the horn continues unchanged. By an amazing economy of means, we know the artist-hero-lover (horn) is alone—the romantic *mal de l'isolement* (pain of isolation). This simple gesture closes the movement.

Mvt 4: *Marche au supplice* (March to the Scaffold)

Allegretto non troppo (pulse = 72) in 4/4 meter; 7 minutes

Movement 4 emerges out of the distant thunder and aloneness of mvt 3 with, again, timpani playing softly. (An effective performance strategy is to "hold the moment" at the end of mvt 3 and, without lingering or distraction, seamlessly begin mvt 4.) In a dramatic shift, timpani and additional percussion instruments play a tattoo, a distinctive rhythmic pattern played by military and marching bands. Cellos and contrabasses play pinprick pizzicato chords on strong beats, like delightful pointillist "pops." Two muted horns lock into those "pops" by playing a syncopated three-note gesture, also very softly. Nothing is vague now, time is rigorously organized, rhythms are glisteningly clear, and we find ourselves in a stern, inexorable march. A terrifying buildup begins: bassoons join, then clarinets, and then trombones; changing chords and crescendos pull the momentum forward. The flinty, grisly musical unit drives right into a loud CRACK! This is macabre stuff. Berlioz grew up in the country hearing marches played for outdoor celebrations and military processionals, and he became a master at composing them.[12]

The printed program (appendix C) informs us our artist-hero-lover knows his beloved has rejected him. In his opium-ridden state, he dreams he murders her. Convicted and marched to the guillotine, he then witnesses his own execution. At the end, we hear the guillotine blade hit, and with a single pizzicato, his head thuds to the ground. The term *fantastique* was synonymous at the time with grotesque; we certainly have it in ample supply here.

The two prominent themes in mvt 4 are not related to the *idée fixe*. Theme A is a single melodic line played first by the cellos and basses (reminiscent of the cello and bass recitative in mvt 2); its snap, snarl, and swagger begins high and moves low. On repetition, theme A is joined by its countermelody (a simultaneous, different melodic idea) played by four bassoons in their high register; it is superimposed directly on top of the snap, snarl, and swagger. Then first violins take over theme A for its third iteration; the timpani and horn "tattoo" from the opening returns, and a new pizzicato idea in the cellos and basses supports them. Berlioz superimposes, juxtaposes, and dovetails disparate short ideas introduced previously, not unlike playing with bits and pieces of a construction toy set or puzzle.[13] We can only assume that he wanted us to closely follow the course of their transformation, disassembly, and recombination.

Theme B is a brilliant blaze of sound produced by the complete array of woodwinds and brass. It seems preordained because Berlioz already planted the germ, a syncopated rhythm played by muted horns in the opening. Theme B proceeds through four balanced phrases, which is typical of a march. But what a march! Music that was ominous before is now defiant, steely eyed, and full out. We can see the glint of the guards' rifles in the sun and their bright banners fluttering in the wind. Berlioz repeats the entire section because it is far too good to hear only once.

Both themes are manipulated and developed: first A, then B, and then A and A again. Listen for developmental strategies such as alternating groups of strings versus winds; breaking up a theme into fragments; inverting the theme (theme A pitch relationships move in the opposite direction); superimposing a new melody on top of theme B; tossing the timpani's opening rhythm to the strings; and reassigning themes to different family groups of instruments or individual instruments. These all occur throughout the development, recapitulation, and long coda, making already vibrant themes more and more colorful and alive.

Where does the *idée fixe* appear in all this? A solo clarinet begins it near the end. But before the first phrase can finish, a THWAP by tutti orchestra signals the artist-hero-lover's death by guillotine. A massive intensification of sound preceded the execution, and the full force of timpani, winds, and brass follow it, all for a convulsive, grisly close. Watching one's own execution is gruesome indeed, if only in a dream.

Mvt 5: *Songe d'une nuit du sabbat* (Dream of a Night at a Witches' Sabbath)

Larghetto (pulse = 63) in 4/4 meter, *Allegro* (pulse = 112) in 6/8 meter; 10 minutes

From the cataclysmic march into hell's vengeance, our protagonist's dream culminates in a witches' Sabbath—a ritualistic, orgiastic nocturnal gathering of dancing and feasting. In such festivities documented from the mid-fourteenth century, ghosts, sorcerers, and monsters practiced witchcraft to control people or events. Berlioz had gathered inspiration for his scenario from Goethe's recently published epic poem *Faust*[14] and Eugène Delacroix's famous lithograph illustration of an imagined witches' Sabbath. In our artist-hero-lover's dream, it is his funeral, and he is in attendance.

The *idée fixe*, played by the strident, sneering E♭ clarinet in a new meter and faster tempo, is grossly distorted. It is not only a vile witches' dance tune, taunting and hilarious, but also a grotesque parody of his former beloved, who gleefully has joined the other creatures for the sacrilegious debacle. Deep-toned offstage bells toll as if from another world. Hints of the *Dies irae* (Day of wrath) chant tune from the Requiem mass are heard, first in fragments and then finally played in full.[15] In nineteenth-century Europe, every Roman Catholic knew the tune, and today it is a universal musical totem for judgment and death.

If supernatural creatures and witches didn't terrify audiences at the time, then combining the Judeo-Christian judgment day with, of all things, a witches' cabal certainly would. The sacred has been joined, if not equated, with the profane—a worst nightmare come true—and questions abound. Which of the two ill-fated lovers' spirits will be cast into the eternal flames of hell, or will both? Is the *idée fixe* now the artist's lost lover or the spoiled experience of love gone awry? Is all this incrimination of the artist-hero-lover truly intended by Berlioz, or is he finger pointing in jest at the absurdity of it all—witchcraft, religion, and judgment . . . really? Ha! Two themes, the *idée fixe* witches' dance and the Day of Wrath chant, remain entwined to the end of the symphony.

Remarkable Gestures and Soundscapes in Movement 5

Berlioz's daring sound effects were precedent-setting in 1830; even experienced musicians today assume *Symphonie fantastique* was written much later. His goal was to imply or respond to a perceived narrative and incite an array of emotional responses akin to his own. Here are a few remarkable gestures and soundscapes in mvt 5 and a brief examination of how they are constructed.

- Shimmer alert chord. The very first sound in mvt 5 is a soft, pungent chord in the upper strings; eight separate pitches are played simultaneously in high registers. The players use mutes (a wooden damper applied to the strings to muffle their sound) while producing a sustained tremolo (very fast, repetitive flick of the bow on one pitch). Intervals are so close to each other that the agitation causes a noisy, disruptive dissonance—we are enticed and put on high alert. Meanwhile cellos and contrabasses play very low, lumbering chromatic rises. Divided upper strings follow playing quick flicks that slide downward in a sneer. The macabre is undeniably upon us.
- Eerie call from the beyond—flapping of wings, cackling. Flute, piccolo, and oboe repeat stratospherically high notes in a gesture also ending in a downward-sliding sneer. The same rhythms and pitches are repeated by the horn, all the more haunting because

they come from a distance. (The horn player puts his hand into the bell to muffle the sound.)

- Rips and whirls. Very fast, brief, scale-like or chromatic jolts jump out to terrify. Strings or woodwinds play them; they rise or fall. Other instruments join to form clouds of harmonies moving in either parallel or contrary motion.

- Screamy and taunting *idée fixe*; a burble. Clarinet in C first plays an incomplete, broken-off *idée fixe* statement; soon the complete theme is played by clarinet in E♭, an instrument known for its potentially ugly tone and sounding out of tune. Nastier and more demented, the full statement is set higher to have more tension in the sound, and this time it is in a new and more contorted rhythm. Four bassoons are added to play burbles—repetitions of quick and upward four-note sweeps. Something really good must be cooking in the cauldron.

- Eternity calling. For at least one performance Berlioz borrowed authentic church or town-hall bells made of iron (two pitches, C and G) from l'Opéra. Played from offstage, their deep, low, and un-concert-like sound conjures up the supernatural far better than tubular bells used today.

- *Dies irae* melody. Berlioz specified a serpent, the ugliest-sounding instrument available, to play the Day of Wrath chant. The serpent was familiar to contemporary churchgoers because it accompanied the singing of Gregorian chants in religious services. Often it sounded out of tune, and some notes uncontrollably stuck out more loudly. Apparently singers were negatively influenced by its timbre and learned to bellow, perhaps hoping to suffer less by hearing themselves more. Period instrument performances of *Symphonie fantastique* today will employ the serpent alongside the ophicleide, as Berlioz directed, both of which produce the more flavorfully weird sounds that he had in mind. Modern substitutions of bassoons (for serpent) and tubas (for ophicleides) may sound civilized but not nearly uncomfortable enough for Berlioz.

Some Compositional Strategies in Movement 5

Berlioz manipulated musical materials to achieve his desired dramatic goals. Here are several strategies he used in mvt 5.

- Diminution and augmentation. The *Dies irae* chant moves from a sense of foreboding to wild frenzy by diminution—playing it twice as fast. Horns, trumpets, and trombones play in the new speed, giving it a muscular but still ominous effect. By also crafting a new, weird harmonization, Berlioz may have been thumbing his nose at the idea of judgment. Augmentation of the chant (twice as slow), heard in leisurely paced long notes played by four bassoons and two ophicleides, invokes sureness, eternity.

- Playful false starts and fugue as a dance. Berlioz was annoyed by his failure to write an acceptable fugue on his first Prix de Rome attempt. By the time he completed *Symphonie fantastique*—a few months *before* his successful fifth attempt—the technical proficiency was well in hand. And he was ready to have a little fun with the theme of the witches' dance, which is the basis of a fugue. Playful and naughty, the theme starts off with three short frisky ascending glides as if revving up to get started, and they end with a wonderful loud "pop" on a weak beat. The glides occur a total of four times in alternation, variously, with downward string patterns and knelling of bells. After three *Dies irae* phrases in bassoons and ophicleides, a second introduction begins with yet another series of playful false starts, this time three and a half of them and closer to each other. Eventually, about five minutes into the movement and with a loud tutti pounce by the orchestra, the suspense is finally dispelled: the fugue proper of the witches' dance begins.

- Thematic transformation and thematic combination together. The *idée fixe* near the opening of mvt 5, played by the clarinet in C, is so wildly different from the one in the first movement as to be hardly recognizable. Now it embodies Harriet's rejection of the artist-hero-lover and his total disaffection with love itself. The melody is utterly deformed—that is, transformed into a witches' dance. Then it is superimposed over the *Dies irae* chant in thematic combination—a compositional double whammy! It is a brilliant tour de force.

- Quick surge-and-recede dynamics. Near the end, only tutti strings with bass drum, a particularly novel combination of instruments, play minor chords, and dynamics change very quickly from extremely soft to extremely loud. These convulsive surge-and-recede gestures repeat over and over again underneath the *Dies irae* tune when it is played in augmentation by bassoons and then in diminution by brass. The technique is original; and the effect, quite horrifying.

- Structural arc of movement tempos (see table 3.2). Tempos of conventional four-movement symphonies were usually fast–slow–dance-like (minuet or scherzo)–fast. To tell his *Symphonie fantastique* story, Berlioz expanded the format to five movements and put the slow movement in the center. Outer mvts 1 and 5 have slow introductions followed by fast main sections. Inner ring mvts 2 and 4 are fast and somewhat fast, respectively. Slow and deeply meditative, mvt 3 *Scène aux champs* is the musical and dramatic axis; it is also the longest. Our artist-hero-lover has fallen in love in 1 and 2, discovers his rejection in 3, and in 4 and 5 finds himself subsumed in a twisted, horrible nightmare.

Table 3.2.   Movements, tempos, and durations in *Symphonie fantastique*

	Reveries—Passions	Un bal	Scène aux champs	Marche au supplice	Songe d'une nuit du sabbat
Mvt	I	II	III	IV	V
Tempo	Slow-fast	Fast	Slow	Somewhat fast	Slow-fast
Duration	14'	6'	16–17'	7'	10'

Unconventional: *Lélio*, a Sequel

Just about everyone knew Berlioz was the artist-hero-lover in his *Symphonie fantastique*. But with the artist guillotined, if only metaphorically in a dream, Berlioz was obliged to bring him back to life—he couldn't kill himself off in his own composition. Early on Berlioz planned for the symphony to be the first of two extended works performed back to back in one evening: (1) Episode in the Life of an Artist (*Symphonie fantastique*); and after intermission (2) its sequel, Return to Life, a melologue later entitled *Lélio*. He composed *Lélio* soon after the symphony during his sojourn in Italy in 1831–1832 and planned to perform them together on his return to Paris.

Lélio is not a symphony but rather an odd mishmash of solos, choruses, and orchestra movements linked together by an actor-narrator. It never gained traction even after revision and quite successful performances in 1855. The novel two-part, full-evening concept of symphony-melologue foreshadows present-day sequel movies (most of which are also not as good); not even opera composers had thought of such a thing yet. But for audiences today, nothing can successfully follow the last two movements of *Symphony fantastique*. That said, several portions of *Lélio* are particularly wonderful, notably the last, *Fantaisie dramatique sur la Tempête de Shakespeare* (Dramatic fantasy on Shakespeare's *The Tempest*) for chorus and orchestra. The effect of twelve harps positioned at the front of the stage, six on each side facing sideways to the audience, is unforgettable. Interestingly, *Lélio* is another reminder of the importance and frequent recurrence of text, singing, Shakespeare, and reconciliation in Berlioz's music.

Reception, a Real Start

Important composers and notables attended the first performance in 1830, among them Franz Liszt, the eminent pianist and composer eight years Berlioz's junior. They met for the first time that evening, starting a deep friendship and mutual advocacy that proved pivotal for Berlioz. Waiting to publish the full orchestra score until hearing it several more times, Berlioz gave Liszt a revised full-score manuscript, which Liszt then transcribed for piano in 1834. In 1835, composer and writer Robert Schumann favorably reviewed the symphony in the most important international music journal using Liszt's transcription, still the only published score available. Schumann's detailed analysis launched Berlioz's European career.

Symphonie fantastique was performed either in full or as excerpts a remarkable fifty-two times during Berlioz's lifetime. Of those, the complete work was performed twenty-nine times; only three of those were with *Lélio* as the concert's second half. Berlioz conducted it, complete or just excerpts, thirty-eight times beginning in 1835—it became a vehicle for honing his exemplary skills as a conductor. Excerpts performed, in order of frequency, were mvts 1 to 4; 2 to 4; 2 and 4; and either 3 and 4 or 2 alone. It may seem odd to us, particularly considering the work's narrative and architectural coherence, that most listeners heard only one or several movements.

Berlioz was only twenty-seven when he wrote *Symphonie fantastique*. By 1830, after only nine years living in Paris, he had become a fully formed composer. He had not, however, entered the hallowed halls of the opera house. But Berlioz could be proud: in writing his first symphony he had been utterly honest and transparent personally and amazingly original musically.

VIGNETTE 3.1. *SYMPHONIE FANTASTIQUE:* TWO VIOLINISTS IN REHEARSAL

The first rehearsal of Berlioz's new work, Symphonie fantastique, *planned for performance on May 3, 1830, at the Théâtre des Nouveautés, Rue de Vivienne, in Paris, Nathan Bloc, conductor. (The concert was cancelled and rescheduled for December 5, 1830, at Salle du Conservatoire, François Habeneck, conductor). Jacques and Étienne are violinists employed by several opera houses and Société des Concerts.*

Jacques: *Mon Dieu*, there is not enough room for my bow arm; *s'il-te-plaît*, will you move to the left? Look, why is the rest of the orchestra up on stage and just us violins down here in the orchestra pit? We won't be able to hear anything but ourselves, and there's still not enough room for all thirty of us. Nouveautés is simply not big enough for all 130 players; this is absurd. Not enough platforms, not enough music desks, and workmen still hammering on this and that. Unbelievable. What were they thinking?

Étienne: I heard M. Berlioz wanted 220 musicians! These grandiose ideas; he needs to get practical. I, for one, cannot believe we're rehearsing a symphony in a theater that presents vaudeville and *opera-comique*! We should be at the Odéon where new works are normally performed, or at the Conservatoire; both have enough room and a proper stage.

Jacques: You know perfectly well, getting started is all about who you know. I heard Berlioz secretly sang in the opera chorus here for a few months. He even walked to rehearsals disguised with a false nose, afraid people would think he was cavorting with low life and his family would find out. But he got to know the conductor, Bloc, and *voilà*, here we all are—it's the only place he could find. The ministry of the interior still isn't allowing new works at the Odéon, and the Salle du Conservatoire season was already booked. Besides, even though Berlioz flunked the Prix de Rome four times, I think there's something to him. Bloc is completely on his side. When Berlioz sat next to me in the Opéra pit last week and turned pages, we had a phenomenal conversation about string technique. He even had me over to his apartment to play a few passages he had composed to see if they worked. He approaches sound meticulously, like a scientist!

Étienne: *Hélas*, when *are* we going to begin? Stagehands are *still* running around, and the trumpets and bassoons have no place to sit. Really, careful of that candle.

Jacques: Well, at least our parts were copied correctly this time. Did you play that first performance of Berlioz's *Messe solennelle*? When was that, let's see, two years ago? There were unbelievable errors—key signatures were missing; rests were wrong—everyone was lost. Never trust a choirmaster who thinks his choirboys are capable of copying out orchestra parts from a conductor's full score. After today, Berlioz probably isn't going to trust stage managers either.

Étienne: *Oui*, I played for that performance. The conductor, Valentino, treated Berlioz with such class. When he heard Berlioz immediately revised the parts and recopied them himself, Valentino loaned him money to pay musicians for a second performance. *Incredible!* And Berlioz conducted it! I heard this was his first time conducting a performance. If Beethoven and Mendelssohn can do it, well so can Berlioz! He knew how to get the phrasing he wanted and how to rehearse instead of just running through things. Plus, his gestures were clear. It certainly helped that he faced us and not the audience for a change.

Jacques: Hmm, I hear it's quieting down up there. Have you played through this first movement yet? *Très difficile*. Better get to work.

ROMÉO ET JULIETTE

Reading Shakespeare's play is certainly not a prerequisite for enjoying Berlioz's rendition of *Romeo and Juliet*; after all, most listeners will already be familiar with the story more or less. But just as with any play, opera, or musical, reviewing a synopsis (provided here) is a good idea. Then while listening to Berlioz's marvelous retelling we can revel anew and experience more deeply the tumultuous feelings brought on by this ill-fated love.

Conception of the Work

Writing *Roméo et Juliette* had been on Berlioz's mind since 1827, when he first read Shakespeare's play, which had recently been translated into French. He attended a Paris performance given in English; his future wife, Harriet Smithson, was in the title role. Poet Emile Deschamps noted in his memoir that he and Berlioz began working on the libretto at about that time. Five years later during his residency in Italy, Berlioz attended Vincenzo Bellini's opera on the same subject, *I Montecchi ed I Capuletti*. Berlioz amusingly recounted the experience in his *Mémoires* and wrote a review listing all the things Bellini should have known better than to do in his opera. In his deconstruction Berlioz outlined a plan of his own for what he later described as his "choral symphony."

So, while Berlioz's obsession with Harriet and his state of *vague des passions* prompted completion of *Symphonie fantastique* in 1830, *Roméo et Juliette* enjoyed significantly more time to gestate. By 1839, he had gained much more experience composing, conducting, and reviewing concerts. He had also seen four new major works through to performance: *Lélio*, the sequel to *Symphonie fantastique*; *Harold en Italie*, his second symphony with viola solo; *Grande messe des morts* (*Requiem*), the work upon which his fame as a composer of choral music is based; and *Benvenuto Cellini*, his first opera to be staged. Berlioz's focus during these incredibly productive years was mainly on extended works, but he also composed smaller gems for voices and orchestra, including *Sara la baigneuse* and *Le cinq mai* discussed earlier.

Fortunately for Berlioz, a substantial gift from the internationally famous violin virtuoso Niccolò Paganini supported him and his family during the seven months of composition. To date and for the most part Berlioz had been supporting himself and his family by writing music reviews and topical articles, known as *feuilletons*, for the Paris journals. Composing and producing his own concerts, his *raison d'être*, had proved to be risky business on many levels, and only *Grande messe des morts* had been commissioned. The gift from Paganini came in a fortuitous and roundabout way. Previously Paganini asked Berlioz to write a symphony with a viola solo for him to play, but upon seeing that *Harold en Italie* lacked a prominent solo part, Paganini declined to perform it. Hearing a performance played by another artist a few years later, however, Paganini reversed himself. Full of new admiration, he knelt at Berlioz's feet declaring him the greatest living composer and Beethoven's only possible heir; he subsequently gave Berlioz twenty thousand francs to compose *Roméo et Juliette*. Sadly, Paganini died in 1840 having never seen the score or heard the work he fostered and of which he was the dedicatee.

Thanks to Paganini's generosity, Berlioz had ample time now to work on the piece he first had in mind twelve years earlier. Learning from the many performances he conducted of it, he revised it repeatedly until publication in 1847.

Overview

Berlioz based *Roméo et Juliette* on the events in the play that most ignited his imagination: swordplay between the quarreling families and the entrance of the Prince of Verona to dissuade conflict that opens mvt 1; Queen Mab speech by jokester Mercutio and *Scherzo* in mvts 1 and 4;[16] *Grande fête* (Grand party) at the Capulet's villa where Romeo first sees Juliet in mvt 2; and the balcony and tomb scenes of mvts 3 and 6, respectively. Juliette's funeral procession and the solemn oath of reconciliation insisted upon by Le Père Laurence, in mvts 5 and 7, respectively, were invented by Berlioz.

The concert-length work is in seven movements within which are a total of nineteen titled sections.[17] Singers are in mvts 1, 3, 5, and 7. Movements, large section titles, durations, and total number of sections are as follows:

1. *Introduction* (orchestra only), *Prologue* (petite chorus), *Strophes* (a *romance* for contralto solo in verses with refrain), *Scherzetto* (Mercutio, tenor, and a petite chorus foretelling mvt 4); approximately twenty minutes in four sections.

2. *Roméo seul* (Romeo alone) through to *Grande fête chez Capulet* (Grand party at the House of Capulets); approximately thirteen minutes in five sections.

3. *Nuit sereine* (Serene night), *Le jardin de Capulet* (Capulet's garden), and *Scène d'amour* (Love scene); approximately twenty minutes in three sections.

4. *La Reine Mab, ou la fée des songes—Scherzo* (Queen Mab, or the fairy of dreams—fast dance); approximately eight minutes in one section.

5. *Convoi funèbre de Juliette* (Funeral convoy of Juliet; sung by Capulets); approximately ten minutes in one section.

6. *Roméo au tombeau des Capulets* (Romeo at the tomb of the Capulets) and *Invocation*; approximately eight minutes in two sections.

7. *Final* (sung by chorus of Montagues and Capulets), *Air* (Le Père Laurence), and *Serment* (Friar Lawrence and three choruses: petite chorus from the *Prologue*, Montagues, and Capulets); approximately twenty minutes in three sections.

Mvts 1–4 are approximately sixty-one minutes; mvts 5–7 are approximately thirty-eight minutes. Total 99 minutes.

Singers and Text in a Symphony; Plot

Roméo et Juliette is, consequently, a sectionalized tableau reenactment of portions of the play. Singers participate but do not fulfill the principal roles of Romeo or Juliet as they would in an opera, oratorio, or cantata. While we might expect Roméo and Juliette to each be portrayed by a single instrument or theme, throughout the symphony Berlioz uses different instruments or groups of instruments and themes to enact the lovers. The two characters who do have singing roles, Mercutio (tenor) and Le Père Laurence (Friar Lawrence; bass), are supporting cast, plus the two separate mixed choruses of Capulet and Montague families.

The mezzo-soprano in the *Prologue* is a commentator rather than a character from the play.

The seven movements are in an overall arc format, like *Symphonie fantastique*, in that a slow movement, mvt 5, is near the middle. But in other ways *Roméo et Juliette* doesn't behave like any other symphony, or oratorio for that matter. Rather, it reflects Berlioz's penchant for fitting the music to the narrative rather than to previously conceived forms. For example, compared to *Symphonie fantastique* and *Harold en Italie*, there is no recurring *idée fixe* and there are seven movements rather than four or five. In other extended choral-orchestral works, the chorus is front and center, but here the two large choruses of warring Montagues and Capulets are positioned on each side of the stage and the Capulets must wait until mvt 5 to sing a funeral-march-like lament.[18] Then all the choristers must wait again until mvt 7 to join Le Père Laurence to reflect on the profound lessons learned from the two lovers' deaths. Instead of a single narrator, a tenor as is often the case, a petite *Prologue* chorus of twelve to sixteen voices and a mezzo-soprano soloist function like a Greek chorus in a play or opera. The singers orient the audience to previous and future events in an unusual choral recitative—block chords as much spoken as sung—and the mezzo-soprano sings a *romance*, something unheard of in a symphony. Finally, as often occurs in opera productions, a backstage men's chorus sings briefly as they leave the ball in mvt 3. In sum, Berlioz's *Roméo et Juliette* offers a bit of everything from symphony, oratorio, and even opera. But his mixing of genres (so-called genre manipulation) is all for a good cause: retelling a great story in his own way.

Changes in the Plot

Shakespearian experts will spot three incidents in the symphony that are not in the play. Berlioz used changes made by the great English actor David Garrick and later expressed surprise he had not been criticized more for the liberties taken. But the shift from spoken drama to symphony opens a story up to different perspectives—as is often said, don't expect the film to be like the book. The differences may be inconsequential to some listeners; for others perhaps, quite important.

1. The funeral procession for Juliet in mvt 5 does not exist in Shake-speare's play, where it is only implied. Berlioz used the reference as an opportunity to elaborate musically on the experience of sorrow.

2. The tomb scene in mvt 6 is altered. In both the play and symphony, Friar Lawrence marries the two lovers and instructs Juliet to take a sleeping potion. In the play, Romeo arrives at the tomb first and, thinking she is dead, kills himself with a dagger. Juliet awakens, discovers him dead, and takes her own life with the dagger. In the symphony, based on the play adapted by Garrick, Juliette awakens to discover Roméo is alive, but he has already taken the poison. The lovers have a few moments for farewells before he dies. Then Juliette takes her own life. In Shakespeare's version, there is no final dialogue; in Berlioz's, their shared love is prolonged in music.

3. In mvt 7, Berlioz avoided the final, disconsolate six lines of the play spoken by the Prince, the last of which reads, "For never was a story of more woe / Than this of Juliet and her Romeo." Instead, he composed a magnificent finale of grandeur and hope in which Le Père Laurence calls for forgiveness, reconciliation, and peace. The Capulets and Montagues at first resist but then swear to create a "perpetual chain of loving charity and brotherly affection."

Composition Strategies

The following is a detailed look into how Berlioz used musical materials to evoke listeners' perception. To benefit most, first read about the strategy, listen to the example passage, and then listen again. Choose strategies and passages of interest from among the thirteen provided. Audiences today are not likely to make a ruckus demanding to hear a movement played again as they did in the nineteenth century, but we can certainly utilize present-day technology to repeat passages we like and want to understand better.

1. Never a Predictable Melody, and Long

Berlioz's sketches show that he usually composed a melody first. If setting a text, he designed the melody to fit hand in glove with the syntax of the poetry. Generally, next or nearly concurrently he wrote a bass line and indicated the harmonies above it by writing in figured bass chord symbols. Considering we know his earliest compositions were *romances*, which he sang and played on guitar, all of this makes perfect sense—melody and harmony went hand in hand. It is very unlikely that he would lay out a sequence of chords and then find a melody to fit them; rather, the melody came first. In *Symphonie fantastique*, the *idée fixe* melody is uncommonly long in four uneven phrases, and its sub-phrases are pulled out and manipulated into regular and irregular lengths. When listening to it we are constantly intrigued by its progress. In the "Roméo alone" theme (*Roméo seul*) at the beginning of mvt 2, much is the same. Table 3.3 shows how its phrases A, B, and C are also uneven in length (14 + 3 + 9 measures) and their interior melodic ideas are constantly new.

Table 3.3.   Phrases of Roméo *seul* theme, mvt 2

A	B	C	
a (6) b (4) a' (4)	c c' c" (3)	d (3) e (3) f (3)	
14	3	9	= 26 measures

2. Pizzicato Notes and Chords

For what purpose does Berlioz write pizzicato notes and chords? In the *Prologue*, they usually respond to what has just happened. What could they possibly be signaling? Perhaps they are showing a wide-eyed wink of understanding, or an "oh, no, what will happen next?" Or perhaps they're indicating a pop of the fizzy, the sting of an unsettling thought, or a cleansing of the palette. To create urgency they accelerate; they slow to have us relax. Berlioz uses them to shape both our expectations and our responses.

3. Convulsed-Emotion Gesture

In the opening fugue subject of mvt 5, *Convoi funèbre de Juliette*, Berlioz uses a sudden "surge-and-dissipate" gesture—a crescendo or a sudden *forte* on one pitch or set of pitches that is swiftly followed by a diminuendo. The gesture signals great urgency.

4. Pianissimos

Berlioz's full force *fortissimos* (*ff* to *fff* = extremely loud) are universally applauded, but his *pianissimos* (*pp* to *ppp* = extremely soft) are passed over. Yet they lure us into his audaciously delicious sound world almost unawares. In the opening of mvt 2, violins play the *Roméo seul* theme extremely softly (*ppp* is the dynamic marking). If the line were to be played any louder, it would not sound nearly so alone and dejected. Consider the even softer string passage at the beginning of *Scène d'amour* (*pppp*), which low flutes and horns also enrich. Ultra-soft passages put us in touch with our most private, previously unacknowledged feelings.

5. Chromaticism

Harmonic chromaticism (colorful chords moving by step or half step and creating dissonance) is used for narrative and emotional expression. The instrumental passage opening *Scène d'amour* (in mvt 3 prior to the entrance of the men's chorus) is an example. Nothing is pedestrian about the music, although it is just a series of chords with no melody. One note changes here and another there, usually by an adjacent step, while others stay the same. If we describe the harmonies, they are crunchy, incomplete or complete, or on the way somewhere. Our responses are perhaps perplexed, unsettled, calm, or expectant. We have entered the Capulet garden, the sky is clear and starry, and all is silent and deserted.

The *Roméo seul* (alone) theme at the beginning of mvt 2 is striking for its melodic chromaticism. At the outset first violins play it without accompaniment; the effect is stark, brooding, and plaintively tortured. Chromatic pitches—those notes in between the more predictable consonant ones—are positioned to be pointedly dissonant at puzzling or poignant moments.

6. Harmony

In the very next passage of *Roméo seul* in mvt 2, Berlioz's restless and utterly engaging use of harmony stands out. Oboe and clarinet embark on a brief idea of leisurely, sustained notes (three pitches, the second of which is repeated); it is the beginning of Roméo's *tristesse* (sadness) theme. So simple as to seem insignificant, nonetheless it is repeated four times in a row. But each time Berlioz intensifies the harmony, prompting the violins and woodwinds to unexpectedly take off with new heartrending inflections. By grouping oboe and clarinet in a high register and juxtaposing them against a far-below and isolated walking bass line, Berlioz sets up the framework for one of the most exquisite moments in the work. Strings and other winds delicately, discreetly fill in between this high-low polarity to generate yet another masterful accompaniment. As the passage slowly unfolds, the harmonies surrounding Roméo's theme are mysteriously manipulated; all becomes incredibly poignant. The nineteen measures of music are in seven short phrases; at phrase *f*, the momentum turns homeward (see table 3.4).

Table 3.4.   Phrases of Roméo's *tristesse* theme, mvt 2

Intro	A	B	C	
a (2 + 2)	*a* (2 + 2) + *b* (2)	*c* (2) + *d* (1.5)	*e* (2.5) *f* (1.5) *g* (1.5)	
4	6	3.5	5.5	= 19 measures

Scène d'amour in mvt 3 is the pinnacle of harmonic expression. It took the most time for Berlioz to compose, and he believed it to be his best composition of all his offerings. Our ear is drawn in by each new inflection of one note or two, here or there, in the vertical alignment. Berlioz never releases us by becoming predictable; nonetheless, the harmonies are smooth, evenly flowing.

7. Not Quite a Fugue

Although at times Berlioz claimed to dislike fugues, he frequently used fugue-like procedures as a compositional strategy. The very beginning of *Roméo et Juliette* opens with a fugue subject played by violas; it is a furiously fast, loud, and urgent "scurry idea." With the nearly immediate entry of cellos and then violins on the same subject, we find ourselves in a fugato, a less strictly constructed variety of fugue. What better way could there be to depict swordplay and angry shouts back and forth between the two warring houses of Verona? The tempo is so fast (pulse = 116) that players can hardly play it cleanly or stay together, which indeed may be the point—to evoke confusion, distress, and chaos.[19]

In Juliette's funeral march, mvt 5, Berlioz uses a fugal procedure for a completely different effect; it is similar to his approach in (7) *Offer-*

toire of his *Requiem* (see chapter 4). Here cellos alone play a long theme as the Capulets (Juliette's family) sing *Jetez des fleurs* (throw some flowers) on a reiterated single pitch. Instruments add in to form a three-part fugato texture underpinning the singers' disconsolate incantation. Later the orchestra and singers trade: violins play the same plaintive single-pitch incantation as though speak-singing *Jetez des fleurs*, while the chorus in three parts (sopranos, tenors, and basses) sings the melodic fugue material. While doing so the singers deliver the complete the sentence: *Jusqu'au tombeau, jetez des fleurs pour la vierge expirée* (All the way to the grave, throw flowers for the dead maiden).

8. Preview

The *Prologue* is quite a clever construction. First the petite chorus explains in recitative what just happened in the prior orchestral *Introduction*: there are two warring houses in Verona, Roméo's Montagues and Juliette's Capulets (we just heard the fugato fighting). The Prince of Verona has forbidden any more fighting and threatens death to those who act against his orders (we heard this too, with lots of brass). Then the events in mvts 2–5 are briefly foretold in text and music. Berlioz wanted the music of each event to be introduced and familiar when it reappears later, similar to the function of an overture introducing important themes that will appear in an opera.

But such short wisps are hard to remember as the important musical monikers he intended. Below is listed each of the *Prologue* events in order and the movement and section in which the music is fully presented later. The one exception is the *Prologue*'s opening (1), which is an explanation of events that just happened in the preceding orchestral *Introduction*; there is no reprise. The rest of the *Prologue* does indeed predict the future. Having text in hand to follow the translation is essential. That said, the character of the music for each event matches its subject.

1. Warring families and Prince's declaration forbidding fighting in previous orchestra *Introduction* (text only, no reprise of music); mvt 1
2. Dance-like party theme of the *Fête* (party); mvt 2
3. Dreamlike men's choral passage ending the *Fête*; mvt 2

4. *Roméo tristesse* (sadness) theme: slow, three pitches in long notes, here sung and played; mvt 2

5. From *Scène d'amour*, the halting, hesitant transition and ecstatic second half of Roméo's love theme (sung and played); mvt 2

6. Following the mezzo-soprano's *Strophes*, preview of Queen Mab Scherzo in mvt 4. Entitled *scherzetto* (little joke), it is sung by Mercutio (tenor; his only appearance) and the petite chorus joined by only piccolo, flute, violas, and cellos.

7. *Convoi funèbre* (funeral procession) rhythm in upper strings and opening phrase from the fugue subject in mvt 5.

9. Recitatives: Choral and Instrumental

The use of choral recitative in the *Prologue* is novel and makes perfect sense because it can deliver a large amount of information swiftly. While using a soloist would have been easier (less rehearsal time), Berlioz used a small, mostly a cappella vocal ensemble possibly for three reasons. First, it announces that singers and sung text are in the work despite all of the choristers not appearing until more than an hour later. Second, use of an ensemble emphasizes unanimity of attitude and inclusiveness, which are important messages in the story. Third, by having only a few voices in the *Prologue* and a full-out triple chorus in the finale, a marvelous textural crescendo occurs from beginning to end.

Interestingly, Berlioz also composed instrumental recitatives. Aware of his grounding in literature, we should not be surprised by his use of instruments to "speak." Already Beethoven, one of Berlioz's idols, composed an instrumental recitative near the opening of his Ninth Symphony, fourth movement. Do we miss the words? Well, maybe, but implying them can be magical. The Prince of Verona speaks via trombones and horns in the *Introduction*. The passage occurs after (a) the opening string tumult/swordplay fugato; (b) the appearance of muscular trombones in a passage resembling a victory march (as in the play, the Prince and his entourage walk into the courtyard to stop the fighting); and (c) the breaking apart of motives, which causes a momentum slowdown. A sustained chord and pause of silence pique our anticipation, and then trombones/horns declaim as though making a pronouncement. Rhythms and phrase contours are irregular, and pacing is start-and-stop like the speech patterns of a good actor. The Prince threatens death to anyone who fights by the sword.

In mvt 6, at the tomb, the deaths of both Roméo and Juliette are framed in recitative-like instrumental passages. The first occurs after a fast opening followed by a series of sustained chords and pauses, and then a slow section. Now a low, agitated rumble of cellos alone is followed by very high clarinet: Roméo has taken the poison, and Juliette is awakening. The musical delirium that follows is like a flood of passionate words. In a second recitative-like passage, violins in a very high register play falling patterns interspersed with full orchestra *forte* punctuations; these punch-in-the-gut chords may be Roméo's death throes. A lone, falling oboe line and two lone cello pizzicato notes mark his end. The action is so crucially "in the moment" that only the most free-form compositional strategies can be used. There is no rhythm establishing time, no melody, and hardly any harmony. The music is wordless but speaks.

10. The Romance, Strophes

Strophes: Premiers transports (A song in strophic form: first feelings of love) is the musical anchor of the *Prologue*. The nameless, idealized mezzo-soprano tells of unforgettable first raptures under the Italian stars, the scent of orange blossoms, a first love that is above all poetry, and passion so pure that its words are tears. What king could fancy he knew a joy equal to such radiant ecstasy? But what is this, a song in a symphony? How bizarre that it is so simple, just two verses with a refrain; and the accompaniment is so spare, only a harp, six cellos, and occasionally a few woodwinds and petite chorus. Berlioz sets a *romance* within a symphony to stop time for a few moments and distill the quintessential feeling of being in love. At one point the cello line goes up to its highest register in an ecstatic duet with the singer—an ecstasy of two as one.

11. Thematic Combination

Appearing to be in no way compatible, two disparate melodies are combined as if preordained. It seems to be a miracle. In mvt 2, right after the first appearance of a tambourine, a solo oboe plays the Roméo love theme accompanied by pizzicato cellos sounding like harps. The melody is slow and noble, as though saying, "I will wait for you and love you forever." Later the sparkly, jaunty *Fête* (party) theme, a wild and rhythmically captivating dance, appears in violins and violas. After passages of transition and restatement, the two themes are superimposed, one upon the other. Roméo's slow love theme, now played by piccolo, flute, oboes, clarinets, bassoons, and horns, is rendered in notes twice as long as before (I'll love you *beyond* forever!) while violins and violas continue playing the *Fête* theme. Trumpets, timpani and tambourine, harps, cellos, and contrabasses add generous glitter so that ebullience is magnificently joined to pure happiness. We can almost see the rapture of love in his eyes.

12. Fascinating Bass Lines

Like most composers, Berlioz used descending bass lines to unwind momentum and ascending lines to intensify it. But he went a step further by writing repeating melodic gestures in the bass. One such instance is in the passage leading up to Roméo's *tristesse* theme in mvt 2. Bassoons, cellos, and contrabasses together play a repeated four-note pattern moving by skips of up-down-down. It sounds like a lumbering, cautious walk. So, instead of a bass line functioning solely as harmonic foundation, the bass provides an additional motivic layer at the very bottom of the texture. The entire gesture can and does move in any direction.

In other passages, Berlioz uses a sustained bass pedal tone (as in the foot pedals of an organ), a nearly universal compositional technique. Like a ship's anchor, the bass tone stays in place for a long time while independent events evolve above it, some consonant with it and some dissonant. In mvt 2, when the *Fête* theme and Roméo's love theme combine (discussed above), the bass line stabilizes onto a pedal tone. Finally when it moves off its mooring, the most delectably crunchy and wonderful sonorities of the movement are heard.

13. Gestures

Berlioz generously employs gestures: discreet units of pitches, instrumental colors, and rhythms that imply thoughts and feelings—it is up to each listener to decide just what those are. Gestures are layered, interlocked, juxtaposed, and added in or taken out like building blocks or pieces of a jigsaw puzzle. In *Scène d'amour* (after the opening calm and men's chorus), the following gestures appear:

a. Sustained notes played by flute and clarinet, which hold over beyond the opening calm.

b. A repeating accompaniment pattern in violas, cellos, and basses; the same rhythm continues while intervals between pitches expand or contract. The first three notes of the gesture are in leisurely falling intervals followed by a wide ascending leap.

c. A violin "nudge"— five clearly articulated notes squeezed together rhythmically and seemingly trying to summon the courage to speak. The gesture appears irregularly, never expectedly.

d. A repeated bass pizzicato pattern that was initially a bass pedal tone (referred to above in discussion of bass lines).

Following these gestures, a crescendo leads (after a brief, halting interlude) to the fully formed love theme played by solo horn with violas. An incredible sum of the parts has emerged: a mannered, slow-motion dance that feels both inevitable and ecstatic.

Innovative Instrumentation and Orchestration

Berlioz chose instruments and combinations of them for optimal dramatic effect. Imagining the reasons that prompted his choices is enticing. Here are just a few of many situations where his decisions invite our curiosity.

1. Harp. Berlioz said he had a "vague feeling of romantic love" whenever he saw a harp. Traditionally it had been used only in operas for pictorial and evocative purposes. Berlioz was the first composer to use it in a symphony, which was in *Un bal*, mvt 2 of *Symphonie fantastique*. For *Roméo et Juliette* he wanted eight to ten harps, although he said he would be happy with four; two was his absolute minimum. They were to be placed at the front of the stage where the audience could comfortably hear them. Only one harp, though, plays the single chord at the beginning of the *Prologue* in *Roméo et Juliette*. Its ring and jolt of plucked strings is a cleansing of the palette. It follows warm, bowed strings heard just before and is meant to both startle and announce, even though the harmony remains the same. Joined by only a small chorus singing in recitative style, the harp also evokes an intimate atmos-

phere. Later it will step up into a prominent accompaniment role in *Strophes*. In *Fête* (mvt 2), Berlioz calls upon all harps (please, all ten!) precisely at that miraculous moment when the two themes combine. Their lushness and sparkle creates nearly unbearable joy.

2. Winds as actors. In general, woodwinds and French horns provide a core of color to the string sound, such as in the opening of *Scène d'amour* where only flutes and horns join the strings in sustained sonorities. Winds also add glow to lyric themes played by violins, such as in the repetitions of the *Roméo seul* theme. But woodwinds and French horns also function like character actors. The piccolo may be used for surreal, mysterious, or satanic music: in the Queen Mab *Scherzo*, piccolo and flute throw out lightning-fast flicks like fairies flitting about. In the same movement, four bassoons and two horns every so often play an oddly sounding low tone somewhat resembling a honk. Here the queen fairy has driven her magical chariot into the nose of the slumbering dreamer so he will have fulfilled dreams. He is happily snoring! At first the low note fits pleasingly into its surroundings, but as the chords change, it does not. The snoring becomes more evident, strident, and humorous with each unpredictable repetition.

3. Violin special effects. Roméo's sense of isolation is aptly depicted at the beginning of mvt 2 simply by the construction of the melody. But aloneness is further magnified by the violins playing the theme by themselves. There is no accompaniment or doubling, just solitude and a heartrending tune. A quite different and special instrumental effect is in the Queen Mab *Scherzo*. There are passages in which the composite string sound is very high, still and thin—ethereal. The technique called for, playing harmonics, is achieved by the violinist's left hand lightly touching a string but not pressing it all the way down to the fingerboard. The resulting sound is a high frequency and timbre not customarily heard. In Berlioz's setting we find ourselves transported into magical otherworldliness.

4. Percussion. Antique miniature cymbals delicately ring out a high, sparkling, tinkling sound that the customary modern orchestral cymbals do not resemble. Notably in the Queen Mab *Scherzo*, Berlioz clears away other instruments so they function as a pal-

ette cleanser or an "ahem" call for attention. The four sets of cymbals are to be played from a location near the front of the orchestra so that, like the harps, they may be heard clearly.

Berlioz, English, and Shakespeare

Much has been made of Berlioz falling in love with Harriet when he saw her act in two Shakespearian plays. He did not know a word of English at the time, according to his *Mémoires*, and "could only glimpse Shakespeare darkly through the mists" of a "pale and garbled" transla- tion."[20] David Cairns tells us that Berlioz took an evening class in Eng- lish in 1828, after he saw Harriet act. He evidently became a fluent reader, and over the years, due in part to his marriage, he was able to speak it reasonably well. On one of his trips to London he even gave a speech in English.

Further research by Peter Bloom has revealed Berlioz became com- fortable enough with English that he read the bard's plays over and over, reciting numerous passages from memory; he knew and quoted from twenty-three of the thirty-eight plays. In several scores, Berlioz quoted Shakespeare in epigraphs placed beneath the title or a move- ment, hoping the performer would gain insight into his state of mind or objective when composing the work. Most of the quotes came from *Hamlet*. Berlioz was regarded by Shakespearean admirers at the time as an authority, and he became an ardent advocate, joining a planning committee in 1864 to celebrate the three hundredth anniversary of Shakespeare's birth. Amazingly, only two on the committee were ca- pable of reading Shakespeare in his own language: Hector Berlioz and Victor Hugo.

Berlioz's first encounter with Shakespeare "darkly through the mists" was due not only to his limited English at the time but also to Harriet's artistry as a mime. Her onstage presence, posture, gestures, and timing were the basis for her fame, far more so than her delivery of lines. Would understanding every word of *Romeo and Juliet* in 1827 have obstructed his receptivity? Possibly. When both watching and lis- tening, there's simply too much information coming all at once for a nonnative speaker. Was he also in the swoon of an inexplicable love? Yes. It was probably for all these reasons—lack of English at the time, her effective miming, and the enthrallment of love—that Berlioz was so vulnerable to his imagination and why he chose to convey the two leads with only instruments.

New Rehearsal Procedures, Performance, and Reception

At his own expense, Berlioz organized three performances in a row of *Roméo et Juliette* under his direction. No one before had dared to give three concerts close together consisting of a symphony by itself. It was presented in Paris on November 24 and December 1 and 15 of 1839, all Sundays at 2:00 p.m. at the Salle du Conservatoire. Performers were one hundred instrumentalists, about a hundred choristers (more than forty singers in each of the two choruses and twelve singers in the *Prologue* chorus), and three soloists. The music was more difficult than the tried-and-true offerings of his contemporaries. But Berlioz knew which technical challenges and special effects had to be rehearsed in sectionals; his music needed him to conduct it. Hoping his father would come to Paris, Berlioz wrote that he would hear *Roméo et Juliette* under the composer's own direction, and there was no way it would be disfigured.[21]

Violinist-conductor François Habeneck, who introduced Beethoven's Symphony no. 1 to Paris in 1811, and nos. 3 and 5 in 1828, influenced Berlioz's rehearsal strategy. To understand Beethoven's innovations, Habeneck had methodically rehearsed his Conservatoire students over several months, even holding evening sessions in his home. His inquiring, unheard-of approach resulted in an excellence rarely experienced in the city of under-rehearsed operas. The rehearsal custom was to play through without stopping and hope the players would fix anything wrong on their own (if they knew what was wrong) the next time.

The rigorous approach Berlioz applied to *Roméo et Juliette* incited a display of advocacy from musicians unheard of in the professional music community; they were so positive at the dress rehearsal that he believed success was ensured. Writing to his father after a performance, he reported the orchestra and choruses "stood and filled the hall with cheers while the public offered shattering applause from the parterre and gallery."[22] His efficient, custom-made rehearsal scheme resulted in an unusually polished performance.

Having made a career of conducting since the mid-1830s, Berlioz codified rehearsal procedures and stage setup, and he raised performance standards to the highest levels yet known. He wrote one of the earliest guides for conducting and rehearsing, located in the last chapter of his orchestration treatise, *Grand traité d'instrumentation et d'orchestration modernes* of 1855. Topics include conducting patterns, chorus masters, subconductors, and positioning of players in the concert hall. Among his axes to grind were the conductor facing the audience rather than the orchestra, players adding uncalled-for ornaments, and bass players opting out of playing all their notes.

Berlioz usually had numerous sectional rehearsals, which he led or had others lead, and one full rehearsal: violins alone first and then violas, cellos, and basses all separately. Then the woodwinds joined by a small group of strings to fill gaps and play cues for next entries. The brass sectional proceeded in similar fashion, and the percussion and harps also rehearsed separately. With such thorough groundwork, subsequent tutti rehearsals were far more productive. Berlioz achieved performances that were true to the score, and the players understood their role at any given moment. They played "in character" as opposed to just correctly, together, and in tune. By the time he published *Roméo et Juliette* in 1847, Berlioz decided a chorus subconductor was needed to conduct the behind-the-scene men's chorus at the beginning of mvt 3. He also knew that the only way to guarantee success in that specific circumstance was for the onstage orchestra conductor to follow the chorus by ear, and he put those instructions in the score. It was a highly unusual strategy then and today, but it makes perfect sense.

Performances

During Berlioz's lifetime, the complete *Roméo et Juliette* was performed fewer times than his other symphonies—only nine; he conducted six of them. *Symphonie fantastique*, by contrast, had twenty-nine complete performances. The additional time and effort required to coordinate and rehearse double chorus, prologue chorus, and backstage men's chorus, plus the difficulty of the music, certainly contributed to its limited exposure.

That said, excerpts from *Roméo et Juliette* were performed quite a bit, and of the total sixty, Berlioz conducted forty-three. The movements most often performed were, in order, as follows: from mvt 2, *Fête*; from mvt 3, *Scène d'amour*; from mvt 4, Queen Mab *Scherzo*; from mvt 7, *Final*; from mvt 2, *Roméo seul*; from mvt 1, *Strophes: Premiers transports*; and *Serment* from mvt 7. Of all his four symphonies, *Harold en Italie* enjoyed the most complete and excerpted number of performances, even more than *Symphonie fantastique*. Today, due in part to unfamiliarity, *Roméo et Juliette* and *Grande symphonie funèbre et triomphale* are heard the least; and *Symphonie fantastique*, the most.

On several occasions, Berlioz confessed that *Scène d'amour* from *Roméo et Juliette* was his favorite composition. Players and audiences have always adored it. Hearing Colin Davis's London Symphony Orchestra Live recording, in which the conductor's passionate and sometimes audible creature noises slip in, is further affirmation of its sublimity.

Berlioz wrote his four symphonies to relive and share feelings he encountered in stories, whether based on his own loosely devised narrative, a Lord Byron epic poem, or a Shakespeare play, or remembering those who died in battle. Was he on the precipice of writing an opera? Yes, continually. Numerous projects were contemplated or started and left unfinished. Two completed operas had already failed by late 1838: *Les francs-juges* (1826) was rejected by l'Opéra on the basis of its libretto; and *Benvenuto Cellini* closed in fall 1839 after only four performances. Both were crushing disappointments. But Berlioz's response was to write symphonies, choral works, and songs instead. Fortunately, he usually conducted them and thus positively shaped their fate. During those years, Berlioz established himself as among the most preeminent composer-conductors of the nineteenth century.

VIGNETTE 3.2. *ROMÉO ET JULIETTE*: TWO SOPRANOS BEFORE REHEARSAL

Colette and Marie are choristers sitting on stage in the dress rehearsal of Roméo et Juliette. *It is late November in 1839, Salle du Conservatoire, Paris, and rehearsal is soon to begin.*

Colette: *Hélas*. I wish Berlioz had written more music for us to sing; after all, we *are* the Capulet and Montague families; it's not as if we're not important. Since we're not in the *Prologue* chorus, we only get to sing in mvts 5 and 7. I guess I should have brought my knitting.

Marie: True, the orchestra plays everything, and the first thing we get to sing is a funeral procession, of all things. *Mon Dieu!*

Colette: Well, we do get to make peace with everyone at the end; that's pretty special.

Marie: Yes, *Final* is so glorious! All three choruses—*petite chœur*, Capulets, and Montagues—and that luscious Père Laurence singing the *Serment*. I keep on hearing that melody in my head. What a tremendous wrap-up.

Colette: I like that we sit between the audience and the orchestra, just like the three soloists, *très bien*! But I wish I could see M. Berlioz conducting. Anyway, our chorus master over there gives us a pretty clear beat and thank goodness he cues us!

Marie: By the way, have you heard the contralto soloist in *Strophes*? Now there's a song if I've ever heard one. I tell you, I'm right there in Italy with her—the breezes, smell of orange blossoms, and the glittering, starlit sky. And those gorgeous six cellos in the second verse! They move in parallel motion with her melody all the way up in the same register with her. *C'est incroyable*. Strange, though, a song in a symphony and she isn't even a character in the play.

Colette: Hmm, strange that Berlioz didn't give Roméo any arias, poor guy. Juliette was so in love with him, so *fidèle*. She never gets to sing a word either.

Marie: You know, I've been thinking about that. In a way, we choristers are sitting here onstage like real people, as in a play or opera. But Roméo and Juliette have this special wordless halo around them as if they're in a different reality. If they were singing they would be too distracting, too *real*. Maybe Berlioz did want the instruments to say it all.

Colette: Now that you put it that way I'm really glad I'm *not* singing the whole time. I can sit right here and listen to everything from the best seats in the house.

Marie: Back to practicalities: what are you going to wear?

Colette: I think the two choruses should wear different colors. Then the audience will know which family is on each side of the stage and be able to spot who's singing when!

Marie: Yes! My red scarf is perfect for the Montagues, Roméo's family; the Capulets can be blue.

4

EXTENDED CHORAL-ORCHESTRAL WORKS

Hector Berlioz composed seven extended choral-orchestral works, more than his symphonies or operas. Like his symphonies, none resembles the others in organization or scope.

EXTENDED CHORAL-ORCHESTRAL WORKS

1. *Messe solennelle* (1824; *Resurrexit* revised in 1828): fifty minutes; nine movements; soprano, tenor, and bass *divisi* chorus; soprano, tenor, and bass soloists; orchestra.
2. *Huit scènes de Faust* (1829): thirty minutes; eight individual scenes; soprano, tenor, and bass *divisi* chorus; bass, tenor, and mezzo soloists; orchestra plus harmonica and guitar.
3. *Le retour à la vie: mélologue en six parties*, sequel to *Symphonie fantastique*, later called *Lélio, ou le retour à la vie* (1831): fifty minutes; six movements; soprano, tenor, and bass *divisi* chorus; reciter, two tenor soloists, and a baritone soloist; piano and orchestra.
4. *Grande messe des morts* (1837): ninety minutes; ten movements; soprano, tenor, and bass *divisi* chorus; tenor soloist in one movement; expanded orchestra.
5. *La damnation de Faust* (1846): two and a half hours; parts 1–4; soprano, tenor, and bass *divisi* chorus; mezzo-soprano, tenor, and

two bass soloists; children's chorus and soprano solo in final movement; orchestra.

6. *Te Deum* (1849, rev 1852 and 1855): sixty minutes; six movements (plus a prelude before mvt 3 when performed for military ceremonies, which he withdrew, and a final march); two antiphonal soprano, tenor, and bass *divisi* choruses; tenor soloist in one movement; children's chorus (added 1852); organ at opposite end of building from orchestra, chorus, and soloists.

7. *L'enfance du Christ* (1850–1854): ninety minutes, parts 1–3; soprano, alto, tenor, and bass chorus; soprano and alto *divisi* backstage choruses at the end of each part; mezzo-soprano, tenor, baritone, and bass soloists; small orchestra.

Much has been made of Berlioz composing choral-orchestral works for large forces in large places, known as *style énorme* or monumental architectural style. But surprisingly only two of his seven extended choral-orchestral works reflect this approach: *Grande messe des morts* (*Requiem*; High Mass for the dead) written for performance in L'église St-Louis des Invalides, the official chapel of the French military services; and *Te Deum* (We praise thee, o God) for L'église St-Eustache. In these instances, outsized forces were intended to exploit the uniquely expressive sound possibilities of expansive sacred spaces. Berlioz's breadth of imagination and subjects of universal truths warranted no less. A number of shorter individual works for chorus and orchestra are also for large forces in grandiose spaces, including *L'impériale* and *Hymne à la France* (see chapter 2), but these were generally intended for open-air pavilions or large exhibit halls. To be sure, experiencing the transformative power of compositions such as these requires hearing them live and in an appropriately large space. No recording can possibly replicate the multidirectionality of melodic ideas and textures refracting off and across a myriad of widely spaced surfaces. The sonic ambience and emotional impact, from tumult to lingering echo, is without equal.

Berlioz was commissioned to compose *Grande messe des morts* (*Requiem*) for a national commemoration of the death of King Louis-Philippe's commander-in-chief. Fortunately, themes and strategies had been occurring to him for some time, and he wrote it quickly. He composed *Te Deum* of his own volition eleven years later, perhaps in honor of Napoléon I, for whom he felt great affinity his entire life, and in solidarity with Napoléon's nephew, Napoléon-Louis, who was enjoying a controversial political ascent. Berlioz considered mvt 6, *Judex crederis* in *Te Deum*, to be the brother of mvt 6, *Lacrymosa* in the *Requiem*—both are overwhelming in scope, originality, and power. Passages with massive tutti forces are made even more striking by their juxtaposition with other passages played by just a few instruments. Based on traditional Latin texts used for special occasions, both works have an aura of ritual.

Berlioz composed *La damnation de Faust* (The damnation of Faust) and *L'enfance du Christ* (The childhood of Christ) for the concert hall; they are his oratorio-style works, which he described, respectively, as a dramatic legend and a sacred trilogy. Opera companies have produced them, but such efforts have had mixed results. As with *Roméo et Juliette*, Berlioz intended for the music and narrative to probe and ignite the listener's own imagination; intervention of visual augmentation, such as costumed characters on a stage with sets, misses the point. The music needs nothing more than, well, the music.

MESSE SOLENNELLE

A brief word about the toddler in the group, *Messe solennelle* (Solemn High Mass), composed when Berlioz was twenty-one. It was considered lost, except for the single movement *Resurrexit*, until discovery of a complete autograph score in Antwerp in 1991. A profusion of ideas—distinctive melodies, rhythms, motifs, and instrument combinations—seem to pile up, one on top of the next in a furious, ecstatic rush. Some are enticing; others we might take or leave. In hindsight it served Berlioz well as a research and development training ground, as did *Huit scènes de Faust*. While he may not have been satisfied with how some ideas played out, Berlioz never let the good ones slip through his fingers. He held on to useful themes and textures from *Messe solennelle* and reframed them in later sacred works, *Requiem* and *Te Deum*. Not viewing musical ideas as exclusively sacred or secular, Berlioz also lifted some for *Symphonie fantastique*, *Benvenuto Cellini*, and *La damnation de Faust*.

Messe solennelle is a fine stepping-off point for gaining insight into Berlioz's compositional learning curve while composing for an expansive acoustical space. In *Kyrie* (mvt 1) of *Messe solennelle*, entries by the chorus and the weird instrumental "pops"—sudden *forte* woodwind jolts that immediately die away—appear predictably. But in the companion passage, *Offertoire* (mvt 7) in *Requiem*, similar choral entries and "pops" seem to be in an eerie stream of consciousness. We can guess when they might happen, but truly it's guessing, and so the music is far more mysterious and alluring.

Similarly, the music he wrote in *Messe solennelle* for the text *Et iterum, venturus est* (and he shall come again with glory to judge the living and the dead; and his kingdom shall have no end) is clearly a trial run for the remarkable, famous *Tuba mirum spargens* passage of the *Requiem*. Listening to both passages back to back is time well spent. In *Messe solennelle* the textual phrase is sung by only a solo bass. By contrast, the similar line in *Requiem* is much more alive, and the slower tempo allows the sound to roll out magnificently into a cavernous liturgical space. Choosing not to harmonize it, all seventy basses (yes, as per his instructions in the score) thunderously sing the *Tuba mirum spargens* line in unison as though preordained from another world. He knew, based on his prior experience, that the characteristics of that unison line, sung by so many in that particular vocal register and in that expansive space, would indelibly penetrate the audience's psyche. Likewise, the fantastically elaborate brass buildup preceding *Tuba mirum spargens* is eternally memorable and far more spectacular than in *Messe solennelle*.

Berlioz also realized *Messe solennelle* contained too much fast music to work well in a large cathedral space. In a similar hall today, such as the National Cathedral in Washington, D.C., those passages would be a blur—waves of sound folding over one another and quickly becoming indistinguishable. Some music even resembles the elegant, filigree writing of the young Mozart, which was intended for intimate spaces, more so than the *grande ligne* (long, expansive line) one generally hears from Berlioz. Other passages sound like attempts to be traditional to please his instructors at the Conservatoire. When Berlioz heard *Messe solennelle* performed, he immediately recognized its flaws.

Despite its formative attributes, the initial performance of *Messe solennelle* marked a critical turning point. His composition teacher, Jean-François LeSueur, gave him the imprimatur of future success, and for its second performance Berlioz conducted an orchestra and chorus for the first time. After the *Et Resurrexit* movement, the orchestra players applauded louder than the audience, just as they would at the first performance of *Roméo et Juliette* and during rehearsals of *Symphonie fantastique*. From this moment on, players and singers were often the first to recognize his genius.

Importantly, too, and because of a disastrous first rehearsal, Berlioz learned to take full control of preparing and proofreading performance materials. To save on costs, choirboys had been assigned by their director to write out the solo, chorus, and orchestra parts, and they contained innumerable errors. Having learned the hard way, never again was a Berlioz rehearsal crippled by inadequate preparation of the music materials.

Before deciding to dismantle, borrow from, and abandon the score of *Messe solennelle*, Berlioz gave the autograph to a colleague in Belgium as a gift. He forgot about it and claimed later to have burned the work. Lucky for us the gift copy was found 173 years later in an Antwerp organ loft.

GRANDE MESSE DES MORTS (REQUIEM)

Upon publishing a new edition of *Grande messe des morts*, Berlioz wrote that, if he were threatened with seeing all his works burned except for one score, he would beg exception for the *Mass for the Dead*. Its significance to him lay in the ways he captured the expressive possibilities of the text, opportunities that had gone unrecognized or avoided by composers before. Known for its force and originality, *Grande messe des morts* is remarkable for its compositional strategies. Composed to reflect nationalistic-patriotic ideals, no similar work matches its brilliance in scale, orchestration, or drama. It was one of his few government commissions, and he was rightfully proud of it. The space where it was first performed, L'église St-Louis des Invalides (Saint Louis Church of the Invalids),[1] continues to host commemorations of the nation's war heroes.

Longer than its Requiem mass predecessors, *Grande messe des morts* is a complete concert unto itself, offering ninety minutes of choral-orchestral music in ten separate movements with no intermission. Breaking with the tradition of using a solo quartet of soprano, alto, tenor, and bass, Berlioz writes for only one soloist, a tenor, who sings in just one movement, the *Sanctus*. Using the traditional text (with some omissions and reordering), he also emulated his French predecessor composers, particularly François-Joseph Gossec (1734–1829) and his teacher Jean-François LeSueur (1760–1837), by expanding the forces beyond a standard-sized orchestra and chorus.

A walk through the amazing assemblage of performers is a worthwhile endeavor. In addition to the solitary tenor soloist, the score specifies at least eighty sopranos, sixty tenors, and seventy basses. The chorus, therefore, in addition to being quite large, was slightly more than one-third first and second sopranos, which is a significant contrast to the ideal fifty-fifty balance of women to men in mixed choruses today. Berlioz's three-part voicing, often divided into six-parts, was typical of French music at the time, in contrast to four-part soprano-alto-tenor-bass (SATB) or five parts (first and second sopranos: SSATB) customary in other countries then and today.[2]

For the immense orchestra, Berlioz designed the woodwind section as follows: four flutes, two oboes and two English horns, four clarinets, and eight bassoons. Each section was double the norm. The brass section includes twelve French horns seated in the main orchestra plus four distinct brass choirs, each positioned at one of the four corners of the performing forces in a cathedral or concert hall. They include four cornets à pistons, twelve trumpets, sixteen trombones, two tubas, and four ophicleides for a grand total of fifty brass players, thirty-eight of which are grouped in their own four units. Percussionists number an extraordinary eighteen individuals to play eight pairs of timpani, two bass drums, four tam-tams, and ten pairs of cymbals. Berlioz required, ideally, 108 strings: twenty-five first violins, twenty-five second violins, twenty violas, twenty cellos, and eighteen double basses. The performer total is roughly two hundred singers and two hundred instrumentalists. Rarely, however, do they all sing or play all together.

The performance space, L'église St-Louis des Invalides, is a later addition to a complex of buildings constructed 1670–1676 in central Paris. It originally included a retirement home for veterans (Hôtel nationale des invalides) and later a museum and monuments relating to the military history of France. The domed structure first seen upon visiting the site, Église du Dôme (Dome Church), is a private chapel that was added in 1708.[3] Berlioz's *Requiem* was performed in the larger, long, and narrow chapel, L'église St-Louis des Invalides, where the resident military veterans worshipped. This structure was added to the complex in 1679 and, unfortunately, no longer exists as it did in 1837. To see a still-existing space in Paris where Berlioz performed *Requiem*, visit the L'église St-Eustache, a gothic church completed in 1637. He organized and conducted performances of it there in 1846, 1850, and 1852, and his *Te Deum* in 1855.

Envision L'église St-Louis des Invalides with a very high ceiling, a fairly narrow nave, marble and stone walls and floors, columns, side chapels, and wooden pews. Plaster frescoes, oil paintings, and cloth banners adorn the walls, and flags of defeated countries, statues, and weapons are on display. Music for such an important occasion in such an imposing, resonant space must not have florid, fast phrases that billow out and over onto the next, as happened in *Messe solennelle*. Berlioz needed music that would unfold clearly. Themes must be simple and deliberate, and there must be not only grandeur but also introspection.

Three Kinds of Part Writing for the Voices

One way to approach *Requiem* is to consider how voices behave and interact in such a resonant acoustic. Here are three chorus textures to listen for.

1. Unison. Singing unison liturgical chants was deeply ingrained in the French-Catholic psyche; it focuses attention, declares unanimity, and somehow calms the soul. But hearing melodies by Berlioz sung by as many as sixty to eighty voices goes several steps beyond. With the exception of *Quaerens me* (mvt 5) and *Hostias* (mvt 8), every movement has an extended passage for one section in unison. The single-line passages of *Te decet hymnus* text in mvts 1 and 10 and the *Dies irae* opening of mvt 2 are particularly memorable.

2. Homophony. By contrast, note the simple, statuesque passages in *Hostias* (mvt 5) and the opening of *Agnus Dei* (mvt 10). These utterly calm homophonic moments have no apparent melody, only harmony, and the stillness amidst changing colors has its own allure. In the forceful *Rex tremendae* (mvt 4), loud calls in

block harmonies move slowly through a turbulent orchestral texture. Here the rhythmic vitality required to declaim the text
clearly serves to amplify the volume.

3. Imitative counterpoint. In a fugue or fugato, a variety of imitative
   counterpoint, the listener focuses on a melody presented by itself
   and follows it as it combines with a secondary idea; lines evolve,
   intertwine, culminate, and cadence to closure. Fugues or fugatos
   are in *Requiem et Kyrie* (mvt 1) and *Quaerens me* (mvt 5). Because interweaving lines can easily blur together in a reverberant
   space, Berlioz designed themes that unfurl clearly. He set them
   in uncluttered textures and chose deliberate tempos to reduce
   unwanted smudging. An egalitarian, he left no voice part out;
   each of the three (soprano, tenor, and bass) sings the melody
   alone, and likewise, everyone harmonizes. When not singing the
   primary melody, the other lines are still melodic in nature or they
   sing an incantation-like patter. Listen for fugues or fugatos also in
   Lacrymosa (mvt 6) and *Offertoire* (mvt 7).

Text and Tradition

The traditional *Requiem* or *Messe des morts* (Mass for the dead; only
Berlioz and his Parisian predecessor Gossec entitled their works
Grande messe des morts) is a spoken and sung liturgical service in
memory of the departed. Its texts derive from ceremonial conventions,
a thirteenth-century poem, and long-held beliefs in the Roman Catholic
faith, which Berlioz grew up in but did not embrace. In this case Berlioz
wrote to commemorate a fallen military hero who, in turn, was a symbol
for all French soldiers lost in battle since 1830. While his *Requiem* was
written for performance in a liturgical space, it functions as a concert
work where no celebrants are required.

Berlioz made changes to the standard text, whether for reasons of
personal conviction, because of the occasion, or for purposes of musical
structure. For example, he ends two movements by repeating the first
lines (mvts 6 and 7) and leaves off the last line or two in three (mvts 2,
7, and 8). The obligatory Sequence poem (mvts 2–6) has nineteen
verses, but Berlioz left out four of them. Most unorthodox for a Mass
setting, there is no Benedictus section in the *Sanctus* (mvt 9). Finally,
he unconventionally concludes *Agnus Dei* (mvt 10) with *cum sanctis*

tuis in aeternum, Domine, quia pius es (with your saints forever, Lord, for you are merciful), which is the last line of the Communion text, *Lux aeterna* (Light eternal). Many in the audience at the time, having grown up attending Catholic services in Latin or through their schooling, would have understood every word and noticed the changes. But no one seemed to mind.

For reference while listening, the Latin title and corresponding English first line for Berlioz's ten-movement work are provided below.[4] Having the complete text and translation in hand is recommended.

Requiem Movements and First Line of Text

Introit:

1. *Requiem et Kyrie*, Grant them eternal rest and Lord have mercy

Sequence (thirteenth-century poem; mvts 2–6):

2. *Dies irae*, The day of wrath, that day will dissolve the world in ashes
3. *Quid sum miser*, What can a wretch like me say?
4. *Rex tremendae*, King of incredible majesty
5. *Quaerens me*, In seeking me, you sat down wearily
6. *Lacrymosa*, That day of weeping

7. *Offertoire*, Chorus of souls in purgatory; Lord Jesus, King of Glory, deliver the souls of all the faithful dead
8. *Hostias*, We offer to you, O Lord, sacrifices and prayers (second part of the *Offertoire*)
9. *Sanctus/Hosanna*, Holy, Lord God of Sabbaoth [*sic*] (tenor soloist)
10. *Agnus Dei*, Lamb of God, grant them rest everlasting

A Few General Characteristics of Note

- Recurring themes. Themes that return in a later movement act as threads of overarching coherence and give comfort in familiarity. For example, in mvts 1 and 10, listen for the beautiful *Te decet hymnus* section (A hymn in Zion befits you, O God, and a debt will be paid to you in Jerusalem. Hear my prayer: all earthly flesh will come to you). The *Dies irae* (mvt 2) melody (newly composed, not the liturgical chant that he already used in mvt 5 of *Symphonie fantastique*) returns at the opening of *Quid sum miser* (mvt 3).

- Key relationships. At times Berlioz intentionally juxtaposed uncomfortably distant tonal areas from one movement to the next. One instance is the end of *Dies irae* (mvt 2) in E ♭ major, which is followed by *Quid sum miser* (mvt 3) in a distant G♯ minor. The new music, played by English horns and bassoons, sounds strikingly disembodied. *Requiem* closes in a radiant G major, having begun in a foreboding G minor.

- Levels of orchestra participation and dynamic contrast. Much is made of the extraordinary decibel level or "sonic boom" of the work, but all forces—two hundred musicians in Berlioz's ideal performance—play and sing only in mvts 2, 4, and 6. Many other passages are soft or fragile, having been scored for just a few instruments. Often these are the most emotionally powerful, particularly in a cathedral. Silences, which are often surrounded by a solitary sustained note or chord, are invariably arresting. In terms of overall levels of instrument participation, the work ends roughly where it began at an intermediate dynamic level. In between there are several quite stunning contrasts between movements. For example, the *Lacrymosa* (mvt 6), among the loudest and approximately halfway through, is preceded by the most quiet, introspective movement, the a cappella *Quaerens me* (mvt 5). Likewise, the loud and fearful *Rex tremendae* (mvt 4) is preceded by the disconsolate, soft *Quid sum miser* (mvt 3). The physical impact of these extremes, from silence to ultra-soft to overwhelmingly loud and everything in between, can only be fully experienced in a live performance of the complete work.

- Levels of singer participation. Men sing the most and are featured by themselves in mvts 3, 8, and the opening of 10; they are often divided into four parts. Tutti textures are usually in the standard three parts of soprano, tenor, and bass for fugal passages, but the voices divide into a five or six parts for special transcendent moments, such as *promisisti, Domine Jesu Christe* (promised, Lord Jesus Christ) at the end of the *Offertoire* (mvt 7) and *luceat eis* (shine on them) near the end of *Agnus Dei* (mvt 10). Women in three parts fulfill their customary angelic assignment for *Sanctus/Hosanna* (mvt 9).

- Transfixing fugue. In *Offertoire* (mvt 7), the surreal, meditative quality of the chant-like fugal subject and its quintessential unfolding into a fugue is transfixing. *Offertoire* was the most performed excerpt from *Requiem* during Berlioz's life.

- Contrast of extreme registers. The spread of pitches from high to low are especially breathtaking in *Hostias* (mvt 8) and *Agnus Dei* (mvt 10). Four flutes high in their register are divided into three or four parts while trombones play in unison and extremely low. Not only different registers are heard but quite different timbres as well.

- New setting for end-of-the-world music. Judgment and the end of the world are announced in the unprecedented *Dies irae* (mvt 2) with music derived from *Messe solennelle* (discussed above). All seventy vocal basses in unison join the richly harmonized tutti brass for an earth-shattering *Tuba mirum spargens sonum* (The trumpet, scattering a marvelous sound through the tombs of every land, will gather all before the throne).

Listener's Guide by Movement

Duration, first tempo, and instrumentation for each movement are provided.

1. Requiem et Kyrie (11:14'; Andante un poco lento, pulse = 69)

For flutes, oboes, English horns, clarinets, bassoons, horns (divided two and three ways), strings, and chorus

The orchestral introduction is full of premonition. String instruments begin a low, slow rise, and upon leveling off they seem to speak the second and third syllables of *Re-qui-em* (long-short-short). Three times the strings rise, each time beginning from the same place but reaching a step higher than before. At the third plateau, we hear a radiant chord rather than the unisons from before. The three phrases are of different lengths and separated by pauses, so organization of strong and weak beats is obscured. With no apparent meter, we are unsettled.

Voices sing a fugue comprised of two themes, each moving downward but in different ways. Basses first sing the subject: long notes descending in varieties of broken chords on *Requiem aeternam* (Rest eternal). Tenors soon follow, singing a countersubject on the same text; it descends haltingly by small neighboring steps. Quite high in their register, the sopranos enter on the subject and carry momentum forward. All three voice parts sing both the subject and countersubject. The text implores God to grant eternal rest to the departed.

Dona eis Domine (Grant them, Lord) has a disembodied, wistful sound; men's voices are in the lead. The sopranos sing a billowing arabesque joined by flutes and oboes, and they move into more plaintive implorations on the text *dona eis requiem* (grant them rest). The *Requiem aeternam* fugue begins again but is transformed: the countersubject now rises and is more rhythmically intense. The subsequent *Te decet hymnus* (To you praise is right), a soaring melody sung at first only by individual choral sections, is ethereal and uplifting. Near the end of the movement, *Kyrie eleison* (Lord have mercy) is sung in an eerie unison, as though in fear of the unknown; the passage is similar to *cum sanctis tuis in aeternum domine* (with your saints in eternity) near the end of *Agnus Dei* (mvt 10). The thematic and textural kinship between the first and last movements gives structural continuity from back to front.

2. Dies Irae (13'; Moderato, pulse = 96)

Orchestra in full with prominent brass participation: twelve horns play from the center of the orchestra, and thirty-eight brass (trumpets, cornets, trombones, tubas, and ophicleides) in four choirs play from the four corners of the performance forces, whether in a concert hall or a cathedral; fifty total brass.

The chorus sings the *Dies irae* text (Day of wrath, that day will dissolve the world in ashes, what trembling there will be) to two separate melodies. The first, played at the opening by cellos and contrabasses alone, resembles a Gregorian chant but was newly composed by Berlioz. Immediately after the opening instrumental statement, sopranos, who are doubled by several woodwinds playing the same pitches, sing the second melody.

Being able to anticipate how the opening five sections of the *Dies irae* unfold will facilitate listening to it. Note the three chromatic surge gestures (loud, brief orchestral ascents) in italics below, each of which ends higher than its predecessor and separates sections 1 through 4.

1. The contrapuntally conceived *Dies irae* (discussed above) opens in a stark minor tonality; eventually the two themes combine.

Chromatic surge 1: moves like a tidal wave; accelerates; agitated string tremolos; ends up a half step to B ♭ minor.

2. Anxiety is intensified: while basses seem chained to the low first theme, the tenor line becomes disjointed and driven. Meanwhile, women intermittently call out single pitches on long notes. *Chromatic surge 2, transition to D minor.*

3. Tenors sing more urgently as baritones and basses continue lumbering through the *Dies irae* chant. Sopranos become increasingly evident and insistent as they sing their single pitch interjections. *Chromatic surge 3 and rise to E ♭ major.*

4. Four brass choirs from the corners of the performance forces[5] and twelve horns from the orchestra center enter in E ♭ major in sequenced waves of overlapping pitches and rhythms. The entire orchestra, including sixteen timpani and four bass drums, join the tutti brass on the last chord, a roar of cataclysmic proportions. The conductor may hold it for as long as inspired.

5. From out of the orchestral tumult, basses sing in unison *Tuba mirum spargens* on E ♭ , which is near the top of their range. All instruments are eliminated except timpani and bass drum as they continue their tremolo roar. The earth is shattering apart, graves are opening, and souls are rising to be judged. "The wondrous trumpet spreading the sound throughout the tombs of all regions will gather all before the throne." There is no escape, we shall all be judged. The loudest moment in the *Requiem* occurs at the next fermata when four tam-tams and ten pairs of cymbals add in (just before *Judex ergo, cum sedebit* [when the judge is seated]). No melody is heard, only a colossal wall of sound. A shock of silence follows, preparation for the contrition that's next.

3. Quid sum miser (3'; Andante un poco lento, pulse = 76)

For two English horns and two bassoons, cellos, and contrabasses; tenors

Seeming as though an afterthought, *Quid sum miser* opens quietly with English horn and bassoons playing both themes just heard in the tumultuous *Dies irae*; one theme is gently superimposed upon the other as though in subdued penitence. Different iterations in shifting shades and nuances seem to reach out listlessly to an unknown entity or place.

Only tenors sing the plaintive second theme; they ask who will inter-cede on their behalf when they can trust no one. Stunningly, the char-acter of the music and the texts of the two movements are diametrically opposite despite the similar thematic material. Here are the texts of mvts 2 and 3 side by side:

Dies irae (mvt 2)	*Quid sum miser* (mvt 3)
The day of wrath, that day will	What can a wretch like me say?
dissolve the world in ashes,	Whom shall I ask to intercede for me,
as David and the Sibyl prophesied.	when even the just ones are unsafe?

4. Rex tremendae (6:15'; Andante maestoso, pulse = 66)

For tutti orchestra and chorus

Gloriously resplendent blocks of sound are heard at the beginning as though we are in an austere yet grand royal procession; the texture then shifts to individual vocal sections singing tender, soaring lines. Both approaches, massive blocks of sound and lyric unison melodies, are Berlioz's most successful strategies for clear sound definition in a reso-nant space.

5. Quaerens me (4:09'; Andante sostenuto, pulse = 66)

For a cappella chorus

The movement is a three-part vocal fugue with no orchestral participa-tion. Austere legato lines in strict counterpoint are set against muttered repeated notes. Likely in homage to Renaissance composers such as Palestrina, Berlioz uses counterpoint here to invoke utter simplicity. The profoundly remorseful supplicants are in a devotional pilgrimage.

6. Lacrymosa (10:20'; Andante non troppo lento, pulse = 60)

For tutti orchestra and chorus

The orchestra is in a nine-beat meter of three large pulses, each pulse of which contains three interior pulses, for example, 3 + 3 + 3. Normally music "in nine" has a gentle, loping feel because beats 1, 4, and 7 are accented: ONE-two-three, FOUR-five-six, SEVEN-eight-nine. Here in *Lacrymosa*, however, this gentle loping is disrupted by different instrument families playing distinctive events on one of the unaccented interior beats, one or several of 2-3, 5-6, and 8-9. Roughly described, bass strings glide from beat 9 into 1, woodwinds lean into a strident chromatic pitch on beat 3, strings literally smack beat 6, and all twelve French horns blast out on beat 7. Horns then diminuendo to the end of the measure, and the pattern begins all over again, measure by measure: nine-ONE-two, THREE-four-five, SIX-SEVEN-eight. The bizarre entries and jarring accents by the three different instrumental families of strings, winds, and brass create a vamp (repeating accompaniment pattern) that is edgy, diabolical, and entirely original. Every possible permutation of accent is exploited to ratchet up grotesque weirdness and make the music even more horrifying, punishing, and therefore more enticing. Traditionally compound meters (6/8 and 9/8) were for naïve and soothing music, but here Berlioz turns that convention on its head. Instead of making the *Lacrymosa* music about weeping, as did Mozart and Verdi among many others, he made it about condemnation of the guilty.

Against, through, and around this bizarre template, tenors alone sing the long, lyrical *Lacrymosa* melody. It functions as a connector from one herky-jerky measure to the next, like sinew connecting muscles to bones. Their notes are high and technically demanding but not out of reach. Fortunately, rests separate the phrases so singers have time to breathe often. At the last and most strenuous phrase of the opening section, the lower female voices and basses join as reinforcements and to sustain momentum.

As it turns out, the tenor's *Lacrymosa* melody is the subject of a massive, vigorous fugue containing multiple expositions and transitions in between. Intensity is heightened by the swaying back and forth between woodwinds and brass and by stern punctuations amidst the increasingly dense walls of sound. In the coda the bass drum, sounding like claps of thunder, pounds away in couplets while chorus and woodwinds call back and forth to the brass three times in three different walls of sound. All arrive to the last sonority together, which the conductor may, again, hold as long as inspired. As the sound slowly dies away, the audience is left to savor and ponder.

7. Offertoire (10'; Moderato, pulse = 84), Chorus of Souls in Purgatory

For flutes, oboes, English horns, clarinets, bassoons, horns, ophicleide, strings, and chorus

During the Offertory in a liturgical service, bread and wine are brought forward for consecration. To give the feel of a solemn procession, Berlioz wrote a long flowing line for the fugue subject and set it in a three-part string texture. In contrast, a unison chorus enters on a single note that rocks back and forth to its upper neighbor tone, and each successive entry is placed unpredictably. Meanwhile woodwinds and horns play ritualistic bell imitations signaling utter solemnity and the sting of sin and death.

> Lord Jesus Christ! Glorious king!
> Free the souls of all the faithful dead from punishment.
> Lord, free them from punishment in the inferno and from the deep lake!

The effect of these three superimposed elements—flowing melodies, rocking unison, and bell imitations—is like cinematic time travel through an imagined and constantly changing purgatory landscape. While the orchestra carries the musical narrative, singers persist with mesmerizingly simple text declamations. A radiant six-voice cadence on *promisisti Domine Jesu Christe* (you promised, Lord Jesus Christ) followed by fragment reminiscences of the fugue subject conclude the movement.

Berlioz used the same procedure two years later in *Jetez des fleurs*, the funeral procession in *Roméo et Juliette*, but he took the idea a step further. At the midpoint of the movement, orchestra and chorus trade roles: the chorus sings the fugue mourning Juliette's death while the orchestra plays the single note rocking back and forth.

8. Hostias (3:47'; Andante non troppo lento, pulse = 56)

For three flutes, strings, and men's chorus; eight trombones from the third and fourth brass choirs play unisons

After three consecutive movements of linear writing, now only choral homophony is heard. Men sing simple, solemn phrases in close harmony and a cappella. Flutes in three parts and an eerily high register, plus unison trombones on very low sustained tones, echo the final chords of the men. The extreme differences in register and timbre between flutes and trombones are a metaphor for the metaphysical distance between heaven and hell. Climaxes in the music are given time and space to linger and clear. We sense an immensity of space, and time seems suspended.

9. Sanctus (13'; Andante un poco sostenuto e maestoso, pulse = 52)

For flutes, oboe, clarinets, bassoons, horns, cornets à pistons, ophicleides, bass drum, three pairs of cymbal, women's three-part chorus and six-part mixed chorus, and tenor solo; strings with four solo violins in four parts, viola section divided into four parts, flute solo

The tenor soloist sings a melody of great simplicity and tenderness set near the top of his range. Multiple layers of celestial strings in thin, fragile harmonics accompany him, and a three-part women's chorus of angels echo him in a radiant cushion of sound. The breath-endurance demands on both tenor and flute at this formidably slow tempo are substantial, and fine intonation is required. Berlioz instructs the quick march *Hosanna*, a straightforward fugue sung by voices doubled by strings, to be sung without heavy accents. This instruction is unusual: perhaps an accented singing style was customary for *Hosannas* at the time. Nonetheless, achieving good singer cohesion in this passage is deceptively difficult despite the straightforward victory march character of the music.

The *Sanctus* returns with the addition of a cello line and majestic, mysterious punctuation from the bass drum and cymbals, a gesture of sanctification. The second *Hosanna* is similar to the first but more festive—celebratory trumpets and horns add in for the march toward a bravura close. Berlioz omitted the Benedictus normally included in a Requiem mass, deciding it was not essential to the drama at that moment.

10. Agnus Dei (13'; Andante un poco lento, pulse = 56)

For standard woodwinds (flutes divide four ways), four French horns, strings (violas divide four ways), and eight pairs of timpani. Eight trombones from the four separate brass groups are used as unison pedal tones; all sixteen trombones and four ophicleides play the closing passage in four-part harmony.

The opening instrumental section begins meditatively. Woodwinds play a statuesque succession of six rich chords at a *piano* dynamic, and violas seamlessly overlap with them in closely aligned four-part chords at *ppp*, like an a cappella men's chorus. All seems timeless because the woodwind chords are in tempo (pulse = 56), but viola chords are held *ad libitum* (at liberty, no tempo). Is this passage perhaps mirroring a mourner's fragile thoughts and deeply private feelings? No melody is present, only tentative vertical sonorities.

In a procession of memories, the remaining music in the *Requiem* brings back passages from three prior movements. A cappella men in four-part harmony sing *Agnus Dei* phrases in slow alternation with interjections by flutes (this time divided four ways) and trombone pedal tones, reminiscent of *Hostias* (mvt 8). The *Te decet hymnus* section, heard first in *Requiem et Kyrie* (mvt 1) through to *lucet eis* (shine on them), and the reprise of the *Requiem aeternam* fugue subject and countersubject are repeated exactly. Once again we enjoy soaring unison melodies sung by single choral sections and likewise recall a short portion of the vigorously alive fugal section.

Near the end of *Agnus Dei*, we hear the return of the *Kyrie eleison* (Lord have mercy) unison chant from near the end of mvt 1, but now it is set to new text, *cum sanctis tuis* (with your saints). Somber timpani pulse between vocal phrases whereas before woodwinds played punctuating chords. Then the music of *fons pietatis* (fount of mercy), from the end of *Rex tremendae* (mvt 4), is heard to the new text *quia pius es* (because you are merciful), as though finishing the thought.

Six ethereal *Amens* close *Agnus Dei* in a mesmerizing unwinding. The last moments of mvt 1 are recalled, but considering all that has transpired, the listener has a much deeper sense of the finiteness of life. Eight incredibly somber timpani in a processional military tattoo replace the earlier movement's pizzicato string chords; they alternate with strings playing gentle halo-like arabesques. In a gently rocking motion, each "a-" syllable is sung on a different chord while the "-men" returns to same chord as the "-men" before, which is also the final harmony of the work. We who remain are in catharsis; those departed are at rest.

Commissioned by Bureaucracy; First Performance

The journey of *Requiem* from commissioning to performance was a bureaucratic nightmare. The minister of the interior charged Berlioz to write a work commemorating the death of Édouard-Adophe Mortier, commander in chief to King Louis-Philippe, and other victims who died while successfully defending the king. An anarchist had attempted to assassinate him as the unit processed through the streets of Paris in July 1835. The commission also sought to remember those who died in battle since 1830 and to restore the prestige of sacred music in France. To compose for such an important occasion was an honor and just the career break Berlioz had hoped for.

He composed quickly, having already thought about music for a Requiem mass for quite some time. Following completion there was only a month for preparations before the concert on July 28, 1837: copy and produce lithograph orchestra and choral parts, contract players and singers, schedule rehearsals, and oversee construction of the scaffolding in L'église St-Louis des Invalides for all four hundred performers. But due to the cost of a royal wedding, the government cancelled the concert for lack of funds. Berlioz had already incurred major expenses— copying alone was 3,800 francs, and his commission of 4,000 francs had not yet been received. Only after repeated, humiliating appeals and delays following the eventual performance was Berlioz paid his commission and reimbursed for expenses.

When another important general died a short time later, a new performance date was set, December 5, 1837, and François Habeneck, the royal chapel master and violinist leader of the Société des Concerts (Conservatoire orchestra), was appointed to conduct. Berlioz, as one of several subconductors, oversaw the percussion and four brass choir section rehearsals. He also stood near the players during the performance to provide a beat if necessary due to poor sight lines.

While a complete success, the performance was also eventful, to say the least. In *Dies irae* (mvt 2), at the transition measure into *Tuba mirum*, Habeneck became distracted or, more likely, uncertain. At this precise moment, every player in the massive orchestra needed him to set the new pulse = 72, half as fast as before. They all knew Berlioz's plan for staggered entrances by the four separate brass choirs; they also knew the passage would fall apart without four clear gestures in the new tempo so they could accurately count their beats of rests before playing. Instead of doing his job, Habeneck paused to take a pinch of snuff. To divert catastrophe, Berlioz jumped up to the stage and conducted to the end of the movement. Afterward, Habeneck profusely thanked him. Other distracting situations occurred as well: a chorister fainted while standing on the tiered risers, a group of clergy kept on audibly chanting the liturgy during the performance, and another priest had to be led away having burst into tears. Nonetheless, the resounding success of *Requiem* established Berlioz's importance and paved the way for *Benvenuto Cellini*, the first of his operas, to reach the public.

As for publication of the score, *Requiem* is an exception to the rule; immediately after the first performance it was publicized for sale as a subscription and was soon issued. Sales in 1838 bolstered Berlioz's income and reputation throughout Europe. He later published second and third editions with some changes made after more performances, most of which he conducted himself.

Reception

If the popularity of *Requiem* is measured by repeat performances of the complete work during Berlioz's lifetime, there is not much to celebrate. During the next thirty years, it was performed in its entirety only five times. Berlioz conducted the last three in L'église Saint-Eustache: the first in 1846 in memory of Gluck, his most revered musical hero; and in 1850 and 1852.

While on concert tours in France and abroad, he conducted excerpts. *Offertoire* (mvt 7) was performed most often, thirteen times. Schumann was "electrified" when he heard it in Germany in 1843 during Berlioz's first concert tour there. In terms of organizing singers and players in each new city, *Offertoire* was the easiest. The chorus could learn their parts in a brief rehearsal, and fewer orchestra forces were needed, which saved valuable rehearsal time and cost.

Six performances on tour of *Dies irae* (mvt 2) and five of *Lacrymosa* (mvt 6) advanced Berlioz's reputation for cataclysmic music, although those movements were rarely performed in cathedral-like acoustics. Never excerpted were *Rex tremendae* (mvt 4), *Hostias* (mvt 8), and *Agnus Dei* (mvt 10). They made the most sense only in context of the music surrounding them; the latter two benefit most from a large reverberant acoustic. Other movements were excerpted only two or three times.

Today Berlioz's *Requiem* is performed, but not as frequently as Mozart's, Verdi's, or Brahms's Requiems. The requirements for large forces and a resonant performance space present daunting costs and logistical challenges, and the chorus master and conductor must open themselves to Berlioz's unique musical "take," for it is like no other. Courage is required to perform this remarkable *style énorme* work, but very rarely, if ever, does it disappoint.

Referring to his monumental architectural works, Berlioz wrote in the postscript to his *Mémoires*,

> To perform them well, everybody concerned, the conductor most of all, must feel as I feel. They require a combination of irresistible verve and the utmost precision, a controlled vehemence, a dreamlike sensitivity, an almost morbid melancholy, without which the essential character of my phrases is falsified or even obliterated. For this reason, I find it exceedingly painful to hear most of my works conducted by someone other than myself . . . approximately right is totally wrong.[6]

VIGNETTE 4.1: *GRANDE MESSE DES MORTS*: SHOP TALK

The year is 2010. Choral conductor Grant and collaborating pianist Nancy are driving to the last rehearsal before their community chorus joins with a professional orchestra and tenor soloist. The performance will be in St. Marie's, an expansive stone and wood Gothic revival church in Manchester, New Hampshire.

Grant: That descending fugue subject at the beginning is so cool—each time it outlines a seventh chord![7] It's such an unorthodox pattern of notes for a theme yet so singable. Once the singers understood the template, the rest fell into place! Now that's compositional artistry for you.

Nancy: I can't think of another fugue where both the subject and the countersubject move in the same direction, down. Well, given the topic, rest eternal, it makes sense of course. The themes nudge and respond to each other as they reach up, move forward, and descend. Maybe, in a circumspect way, Berlioz is using both musical subjects as a metaphor for the intermingling of two states of mind, such as agony in death and sorrow.

Grant: That is wonderful, Nancy, I'll have to tell the chorus tonight! You know, I can't wait to hear the four brass choirs from the four corners of the stage area—all thirty-eight players! I was so fascinated with what's going on in the *Dies irae* that I mapped out the order of entries and the direction from which they come. Berlioz made a drawing of where he wanted the four brass choirs and other instrument families placed for a concert years later that also included *Harold en Italie.* I even memorized the order! Listen to this, every entrance crisscrosses the stage from right to left and back to front:

1. four trumpets and four trombones from *back right*;
2. four cornets à pistons and four trombones from *front left*;
3. four trumpets and four trombones from *front right*;
4. four trumpets, four trombones, and four ophicleides enter from *back left*, plus four French horns seated in the orchestra; and lastly,
5. two tubas enter to firm up the bottom end of the sound; from *front left*.[8]

At this point all brass choirs are in! The rest of the orchestra doesn't join for a while, but when hearing the additive progression of entries and new rhythms and harmonies, you know they'll be there soon. If ever there was an all-encompassing, surround-sound, cataclysmic depiction of judgment, this is the moment!

Nancy: And what a sound it will be when our basses enter on *Tuba mirum spargens.* Finding that E♭ near the top of their range is easy, just a half step up from the last chromatic surge. Still, it sounds incredibly creepy, as though it comes out of nowhere. No other instruments are in, just our basses and sixteen thundering timpani. I cannot wait to hear it "live" in St. Marie's as the sound ricochets and splinters off the walls. The onslaught will be my undoing!

Grant: Thinking about acoustics, those solemn a cappella phrases in the *Hostias* and *Agnus Dei* work perfectly in St. Marie's. Our guys are going to be so gorgeous in those long, four-part block sonorities. Each "halo moment" is so fragile as it emerges, one after the next. Absolutely ethereal.

Nancy: At first I thought Berlioz should get on with things; there is too much time waiting around on one chord. But these passages teach patience. The instruments intone chords the way people have thoughts. Totally beguiling.

Grant: Yes, but I'm the breath police. Calm introspection must not be disrupted—some men are still taking sneak breaths in just the wrong places. Hmm, those four flutes from the orchestra and eight trombones from the brass choirs coming from the back right and back left corners; I cannot wait to hear those. The cool, wide expanse of their chords seems like extremities of the universe.

Nancy: I'm looking forward to hearing the tenor soloist sing *Sanctus* from the balcony *behind* the audience. More otherworldliness. He'll be close to three stories above the main floor. Our three-part women angels are sounding quite fine, just like a boys' choir.

Grant: You know, I'm surprised at how fast our chorus has learned this work. It's odd to say, but the notes look plain on the page yet they still pose challenges. The miracle of Berlioz's *Requiem*, it seems to me as a performer, is in recognizing how Berlioz's special effects conspire with one another. You have to have the right performance space; St. Marie's is a gem.

LA DAMNATION DE FAUST: LÉGENDE DRAMATIQUE

The music in *La damnation de Faust* (The damnation of Faust: dramatic legend) is splendidly illustrative of the Faust story *if* you know the story and what's happening each step of the way. The work is not complex or opaque, but scenes can seem nonlinear at times. More than one seasoned Berlioz listener has wondered why, all of a sudden, we're in a Leipzig tavern right after being on the Hungarian plains, or why Marguerite is floating up to the heavens when, last we knew, Faust was going to rescue her from prison. A scene-by-scene listener's map is offered below to aid in joining music to story line. But first here's some background.

Context for Berlioz's Adaptation of Goethe's *Faust*

Johann Wolfgang Goethe (1749–1832) is considered a cornerstone of German literary and cultural heritage and of the Romantic era. His epic narrative poem *Faust*, upon which Berlioz's composition is based, is a story of the struggle between good and evil and the search for enlightenment and peace. Goethe did not create the story; rather, it emerged first as a medieval folk legend and then a play by Christopher Marlowe and an etching by Rembrandt, among other realizations. Goethe first developed his own ideas in 1772–1775 and wrote his epic poem in two parts much later. Around 1827–1828, two translations into French of part 1 appeared in Paris, one a reprint of Albert Stapfer's 1823 edition, and another by Gérard de Nerval, and so the essentials of Goethe's narrative became well known in France.

Berlioz's *La damnation de Faust*, composed in 1846, also had a long gestation. His *Huit scènes de Faust* (Eight scenes of Faust) preceded it in 1828–1829, just when the translations of Goethe's *Faust* into French were hot off the press. Berlioz drew upon *Huit scènes* for his greatly expanded rendition, enticingly describing it as a *légende dramatique* (dramatic legend). Other notable precedents were the opera by German composer Louis Spohr, *Faust*, which was based on plays and poems by other authors, and a famous series of seventeen lithographs by French artist Eugène Delacroix.[9] Berlioz composed his Faust based on the translation by Gérard de Nerval, asking his journalist friend Almire Gandonnière to compose the verses for the libretto. Ultimately Berlioz wrote about half of the text himself, at times composing words and music at the same time. *La damnation de Faust* is the first work for which Berlioz contributed much of the libretto.

The Faust story touched an existential nerve in the early to late nineteenth century and took Europe by storm. *La damnation de Faust* was followed by other settings based on Goethe, most notably Robert Schumann's *Scenes from Goethe's Faust*, a rarely performed oratorio written between 1842 and 1853, and *Faust Symphony* by Franz Liszt, which was premiered in Weimar, 1857. Liszt, the colleague and friend most responsible for advancing Berlioz's international career, dedicated his symphony to Berlioz; Berlioz dedicated his dramatic legend to Liszt. The famous opera *Faust* by Charles Gounod debuted in Paris, 1859.

Opera or Oratorio?

The question is often raised whether *La damnation de Faust* is better staged like an opera or left unstaged like an oratorio. Some opera companies believe that, since it is a great story with lots of possibilities for visual reenactment, surely Berlioz's rendition should be staged. Having been virtually barred from all Paris opera houses starting in 1839 (see chapter 5), surely it is his "wannabe" opera! Besides, *Faust* is a secular story like most operas, and oratorios are mostly based on biblical stories. Indeed, *La damnation de Faust* has many features of contemporary French grand operas: ballet music, a march, a fabulous love duet, and impressive depictions of heaven and hell. Years later he did consider reworking it into an opera, although that plan was discarded. But why *not* stage it? Major companies in New York, London, Paris, and many more certainly have.

Believing more is better and questioning a composer's concept can be a mistake. In his correspondence, Berlioz's earliest reference to the work was as a *opéra de concert* (concert opera), which is an opera performed without sets, costumes, or staging; he then settled on *légende dramatique*. Both descriptions make it clear he did not design the music for staging. As a critic in Paris, he attended and reviewed more than enough concerts and opera productions to know what kind of music was best suited for each genre. Instead of giving over his *légende dramatique* to sets and costumed characters, Berlioz wanted his audiences to focus on listening and using their imaginations.

Instrumentation and Stage Disposition in Berlioz's Time

Berlioz wrote for an orchestra of tremendous variety. Originally in *Huit scènes de Faust* he used guitar for *Sérénade de Méphistophélès*, and in the new work he wanted saxophones (a new instrument) in the Epilogue but trimmed those back. He wanted real church bells, as he used in *Symphonie fantastique*, and an extraordinary eight to ten harps for the Epilogue, as used in *Roméo et Juliette*. Five percussionists would be needed, more than normal but less than in *Requiem*. After revisions, his complete instrumental palette includes the following:

> Woodwinds: three flutes (all also play piccolo), two oboes (both also play English Horn), two clarinets, one bass clarinet, and four bassoons
>
> Brass: four horns, two trumpets, two cornets à piston, three trombones, one ophicleide, and one tuba
>
> Percussion: timpani, snare drum, triangle, bass drum, tam-tam, cymbals, suspended cymbal, triangle, and bells (sounding D, F♯, A, or C)
>
> Harps: eight to ten
>
> Strings: fifteen violins I, fifteen violins II, ten violas, ten violoncellos, and nine double basses

As for stage disposition, Berlioz's concerts were quite different from those normally seen today. The cellos and violas were seated in the center with violins I and II on stage right (on the performer's right when facing the audience) and stage left (performer's left), respectively. Behind them on as many as five sequentially taller platforms, each two and half feet in height, were the woodwinds, brass, and percussion. Louder instruments were farthest from the audience on the highest platforms and harps were on the stage aprons closest to the audience.

For the chorus, Berlioz specified at least sixty singers, ten to each part in soprano-tenor-bass *divisi* voicing. They were arranged onstage in two choirs: the first choir of sopranos-tenors-basses in *front* of the violin I section on stage right, women seated and men standing behind them; and the second choir, also sopranos-tenors-basses, in *front* of the violin II section on stage left, likewise men standing behind the seated women. This is a stark contrast to the contemporary convention of having choruses on risers behind the orchestra.

What would be different if Berlioz's approach were used today? When applying his stage disposition principles and using instruments from the middle of the nineteenth century, the strings will sound softer than expected and their timbre more varied from section to section and from top to bottom of their registers. They will play with more articulation and distinctive phrasing and use vibrato only occasionally. Woodwind and brass sections will both sound more burnished, less bright, and also use little vibrato. Up-close proximity to the audience will cause the harps to sound more crisp, full, and more captivating than expected. Choristers will be more confident because potential technical difficulties—vocal register changes, tessitura, endurance discomfort, and intonation—will have been addressed in sectionals, and their phrasing and expression will be more refined. Positioned at the very front, between the orchestra and audience, text will be easily understood, and the risk of singing with a harsh, shouty timbre, often acquired today from trying to project over a large orchestra, is exponentially reduced. Overall, the clarity and immediacy of sound of an orchestra and chorus prepared and positioned in Berlioz's recommended manner will likely be quite appealing.

Composition, First Performances, and Disappointment

Berlioz composed *La damnation de Faust* while on a concert tour through Austria, Hungary, Bohemia, and Silesia in 1846. Returning to Paris in May, he completed it and planned two performances under his own direction for December 6 and 20, 1846. As was the case for most of his Paris performances, he organized everything. First, he approached three possible theaters starting at the top—l'Opéra, Théâtre-Italien, and l'Opéra-comique—and only the last one was available. It was a much smaller facility, so ticket prices had to be doubled to cover expenses. Writing the advertisements, he didn't hold back: he praised the singing of his Faust, tenor Gustave Roger (1815–1879); pointed out passages of extraordinary effectiveness; and reported his performers were all exceedingly enthusiastic. He also noted it departed in style from earlier compositions, thereby distancing himself from his opera *Benvenuto Cellini*, which was performed eight years earlier in Paris and considered a failure.

Reviews of the first performances were quite warm, but the *Pandaemonium* scene had to be omitted due to its difficulty, and Roger was indisposed to sing Faust's tour de force aria, *Invocation à la nature*, in the second performance. Berlioz was fully aware of the production's flaws: he did not have the top-tier soloists from l'Opéra, the orchestra was fallible, and the chorus was substandard. He attributed the poor audience attendance and huge financial loss to the absence of star soloists (he wrote his singers could be heard any day in the same theater) and inclement weather. Nothing in his career as an artist, he wrote, had wounded him more deeply than the unexpected indifference of his public.

Heroes, Characterizations, Arias, Mischief, and Magic

Outcomes for heroes in the three concert-length works discussed in detail so far—two symphonies and now his *légende dramatique*—are extreme and tragic. In *Symphonie fantastique* the artist-hero-lover is spurned, and in a dream, guillotined for killing his lover. In *Roméo et Juliette* the warring families obstruct the entranced lovers, and devastated by Juliette's death, Roméo dies by self-administered poison. In *La damnation de Faust*, Faust is an enticed but conflicted lover, a loner in pursuit of peace for his tormented soul who is subsumed to hell. It is difficult *not* to imagine Berlioz seeing himself in the monumental struggles experienced by all three central characters.

Berlioz's depiction of the leads in *La damnation de Faust* is superb. We pick up from his inventive musical gestures and textures that Méphistophélès is charismatic, suave and mischievous, but underneath he is malevolent. Faust is melancholic, obsessed with his own boredom; he is vulnerable to being led on and therefore easy prey for Méphistophélès. Marguerite is the least complex; she is a passionate lover and innocent victim.[10]

Compelling arias in *La damnation de Faust* are abundant and excerpted in concerts often. The fun arias are in part 2: *Chanson de Brander* and *Chanson de Méphistophélès*. The deceptive, demonic *Air de Méphistophélès* (Song of Méphistophélès; *Voici des roses*), which cools things down, is also in part 2. Conflicted, passionate arias and *romances* are all in parts 3 and 4: Faust sings *Air de Faust* (*Merci, doux crépuscule*) and *Invocation à la nature*; Marguerite sings *Le roi de Thulé* and *Romance* (*D'amour l'ardente flame*).

Mischief and magic largely take place in choruses and dances. In part 2 during the *Chœur de gnomes and de sylphes* (Chorus of gnomes and sylphs) and *Ballet des sylphes* (Dance of the sylphs), Faust falls in love with Marguerite while in a dream. In turn, Marguerite tells of seeing her future lover in a dream, and *Menuet des follets* (Dance of the will-o'-the-wisps) and *Serénade de Méphistophélès* work their magic.

Dramatic demands on the chorus are extraordinary. Choristers are cast not only as gnomes, sylphs, and will-o'-the-wisps but also as stock groups of people that provide scenic flavor. In part 1 they are Hungarian peasants singing and dancing, and in part 2 they are German town folk singing an Easter processional as well as soldiers and students drinking in a tavern. In parts 3 and 4 the list is astonishing: appalled townspeople outside Marguerite's house; students and soldiers singing in the distance; women peasants asking for mercy at a wayside cross as Faust and Méphistophélès gallop toward hell; princes of darkness standing in judgment; the damned and demons who celebrate as Faust is consumed by flames; and celestial spirits. Surely few other nineteenth-century concert works leverage the potential impact and versatility of a chorus to such great dramatic effect.

Overall, *La damnation de Faust* is packed with marvelous musical realizations of a terrific mix of characters, from conflicted hero and a devil to fair maid. Add to this the profound human conundrums, from passionate love, deception, and judgment to ultimate condemnation. What more universally appealing ingredients could there possibly be for a morality tale told in music?

Listening Map

By 1846, Goethe's epic poem *Faust* was revered in literary circles, and Berlioz set portions of it believing audiences in general would be familiar with the story. To ensure listeners stayed with him, Berlioz streamlined the story by omitting characters and side plots and focused exclusively on the three main characters. He printed a complete libretto for the first performances, an approach not prevalent for operas but certainly so for choral-orchestral works. Because gas lighting in halls was insufficient for reading, audiences were expected to have read the text in advance even though the singing was in their own language.

Berlioz took his storytelling responsibilities yet a step further by including stage directions in the printed libretto and score (he did the same in *L'enfance du Christ*). The directions provide essential information for following the story; they include locations and events (e.g., "the spirits of the air hovering around the sleeping Faust" or "Méphistophélès hides Faust behind a curtain") plus exits and entrances. So, a word to the wise: read a good plot summary and the best available translation of the complete libretto of Berlioz's *Faust* (not someone else's *Faust*). Review the listening map below and, even though it's not an opera, pay close attention to stage directions to avoid plot befuddlement.

The following listening map includes brief descriptions of salient plot events and commentary on the music. Berlioz's stage directions and scene titles are provided in italics. Dialogue is condensed and paraphrased. Quotation marks are used to indicate point of view and actor and do not indicate a direct quote from the libretto.

Part I: Scenes 1–3 (16')

1. *Plains of Hungary. Introduction. Faust alone in the fields at sunrise.*
Only violas open the work playing the primary theme of the Introduction (*Requiem* and *Roméo et Juliette* begin similarly). The music seems to signal, "This is me and how I feel; it could be you." Faust sings intermittently throughout the mostly instrumental introduction. He revels in the coming of spring, shimmering morning light, birds awakening, the sweetness of nature while he is away from men and conflict. Having the title soloist sing so early in a work is unconventional; the music is a hybrid of aria and overture just as the overall work is a hybrid of oratorio, opera, and symphony. Of the three main characters, we meet only Faust in part 1; Méphistophélès enters in part 2 and Marguerite in part 3.
Distinct sounds of rustic life and of war begin to disturb the calm of the landscape.

2. *Ronde de paysans* (Peasants' round dance).
Peasants sing a lusty song while dancing. The verses are in a fast three meter in contrast to the "tra-la-la" refrains in duple meter. The music reflects a stark contrast between the joyous camaraderie of the peasants and Faust's gloom. Faust is unaffected; a nonjoiner, he prefers solitude.

3. *Another part of the plain. An army advancing.*
Faust sees flashes of armor as soldiers march by. The Sons of the Danube (Hungarians) prepare for combat; "their eyes are ablaze with fire, their hearts pulse to their victory song." Faust, though, says his heart remains cold; he is indifferent to winning and glory. *Marche hongroise* (Hungarian march), also known as *Rákóczi March*, is the most brilliant

of Berlioz's many marches and most often performed. It is based on a song composed in 1809 to honor Ferenc Rákóczi, a Hungarian military leader and politician who fought for Hungarian independence from Austria. Berlioz had previously written his arrangement on commission and performed it in Pest, later deciding to include it in *La damnation de Faust*. Met with great success as a single work, it ultimately became a symbol of Hungarian national aspiration. To include his arrangement in *La damnation de Faust*, Berlioz changed the location of part 1 from Goethe's Germany to Hungary, much to the consternation of some Germans critics.
Troops pass, Faust moves off.

Part 2: Scenes 4–8 (40')

4. *North Germany, Faust alone in his study.*
"My ennui pursued me in the countryside, so I left and came home. How I suffer melancholy. Where can I find what my life lacks?" Contemplating suicide, *he lifts the cup [of poison] to his lip* but suddenly outside he hears townsfolk sing an Easter hymn while processing: "Christ has risen." Faust: "My wavering faith is reaffirmed and brings me peace. The kiss of divine love has dismissed all fatal desires." Chorus: "Christ transfigured rises to the courts of heaven" (the text is a hint of the final chorus, the apotheosis of Marguerite). The four-part men's chorus is absolutely resplendent; women and Faust join in. Faust, in his closing accompanied recitative, sings, "My tears have flowed, heaven has reclaimed me."

5. Méphistophélès, Faust.
Appearing brusquely, Méphistophélès is represented by a quicksilver trombone/piccolo gesture, like a magical poof of smoke. The gesture recurs similarly throughout the work no matter the circumstance or guise. (In a Eugène Delacroix lithograph, Méphistophélès was a poodle; Berlioz's gesture is similarly deceiving.) Méphistophélès: "You've been marvelously charmed by the pious pealing of silver bells." Faust: "Who are you?" Méphistophélès: "I am the spirit of life, I will console you. I'll give you everything, even happiness, pleasure." Faust: "Show me your marvels." Méphistophélès: "Follow me for a change of air." The text is sung in accompanied recitative, and the twirling strings near the end evoke time travel.

They leave.

6. *Auerbach's cellar in Leipzig.*
Chorus of drinkers (men): "Oh, it's good to sit by a bowl of fiery drink
and fill yourself like a barrel. Who knows a good story?" Brander (baritone) sings a rhythmically captivating song (*Chanson de Brander*) about
a rat that eats poison and hides in the oven: "That rat is really on heat"
(a sensual pun on being "in heat"). In jest, the men respond with a
Requiem and *Fugue on the theme of Brander's song*, singing one word,
"Amen." It is a cheeky reference to Handel's final movement of *Messiah*, also a fugue on "Amen." But Handel definitely would not have
written this! In performance choristers may choose to sound raucous
and ugly, deadpan serious, or sanctimonious, but they must not sound
sincere or attractive—Berlioz intentionally wrote a terrible fugue. It
parodies religious leaders and the low standards of church music. *In a
low voice*, Méphistophélès mockingly tells Faust they are hearing brutality (that is, musical brutality) in all its innocence.

Méphistophélès one-ups Brander and his chorus of drinkers: "I can
top it with another subject no less touching." *Chanson de
Méphistophélès* (*Une puce gentile* [A delightful flea]): "A prince loved a
flea, had it measured by a tailor for court dress—a suit of gold, velvet
and silk. The flea was so proud it sent for all its brothers and sisters, and
they also became noblemen. The prince's courtiers dared not complain
and they scratched all day." Chorus: "Let's squash it." Méphistophélès
to Faust: "Oh, you don't like it, let's leave." (*They leave.*) The flea song
reenacts a popular satire of the eighteenth-century ancien régime in
which animals were substituted for people of certain social types. The
objective was to make fun of their stock class traits (arrogance, fussi-
ness, and odd appearance), highlight drunkenness, or play tricks on
them. The music that follows the flea song conjures up fantastical
traveling through air and increasing detachment from reality.

7. *Groves and meadows by the (river) Elbe.*
A lone clarinet and then bassoons introduce Méphistophélès's *Voici des
roses* (Here are roses), one of Berlioz's most beautiful *romances*. With
accompaniment of luscious brass choir, Méphistophélès comforts
Faust: "Rest on this bed, here roses are blooming. You will hear divine
utterances by spirits of earth and air; now begin your dream." For all
Méphistophélès's apparent generosity, he is pure deception: the dark,

sumptuous, trombone-dominated accompaniment is a decoy for insidious disingenuousness. Do not trust a devil disguised by a gorgeous *romance*.

Faust's Dream: Chorus of Gnomes and Sylphs. Chorus: "Sleep, happy Faust! Dreams of love will at last enchant you." Note the flickering flutes and piccolos in the introduction—Méphistophélès is there somewhere. In triple meter, the pointillist patter of syllables is deliciously delicate and in obvious contrast to the long lines sung in other voices and played by strings. *Asleep*, Faust: "Marguerite!" Méphistophélès: "The spell is working; he's ours." Méphistophélès to the gnomes and sylphs: "All is well, my young elves; I am pleased with you. *Dors, dors* (sleep, sleep)." The magical music that follows, *Ballet des sylphes* (Dance of the sylphs), is a development of prior music but now for instruments alone. *The spirits of the air hover awhile around the sleeping Faust, then vanish one by one*. Fairy dust harmonics played by harps and echoed by delicately soft timpani close the ballet. Faust *waking with a start*: "Marguerite! I have seen a heavenly vision, what an angel! Where can I find her?" Méphistophélès: "Follow me at once to that perfumed bower where your beloved lies waiting for you alone. We'll make our way to her through these young foolish students. Hide your ecstasy and follow my instructions carefully."

8. *Soldiers' chorus and students' song.*
Soldiers sing in a carefree, confident 6/8 meter punctuated lightly by pizzicato strings. Students, meanwhile, sing in a sturdy 2/4 meter in Latin; the text is based on the traditional, light-hearted university song, *Gaudeamus igitur* (So let us rejoice). During all this the orchestra does not double the soldiers or students but plays robustly in dialogue with them, clearing the way for the voices to stand out quite handsomely. Berlioz then simultaneously superimposes the music of the two groups in their two different meters, one over the other, for a stunning and magnificent finale to the first half.

Part 3: Scene 9–14 (35')

9. *Drums and trumpets sound retreat. Marguerite's room, it is evening.*
(There is no explanation of how Faust gained access to her room; surely it was Méphistophélès's doing. He is up to no good.) Faust sings his famous aria: *Merci, doux crépuscule* (Thanks, gentle twilight): "How I

cherish this silence and breathe in pure bliss, how lovely to look upon your virgin bed!" *Faust walks slowly around Marguerite's room, examining it with passionate curiosity*; a solitary line played by violins appears to represent him. To some, Faust's behavior in this scene may appear a bit extreme, erring on the side of prurient stalking.

10. Suddenly the quicksilver "poof" of Méphistophélès is played by trombones and cornets (*Méphistophélès rushes in*).
A melodic fragment played by solo clarinet foreshadows the *romance*, *Le roi de Thulé* (The king of Thulé), to be sung in the next scene. Méphistophélès: "I can hear Marguerite coming." *He conceals Faust behind the curtain.* "Keep calm or you will lose her." To himself: "I and my will-o'-the-wisps will sing to them a fine nuptial song." Pizzicato strings play a foretelling snippet of Méphistophélès's fun-sounding but cynical *Sérénade* in scene 12—he is definitely up to no good, and certainly no wedding vows are on the horizon.

11. *Marguerite enters, a lamp in her hand. Méphistophélès exits.*
Marguerite sings a recitative: *Que l'air est étouffant!* "How oppressive the air is, I'm frightened as a child. While I slept I saw my (unknown) future lover!" She sings *Chanson gothique: Le roi de Thulé* (Song in a gothic style: The king of Thulé) *as she braids her hair.* The story is of a king who received a gold chalice from his wife at her death. He was faithful to her for the rest of his life and, as a sign, always drank only from it. Now nearing his own death he drinks once more and throws it into the ocean just before he dies. The song depicts a man's constancy until death to his wife, and, in like fashion, the naïve, pure Marguerite imagines an idealized Faust committing to her—she certainly is to him. Use of a solo string instrument in a strophic *romance*—here, the viola— is a Berlioz signature previously heard in *La captive* and in *Strophes: Premiers transports* from *Roméo et Juliette*; Berlioz wrote all three for mezzo-sopranos. The beguiling simplicity of Marguerite's *romance* allows her deepest longing to be utterly transparent.

12. *Evocation.*
In an unspecified location, Méphistophélès summons up his will-o'-the-wisps spirits with a disjointed and downward unison woodwind line; three piccolos are his "spirits of fickle flame." Méphistophélès: "Your nefarious gleam is going to bewitch a young girl and lead her to us." The lightning-fast repartee between Méphistophélès and his wisps (fairies)

sounds spontaneous, and the *Menuet des follets* (Dance of the will-o'-the-wisps), a mannered minuet in a three meter (but "feels" in one), is absolutely entrancing. In the lyrical middle section, note how the long melodies in the strings contrast with the impish flickers of the three piccolos. With piccolos still in the lead, the ultrafast closing section is another preview of Méphistophélès's *Sérénade*, which he sings along with the chorus of will-o'-the-wisps in the next scene. What follows is both magical and salacious.

Méphistophélès (*with the gesture of a man playing a hurdy-gurdy*): "Now let's sing Marguerite a 'moral' song to damn her even more surely." *Sérénade de Méphistophélès* (*Méphistophélès's serenade and chorus of the will-o'-the-wisps*): "You will enter this room a fair maid, but you will not come out one." *With a burst of harsh laughter*, the chorus shouts, "Ha!" While the music is entertaining, the message is ironic and raunchy ("moral" means the reverse). A hurdy-gurdy is a stringed instrument played by the right hand cranking a lever in circles in front of the body waist-high or lower; the left hand plucks strings; it is known as a "peasant's lyre" played by itinerant blind men. By imitating a hurdy-gurdy, the orchestral strings imply sexual activity. Then, as if the will-o'-the-wisps were caught being naughty, Méphistophélès sings, "Silence! Vanish!" *The will-o'-the-wisps sink into the ground.* And then to the audience too, "Let's go and see our turtle doves cooing."

13. *Duet.*
Solo oboe plays a reprise of Marguerite's *Le roi de Thulé* melody, signifying both her hope for an enduring love match and dark foreboding. In the bedroom, *Marguerite catches first sight of Faust:* "Can I really believe my eyes; is it really he?" Faust: "Beloved angel, whose divine image lit up my heart before I knew you, I see you at last." Faust and Marguerite meet for the first time and they immediately head toward, seemingly, inevitable consummation. Marguerite: "I don't know what this passion is that leads me to his arms; everything is growing faint . . . I'm dying."

14. *Trio and Chorus.*
With a loud jolt of trombones (no piccolos this time), Méphistophélès *bursts in*; it's just about daylight: "Quick, it's too late!" Faust: "Who said you could come in?" Marguerite: "Who is this man?" Méphistophélès: "We must save this angel." Townspeople are pointing at the house,

jeering, knocking at the door: "A gallant is in the house, you'll soon see
an addition to the family." Faust was ready to open his soul to happiness
just when this public debacle happened. A furiously busy pattern played
by cellos ratchets up dramatic intensity, but unfortunately the dialogue
between characters is often obscured by the wildly fast pace and associated commotion. Marguerite pledges her life and soul to Faust, but
Faust is slipping into Méphistophélès's insidious grasp. Méphistophélès
to Faust: "The time is near when I will seize you. By tantalizing you
without gratifying your desire, your madness will redouble." The townspeople are shouting, and Faust must leave before consummating their
love. Reprises of the passionate love duet temporarily halt the hubbub;
then the furious pace returns as the lovers pledge to see each other
tomorrow.

Part 4: Scenes 15–19 and Epilogue (33')

15. (No location or elapsed time is indicated.) Marguerite sings *romance*: *D'amour l'ardente flame,* "The ardent flame of love consumes
my youth. Being away from him is a life of mourning."
Her melody is first played by oboe solo, seeming to represent her inner-
most thoughts. Of utmost intimacy and beauty, the music alternates
between slow and fast sections and very different orchestra textures;
Marguerite is caught in extreme swings of emotion. The song is a favorite and among the most dramatic that Berlioz composed for mezzo-
soprano. *In the distance*, drums and trumpets play the familiar retreat;
it is evening and time to retire. Chorus of soldiers: "At the trumpet's
sound brave soldiers throw themselves into pleasure or battle," and
students again sing phrases from their Latin song—all music is from the
evening Faust fell in love with Marguerite (end of part 2). But time has
passed, and he has not returned; the promise of "tomorrow" has ex-
pired. Oboe and voice, with pizzicato strings, forlornly close the scene.

16. *Invocation à la nature* (Invocation to nature). *Forests and Caves.*
Faust is in crisis—conflicted and disconsolate: "Nature, immense, un-
fathomable, proud. Forests, rocks, torrents, I adore you! Sparkling
worlds above, to you my longing heart and insatiable soul cry out for the
happiness they cannot seize." Lumbering bass lines simulate dreadful
gusts of hurricane winds and their roar in the forest trees, a metaphor
for Faust's ruptured world. Like Marguerite's *romance* just before, this

aria is among those tenors most aspire to sing. The drama now swiftly careens toward conclusion.

17. *Recitative and Hunt.*

Méphistophélès *climbing up the rocks, calmly* to Faust: "While you dream here, that poor child is in prison, condemned to death for parricide." He goes on to explain: "A brown liquid, harmless poison, which you gave her to keep her mother quiet during your nights of love, has caused all the trouble. While waiting for you, she used the drug constantly, and the old woman died of it." Horns (hunters moving through the woods) play throughout the recitative, framing it harmonically and signaling a remote forest location. Faust *frantically*: "Thunder and lightning! Save her, you brute!" For payment to do so, Méphistophélès requires that Faust sign an oath to be his servant. Faust signs, believing they will ride back to town where Marguerite is imprisoned and set her free. With jittery bouncing of bows on strings, two horses are brought forward for the journey.

18. *La course à l'abîme* (The ride to the abyss).

Faust and Méphistophélès galloping on two black horses. Instead of taking Faust to rescue Marguerite from prison (as in Goethe's poem), Méphistophélès takes Faust to hell. On the way, women peasants *kneeling at a wayside cross* sing a pleading chant: "Sancta Maria, pray for us," accompanied by a wailing solo oboe. . . . *The women and children scatter in terror* when they see Méphistophélès, who brusquely ignores them. A hideous beast bellows (low trombone), and huge night birds swarm around, shrieking (woodwinds). Méphistophélès *reining in his horse*: "The death knell is already sounding for her"; they stop. Méphistophélès: "Are you afraid?" Faust: "No! Hurry!" Méphistophélès *urging on his horse*: "Hup! hup!" *The horses redouble their pace* and skeletons in an endless line are dancing (long trombone notes and trills). *More and more horror-struck and breathless*, Faust: "It's raining blood!" A gigantic crash of tam-tams, and Méphistophélès *with a voice of thunder* cries, "He is ours!" *They fall into a chasm.*

19. *Pandemonium.*

Faust and Méphistophélès enter the underworld to the sound of full-force brass and percussion, and a men's *chorus of the damned and demons* sings in a bizarre, unknown language. As if judges from a secret society, twelve baritones and basses in the role of the Princes of Darkness ask, "Are you master and lord over this proud soul forever?" Méphistophélès: "Yes, forever." Princes: "Has Faust signed to commit himself to these flames?" Méphistophélès: "He signed freely." *The chorus of the damned and demons* sneeringly sing "Has!" in victory and, while *carrying Méphistophélès in triumph*, celebrate by singing more invented gibberish (Berlioz teasingly suggested it was based on a made-up Nordic language). Gargantuan shifts of harmony and dynamics depict ocean-like surges, and towering waves wind down to nothingness. All stops have been pulled out for this graphic depiction of the horrors in hell; it marks a pinnacle for musical macabre. In turn, one of the most celestial passages follows.

Epilogue.

> *On earth.* Six baritones alone (or a soloist, perhaps Brander) narrate: "Then hell fell silent. Only the bubbling of its great lakes of fire and the gnashing teeth of those who tortured souls could be heard; in its depths a horrible mystery was performed." A small chorus of tenors and basses respond dissolutely: "Oh terrors!"

> *In heaven. Chorus of celestial spirits* (sopranos and tenors only; eight to ten harps, divided on each side of the stage at the front; *divisi* upper strings). *Seraphim bowing before the Most High* gently call out: "Praise! Hosanna!" Only sopranos sing: "She is greatly loved, Lord." Four or five harps play delicate, pristine harmonics joined by *divisi* cellos in tremolando. A solo treble voice (female soprano or four young boys, usually positioned in a balcony or from the back of the hall) beckons Marguerite to heaven.

> *Apothéose of Marguerite.* Chorus: "Rise up again to heaven, naïve soul that love led astray. Return to your original beauty that a fault altered."[11] Four violins and woodwinds play leisurely falling intervals in a gentle patter. Children join sopranos: "Come, heavenly virgins! Continue to hope and smile on your blessings." Some performances add a bit of stagecraft: children carrying candles process through the audience while singing and line up across the front of the stage just before everyone's last note: "Viens, viens" (come, come).

Berlioz on Tour, International Fame, an Institution at Home, and an Afterthought

After the failure of *La damnation de Faust* in its Paris premiere December 1846, Berlioz took it on the road. Traveling by stagecoach and train, he carried the autograph full score and orchestra and chorus parts in a trunk to Russia and Germany. Portions were performed in Riga, and its third complete performance was given to great acclaim in Berlin, June 1847. Berlioz commissioned a singing translation into German while *en route* and added it to his autograph score for performances in Germany and later to his 1854 printed full score.

The next year parts 1 and 2 were premiered in English at the Drury Lane Theatre in London, and he conducted it in Paris with the Société philharmonique, an organization he helped found, in 1850. But again, only parts 1 and 2 were performed; he conducted them many times in Germany during 1852–1853 as well. Finally, Berlioz was able to give two complete performances in Dresden in 1854. They were met with resoundingly positive reviews, and he reported never having heard such an excellent orchestra. In declining health, Berlioz conducted all of *La damnation de Faust* for his last public performance December 1866. It was in the Redoutensaal, dance and concert hall of the Hofburg Palace in Vienna, with 400–450 performers including forty violins, doubled woodwinds, and a choir of over 250. The performance was a major triumph; Berlioz called it the greatest of his life.

The most popular excerpts were encored at the first Paris performances: *Marche hongroise* and *Chœur et ballet de sylphs*; today the latter is sometimes preceded by *Voici des roses* sung by Méphistophélès. After Berlioz's death, due to numerous performances at the popular Pasdeloup and Colonne concert series in Paris, the complete *La damnation de Faust* became the most revered of his compositions. By 1898 it had been performed an extraordinary one hundred times at the Concerts Colonne alone. Subsequently, and to the surprise of many, performances of it became an annual tradition not unlike Handel's *Messiah* today.

Despite enormously successful Dresden performances with the best orchestra Berlioz had conducted to date, a reviewer brought up objections to two plot deviations from the Goethe poem. First, Berlioz started with Faust in Hungary although the story was derived from

German legend and written by a treasured German poet. Second, Méphistophélès did not keep his bargain with Faust. Instead of taking Faust to Marguerite's prison cell and both continuing to live, as per Goethe's poem, Faust signs himself into servitude, and Méphistophélès abducts him to hell in exchange for saving Marguerite, who otherwise would have also been damned to eternal fire. Berlioz dismissed the first criticism in the forward to his 1854 edition, writing that Faust could easily have traveled anywhere and the location at the beginning was inconsequential.

As to the ending, apparently Berlioz made no comment. But it is worth noting that it is consistent with his own deep sense of chivalry and right and wrong. While Marguerite made errors—sleeping with Faust and inadvertently poisoning her mother (no mention is made of her giving birth or drowning a child fathered by Faust, which are in Goethe's poem)—she was an innocent compared to Faust. For Berlioz too, replication of the tragic outcomes in *Symphonie fantastique* and *Roméo et Juliette*, where both the hero and his beloved perish, was not an option. In his world, the consequence of Faust's many errors in judgment was condemnation, and for the idealized woman it was redemption, end of story. Well, almost. Berlioz also ennobles Faust by having him forfeit his soul and consequently his life for Marguerite's sake. Meanwhile, in part 2 of Goethe's poem Faust lives to be one hundred and enjoys many pleasures afforded by . . . who else? Méphistophélès.

L'ENFANCE DU CHRIST: TRILOGIE SACRÉE

Berlioz's last major choral-orchestral work, *L'enfance du Christ: trilogie sacrée* (The childhood of Christ: sacred trilogy), represents a path not previously taken. His prior symphonies and choral works were based on fine literature by well-known authors, and they hinged on secular themes, such as love and reconciliation in *Roméo et Juliette* and the search for life's meaning in *La damnation de Faust*. None were based on a biblical narrative, although sacred topics were welcome on the concert stage. But despite having composed two masses (*Messe solennelle* and *Grande messe des morts*) and a *Te Deum*, Berlioz was a professed atheist and had even made fun of religious leaders and church music. Exactly what prompted him to write so gracefully and poignantly about the Holy Family's escape from Herod and exile to Egypt is a puzzle.

David Cairns has suggested the process of composing and sheer beauty of the music answered an inner personal necessity for Berlioz. Surely this is true, for when Berlioz began composing *La fuite en Égypte: mystère en style ancien* (The flight into Egypt: mystery in an ancient style; part 2) in 1850, he was deeply discouraged by his lack of success in Paris. In a rant to his sister Adèle, he wrote, "I am sick with the frustration of my love of art." He had met with "indifference and idiocy, gross materialism, bestial government, ignorance, the philistinism of the rich, the vulgar preoccupations of everyone . . . snakes, hedgehogs, toads, geese, guinea-fowl, crows, lice, vermin. . . . That's the charming population of that earthly paradise Paris."[12] Later, while traveling and concertizing extensively during 1850–1853, he found he had neither the focus nor the time to compose new works. Then in London, where he had established an ardent following and royalty were in attendance, his opera *Benvenuto Cellini* was shouted down at Covent Garden by a political faction wanting only operas composed and sung by Italians performed there. The artistic merit of *Benvenuto Cellini* had nothing to do with the ruckus it caused, and Berlioz felt jinxed and wronged (see chapter 5).

During that long, uncharacteristic period of compositional silence, performances of *L'adieu des bergers* (The shepherd's farewell) and *Le repos de la sainte famille* (The resting place of the Holy Family) from part 2 were greeted with great warmth. His friends encouraged him to expand on them. Finally in 1853–1854, Berlioz completed part 3 and then part 1 of *L'enfance du Christ*. For the first time the libretto, based in part on events in the gospels of Matthew and Luke, was entirely his own. Having complete control over text and music most likely freed him to compose in varied musical styles: part 2 is a gentle scenic tableau while portions of part 1 in particular and part 3 to some degree are more operatic.

The process of composition pulled Berlioz out of that dark, unproductive time, and to his surprise *L'enfance du Christ* was met with immediate success in Paris, quite unlike the initial failures of *La damnation de Faust* and *Benvenuto Cellini*. Upon taking it across Europe, Russia, and on to England, it became by far his most popular composition during his lifetime. The original part 2, with its famous Shepherd's Farewell chorus, *L'adieu des bergers*, appealed to audiences as much then as it does today.

Berlioz focused on events following the birth of Christ and then filled in his own details. Consequently, the drama feels fresh and vivid, as though a well-known story has been magnified and upgraded into high definition. The main characters—Hérode, Marie and Joseph, and the Father of the Ishmaelite family—seem real, even contemporary; they are like us and like people we know. Most importantly, Berlioz understood the angst and desperation of the Holy Family fleeing a paranoid and deeply troubled king. As a nonbeliever, Berlioz also saw himself in the shoes of the Ishmaelite family, who were of a different faith and race and at times outcasts, too. Reenactment of the Holy Family's experiences as unwanted refugees and the Ishmaelite Father's welcome into his home highlight Berlioz's keen sense of empathy for outsiders and those less fortunate.

In his libretto, Berlioz also explicitly refers to anti-Semitism. The Jewish Holy Family not only escapes Hérode, also a Jew, but also is rejected by the Romans and Egyptians for being "dirty Hebrews." In Berlioz's rendition, the Ishmaelites, on the other hand, welcome them, never closing their home to the unfortunate regardless of their nationality, race, or beliefs. Berlioz could well have been concerned about the rise of anti-Semitism in Europe during the 1840s and 1850s. Most certainly the focus of *L'enfance du Christ* is not on a Romantic artist, hero, or lover, as had been the case in previous works. Rather, it is on community, respect, fairness, and kindness.

Listen by Visualization

L'enfance du Christ is an evening-length work (ninety minutes) composed for the concert hall. Berlioz's inclusion of stage directions in both score and libretto, as he did for *La damnation de Faust*, has led some opera companies to stage it. But the descriptive music and minimal verbal instructions stand well on merit alone. Berlioz reaches out to our imagination so that we, like him, will conjure up our own images and elaborations. His strategy works brilliantly if given a chance. The orchestra, onstage rather than in the pit, remains the focal point, and the singers are unencumbered by props, costumes, blocking, supernumeraries, and the like. With few visual distractions the audience may truly listen.

The cast of characters in order of appearance is as follows:

Le récitant (Narrator), tenor
Centurion (Roman soldier), tenor
Polydorus (commander of the Roman patrol), baritone
Hérode, king of the Jews, bass
Marie, mezzo-soprano
Joseph, baritone
Le Père de famille (Father of the Ishmaelite family), bass

Similar to *La damnation de Faust*, the choristers have multiple roles, and at times the actual number of singers is specified. Angels in as many as four treble parts sing from backstage at the end of each part.

Part 1: soothsayers (ten baritones and basses); angels behind the scene with the door open (ten *divisi* sopranos and ten *divisi* altos) sing *Hosanna*.

Part 2: full mixed chorus (SATB) of shepherds in Bethlehem on-stage; angels far behind the orchestra (four *divisi* sopranos and four *divisi* altos) sing *Alleluia*.

Part 3: Romans and Egyptians (twelve baritones and basses); Ishmaelites (mixed chorus SATB); mystical chorus (mixed chorus SATB); angels behind the scene, presumably similar in number to the conclusion of part 1 (sopranos and altos in four parts) sing *Amen*.

A brief listening guide follows; Berlioz's stage directions are in italics (not all are included).

Part 1: Le songe d'Hérode (The Dream of Herod; 42')

Our attention is captured by a single, still chord, its sparse texture, and a solitary tenor voice. If we were expecting an overture or opening chorus, we were mistaken. Use of a tenor as Narrator is reminiscent of the sacred Passions and Christmas oratorios composed by Schütz, Bach, and many others. Here, though, the topic is events between Christ's birth and manhood, not the story of his birth or death. In fact, we are going to hear about the hideous crime that paranoia inspired, as the Narrator describes, and how the Holy Family was driven from Bethlehem. In just a few brief moments of accompanied solo recitative, the scene and time are set. We are ready to hear this ancient story-within-a-story reenacted. No other composers have done this. Bring it on!

A street in Jerusalem. A bodyguard. Roman soldiers on night patrol. Scene 1 *Marche nocturne* (Nocturnal march) begins with halting plucks by contrabasses, alone and muted. The hollow pointillist sounds continue as a fugato unfolds: it is nighttime, and someone is marching; caution is in the air. The passage seems like a delayed overture of sorts but is suddenly cut short. In an offhand exchange between two sentries, we learn of the deterioration of Hérode's mind. He is a rich and powerful tyrant tormented by paranoia. Speaking to himself, the larger-than-life king recounts his horrible dream in one of Berlioz's most magnificent arias. Trombones (reminiscent of Méphistophélès) and dark harmonies based on a made-up scale vividly characterize the distraught Hérode. As he describes his agony and insomnia, an ominous solo clarinet acts as a troubled alter ego and further magnifies the overall sense of confusion and vulnerability. By the end Hérode appears broken, disconsolate.

Hérode asks his soothsayer basses (priest advisors) what to do, and they in turn consult their cabalistic spirits, who are represented by instruments. Exchanges between the soothsayers and their consultants are hilarious—the bumbly-burbly music in 7/4 meter (3 + 4 pulses in each metrical unit) is far from holy or dignified; an aroma of witches' brew is in the air! Berlioz is making a plucky jab at organized religion, rituals, and priests in general. The passage is amusing, and for a while the work seems to be more like a comic opera than a biblical story in an oratorio. After repeats of fantastic exorcist-like twirls, the music repeatedly halts and begins again, never finding harmonic rest.

Referring to the Holy Family and those who might help them escape, Hérode recovers himself and cries, "Let them perish by the sword! Rivers of blood will flow. My terrors must have an end." The brass are unleashed in full force for a call to arms. Fragments from the *Marche nocturne* then return to unwind the scene, and all ends on a sustained, suspenseful dissonance. In a dramatic shift, a nativity scene follows: Marie and Joseph sing a beautiful, loving lullaby to the Child in a gently rocking 6/8 meter. The sublime music embodies every parent's awe at the miracle of birth: sweetness and naïveté, pure happiness.

Framed by the gentle antique sound of a small organ (*orgue-mélodium*), invisible angels sing from backstage to end part 1. They direct

Marie and Joseph to flee to Egypt, and having been assured celestial protection the couple hastily prepares to leave. Part 1 ends softly—so softly in fact that the angels cannot sing quietly enough for Berlioz. He instructed the backstage doors to be closed gradually during the final ethereal *Hosannas*.

Part 2: La fuite en Égypte (The Flight into Egypt; 17')

Overture: orchestra only
L'adieu des bergers à la sainte famille: mixed chorus and orchestra
Le repos de la sainte famille: tenor solo, orchestra, brief backstage
    soprano and alto chorus at the close

As indicated earlier, part 3 and then part 1 grew outwardly from part 2. The three together are comparable to panels of a medieval triptych, with *La fuite en Égypte* as the calm interlude between the two longer more operatic outer parts. Within part 2 resides another triptych: its opening overture and closing tenor solo frame the famous shepherds' chorus, *L'adieu des bergers*, in the center.

No other chorus by Berlioz is performed more often, although it is mostly heard with piano accompaniment instead of orchestra. It was the first music Berlioz composed of the entire *L'enfance du Christ* and the anchoring inspiration. Initially jotted down as an organ piece in a host's guest album while he was at a party, Berlioz playfully attributed it to an imagined seventeenth-century composer. Wanting to hide having written such tender music on a religious topic, he also was sure no one would believe he composed it. Furthermore, Berlioz feared attribution would jinx its reception. Or perhaps he just wanted to see how long his little deception would last.

In the opening *Overture* of part 2, the *sainte famille* struggles through a desert landscape that is dreary with sameness; the mood is desperate yet hopeful. The fugue is in three expositions with a charming, brighter, second theme group; the music closes with a gently unwinding coda.

In *L'adieu des bergers*, oboes and clarinets represent shepherds' pipes in a little refrain at the beginning, between the three verses, and at the end. The meter is in three but "feels" in a lilting one, another touch of the pastoral. In strophic form, every verse is in four long phrases. Each phrase is in two halves, each of which has one line of text.

Phrase 4 begins by repeating the text of phrase 3 but is new music; a partial phrase is added at the end.

The text of the first two verses is in third person and descriptive. Laying out their hopes for the Child, the shepherds sing, "May he grow and prosper . . . may the shepherd's lowly life be ever dear to his heart!" But the third verse shifts to second person, addressing the Child directly: "May you never feel the cruel hand of injustice!" Here a slower tempo and softer dynamic bring more focus to the beauty of each vocal line, the intriguing harmonic progressions, and the significance of every word. In a heartfelt dramatic surge of urgency at the end of phrase 3 in verse 3, the orchestra and chorus crescendo together throughout a fermata into phrase 4. At the same fermata moment in prior verses, though, the instruments increased in volume while the chorus became softer, a rare special effect in music literature. Interestingly, Berlioz placed the stage direction *The shepherds gather in front of the stable in Bethlehem* at the beginning of the preceding Overture instead of at the beginning of *L'adieu des bergers*. If indeed the shepherds watched the family during their journey in the Overture like angels hovering over them, then *L'adieu* is a benediction as well as a farewell. As such it seems even more timeless.

Indeed, to encourage listener visualization and a sense of other-worldliness, at one point Berlioz added the description *légende et pantomime* to the third section of part 2, *Le repos de la sainte famille* (The Holy Family stops for rest). The tenor Narrator is brought back to describe the refugees stopping by a spring for respite. In 6/8 meter, the lilting three-note pattern swings lightly within a duple framework that encourages both forward momentum and pastoral calm. The phrase-by-phrase call-and-respond of winds and strings—a dialogue between instrument groups also in *L'adieu* and the Overture—is quite cinematic, as though the travelers are looking at the passing landscape to the left and then the right. Quite subtly, Berlioz joined *L'adieu* and *Le repos* thematically: the beginning of *Le repos* melody is taken from the soprano melody in *L'adieu* beginning, surprisingly, at the held note concluding phrase 3 and continuing through the first several notes of phrase 4. Their shared melodic fragment gives a subliminal feeling of continuity between the two movements. At the end Berlioz instructs eight angels, who sing *Alleluias* in unison and then in four parts, to be placed far behind the orchestra. Because Berlioz in the 1850s still positioned the main chorus at the front of the stage between the orchestra and the audience, the sound of angels coming from the back would have been strikingly otherworldly.

Overall, part 2 *La fuite en Égypte* is restrained and lightly orchestrated. No recitatives or wild rhythmic events carry the action, and no soloists are in character roles. There is only beguiling simplicity. The archaic hue, attributed first to the imaginary seventeenth-century composer, is achieved mostly by use of a modal scale whereby one (or more) of the seven expected steps is altered, in this case the seventh. In addition, all three sections of part 2 are in varieties of three-pulse meters, often a sign for the holy trinity, and each has its own distinctive melodic and harmonic radiance. In sum, the gentleness in part 2 possesses a kind of gravitas all its own and is no less compelling or dramatic than the controlled chaos and tumult found elsewhere.

Part 3: L'arrivée à Saïs (The Arrival at Saïs; 38')

The last segment of the Holy Family's resolute journey, described by the Narrator, is in a plodding duple meter and minor tonality. A solemn storyteller, he is an equal among equals in the orchestral texture. Their shared melody is derived from the initial melodic turn in the Overture of part 2; in effect the correlation, whether heard or simply felt, signals that the family is still traveling, although now they are quite tired. Berlioz works the melody into a fugue; this is the same strategy he used in the opening *Marche nocturne* in part 1 and the Overture of part 2. Gasping and near death, the family arrives at Saïs in Egypt.

Just as Hérode's aria is the most overtly gripping soloist moment in part 1, so is the duet sung by Marie and Joseph in part 3. Having reached Saïs, they search for food and shelter but are met by a town full of cruel, haughty people. Important components to listen for in the duet include the following:

- unremitting tension caused by the lower strings in tremolo;
- intermittent wail of violas as they echo and embellish the last melodic turn of Marie's first phrase and later fragments—violas too have second thoughts and fears;
- the knock on the door of a Roman home, and later on an Egyptian's, played by timpani; and

- ratcheting up of harmonic, rhythmic, and textural urgency only to be stopped, in an abrupt switch to duple meter, by the men's chorus of Romans and then, in a higher register, the Egyptians: "Get away, you dirty Hebrews, tramps and lepers. We have nothing to do with you."

Quite interestingly the duet, so desperate and imploring, shares the same type of meter and tempo, pulse = 50, with the choral benediction *L'adieu des bergers* despite their entirely different dramatic purposes. The comparison is informative for conductors who must set tempos in performance and want to follow Berlioz's directives. The tendency to take the *L'adieu* tempo too slowly can be mitigated by imagining the tempo of the duet, which is much easier to set.

In the following accompanied recitative, Le Père, father of the Ishmaelite family, graciously welcomes the Holy Family into their home. Events then follow in rapid succession:

- The Ishmaelite chorus *Que de leurs pieds meurtris* (Wash the wounds of their bruised feet) is a fugue. The subject is in 2/2 meter (simple duple) and simultaneously superimposed over the countersubject, which is in 6/4 meter (compound duple); all lines merge into 6/4 toward the end. In addition, a jaunty, perky dialogue between two different syncopated gestures in the orchestra accompanies Le Père and underpins the movement.
- A bristly, hurry-up, orchestra-only fugue delightfully depicts Ishmaelites scurrying about the house to carry out their father's orders.
- In a series of accompanied recitatives, introductions are made between the two families; it is agreed Jesus will grow up with the Ishmaelites.
- The evening's *divertissement* is a charming trio for two flutes and harp (often excerpted as chamber music) that suggests shepherds in a ballet or pantomime. A 9/8 compound meter in a luxuriously slow tempo alternates with snappy swirling fast sections in duple (2/2). If period instruments were used, the sound would be more rustic and plain than with modern instruments.
- Marie, Joseph, Le Père, and the Ishmaelite mixed chorus sing a lullaby. Also in triple meter, it is comforting, radiant, and gracious.

Rather than using viola to echo and comment on the voices, as Berlioz did before in Marie and Joseph's duet, here he assigns a solo bassoon. Elastic changes of tempo within or between phrases, marked as *un poco ritard* (a little slower) and *a tempo* (back to the original tempo), create a beguiling feeling of tenderness and immediacy. The Ishmaelites sing, "May hope and happiness once more gladden your hearts."

Epilogue

Dissipating unisons and silences of unspecified lengths gently dissolve the blissful tableau. Then a deliberately paced series of chords brings us back to the present, and the lone Narrator returns to address the audience, once again in recitative. Lightly scored strings alternate with flutes, oboe, English horn, and clarinets, reminiscent of the spare instrumentation at the very beginning of the work. The Narrator states the irony of the preceding events ever so simply: a nonbeliever saved the Savior. Continuing, he summarizes the well-known story: during Jesus's childhood, his sublime gentleness would flower into infinite love and wisdom. He returned to the country of his birth to accomplish the divine sacrifice that marked the way for salvation. At this moment the orchestra, already reduced to just a few woodwinds and strings, gradually falls away as though to shed everything but the essence of this truth.

In a warm new tonality signaling a change of verb tense from past to present and a new section of music, the tenor soloist solemnly begins the final chorus, *O mon âme* (O my soul). It is known as the "mystical chorus" due in part to Berlioz's tempo marking of *Andantino mistico* (pulse = 60). Turning inward to address himself rather than the audience, he sings,

> O my soul, what remains for you to do
> But break your pride before so great a mystery!
> O my soul, oh my heart, be filled with the deep and pure love
> Which alone can open to us the kingdom of heaven. Amen!

The chorus then repeats the first two lines in a free fugal texture and sings the rest of the Epilogue in dialogue with the Narrator. A cappella to the end, the music is stunning if performed well. All of humanity is represented by single solitary vocal lines, each of which merge together into rich, supple harmonies. The tune seems so naturally fitted to the text: the half-step rise to *âme* (soul) falls back to the original note for the unstressed second syllable (*-e*); the dramatic rise to a higher register, particularly notable for the tenors on *briser ton orgueil* (break your pride); and the exquisite dissonances on weak second syllables such as *fair-e* (to do). At line 3, the descending lines of *O mon coeur* (O my heart) unfold as if they are inverted sunrises. Pride is indeed shattered, and the heart is cracked open to receive love.

The closing *Amens* transfix as they patiently, spaciously unfurl. Backstage angels, an onstage mixed chorus, and the Narrator sing call-and-respond *Amens* three times. In the second, the angels in octaves arrive unexpectedly to a momentarily puzzling nonchord tone. But chorus and tenor answer in enriched, reassuring harmonies. The final *Amen* is the simplest: there is no change of harmony, only a simple revoicing. The singers, all in their lowest ranges and warmest colors, dissipate into silence.

Exactly what is the great mystery for which Berlioz tells us we must break our pride? Is it that Christ made the ultimate sacrifice to save mankind? Or is it that the infant Jesus was saved by a nonbeliever from an outcast race? For the answer, go to the second section of the final chorus and listen to how powerfully lines 3 and 4 of the poem begin (*O mon coeur* [O my heart]) as if each voice is in a cathartic cry. Listen for *emplis-toi* (you be filled) and how the three syllables seem to be more spoken than sung, emphatically, imploringly. Listen to how *seul* (alone) is itself set apart, isolated and sung again, and how the surrounding harmonies launch us up toward *ouvrir* (to open). Surely the mystery lies in the motivation for both consummate acts of giving. The mystery is deep and pure love.

So, from the germ of a farewell chorus and the bare bones of scenes from the gospels, Berlioz's imagination took flight. He filled in missing details with his own poetry and exquisite music. Quietly but firmly standing in solidarity with the Jewish people, he closed each part with beatific offstage angels singing three Hebrew words: *Hosanna, Alleluia,* and *Amen.* Near the end the Narrator, having returned us to the present, speaks directly to us just as he did at the beginning of part 1. In the Epilogue, he then turns inward to address himself, and we as choristers join him in asking what more remains for us to do. With no instruments at all, he and people like us sing passionately in magnificent counterpoint about the mysterious gift of love. Time, faith, race, gender, and station are of no matter.

Reception and Legacy

L'enfance du Christ caught on speedily. Offers to perform it came in from everywhere—Brussels, Weimar, Gotha, Baden-Baden, Aix-la-Chapelle, Bordeaux, London, Strasbourg, and Berlin as well as numerous halls in Paris. All or portions of it were performed twenty-four times during Berlioz's remaining life, and of those he conducted it seventeen times. Pages and pages of his correspondence dealt with performance details such as copying orchestra and choral parts, translations into German and English, hiring soloists, placement of the choruses onstage and backstage, and all the other strategic adjustments necessary for every new venue and performance. He was staggered by the overwhelmingly positive response to his "little sacred work," and the press received it warmly. *L'enfance du Christ* was the first major composition Berlioz had premiered in Paris since *La damnation de Faust* in 1846. What a great comeback.

Some in the press maintained Berlioz had changed his style, implying the sacred topic and new tone in *L'enfance* was an admission of prior compositional missteps. Surely, they wrote, he was not the same composer who, in his monumentally conceived "architectural" works or in *Benvenuto Cellini* or *La damnation de Faust*, was bold and at times even bizarre. This work was conservative, pure, and simple; perhaps he had changed to gain popular acclaim. But in the postscript to his *Mémoires*, Berlioz disagreed with his critics. His use of a smaller orchestra and the prevailing tenderness were simply a matter of matching compositional means to the nature of his subject. He credited the success of *L'enfance du Christ* to his audiences and their newly developed powers of understanding. He had been true to himself.

5

OPERAS

In Paris, where a composer's route to artistic renown and financial security was via the opera house, Hector Berlioz's first successes were in other genres. By the 1830s he was known as an ingenious pathfinder of symphonic music, a repertoire dominated by Austro-Germanic composers Haydn, Mozart, and Beethoven. His reputation hinged on *Symphonie fantastique* and *Harold en Italie*, and his enormously successful *Grande messe des morts*, several overtures, songs, and choruses. But opera was not merely a path to success for Berlioz; it was his passion. The questions became, could he write music well suited to the theater? Were his operas as good as his instrumental and other vocal concert works? Would the audiences come?

The opera composers flourishing in Paris c. 1820–1860 were Italians (Spontini, Rossini, Bellini, and Donizetti) and Germans (Gluck, Meyerbeer, and, later, Wagner). French contemporaries also enjoyed success although they have less name recognition today: Boieldieu, Halévy, Auber, Thomas, Gounod, and others. But unlike Berlioz, all had been actively involved in theatrical productions from childhood. Instead, Berlioz's grounding had been a zeal for classical literature, an excellent start, plus flute and guitar lessons, and arranging *romances* from *opéra-comique* collections. Once he arrived in Paris at age seventeen, his self-designed education strategy consisted of singing in an opera chorus, sitting with players in the orchestra pit during rehearsals, studying scores in the Conservatoire library, taking private composition lessons with LeSueur, and later enrolling in the Conservatoire. He immersed himself in plays by Shakespeare and contemporary literature, attended and soon began reviewing operas, and coached singers preparing their opera roles. Working on librettos with friends and established poets, he began composing operas in 1823.

The trail of works considered and left unrealized, or composed in part but abandoned, is heartbreaking. During 1823–1862, Berlioz contemplated writing at least eleven operas, completed two others in his twenties but abandoned them, and began two more in his thirties and forties but left them unfinished. At one point, Berlioz even worked on four operas at once in different stages of completion. Writing ordinary, merely pleasing music or cranking out formulaic dramas for box office appeal was not his style, yet obviously he had many more ideas than he could see through to realization. His libretto sources ranged from plays and pastorals by Chateaubriand, Flaubert, Hugo, and Scribe to Shakespeare's *Hamlet* and *Othello*; he also collaborated with several literary friends in Paris.

Ultimately, Berlioz completed only three operas that were produced during his life and remain in the repertoire today. The number of operas heard and seen by audiences versus those that were contemplated, completed but abandoned, and unfinished is, sadly, three to fifteen.

Benvenuto Cellini (composed 1834–1838) is a novel hybrid of the comedic and serious, originally in two acts (under three hours). *Les Troyens* (composed 1856–1858), a tragic French grand opera in the lineage of Gluck, Spontini, and Meyerbeer, is his culminating masterpiece, in five acts (under five hours). *Béatrice et Bénédict* (composed 1860–1862), a light-hearted *opera-comique* with spoken dialogue, is his last major work, in two acts (under two hours). Berlioz revised *Benvenuto Cellini* extensively and made only a few changes to the other two. All three are performed today, whereas most of the more popular operas composed by his Paris colleagues have not passed the test of time.

BENVENUTO CELLINI: TWO OVERTURES, CELLINI, PERSEUS, AND THE OPERA'S JOURNEY

Let's start with the spectacular part. The music of *Benvenuto Cellini*, Berlioz's first mature operatic venture to go public, is audacious and dazzling. Later, he wrote that it contained a variety of ideas, a special kind of energy and exuberance, and a brilliance of color that he might never find again. Despite being crestfallen with initial productions and its reception in Paris and London, he never regretted writing it and was immensely proud of later performances.

Two overtures, which are performed more frequently than the opera, showcase what the opera offers musically. Berlioz wrote the Overture to *Benvenuto Cellini* (eleven minutes) upon completion of the opera proper to preview important themes before the curtain went up. Later, to maximize his creative capital, he composed a second overture intended for concert performance, *Le carnaval romain* (eight minutes). It adapted and expanded upon the music in the sparkling carnival scene and became a hit. After twenty-six performances, Berlioz decided to insert it into the opera before the second half, which he first did in London, 1853.

The rhythmic bravura and captivating variety of themes in both overtures is entirely satisfying—the listener does not need to know the story line to truly enjoy the music. At the same time, because themes and textures in the overtures correlate with dramatic narrative as played out in scenes and arias, one delightful way to listen is to connect the overture's music to its musical and dramatic place of origin. Opera-to-overture thematic correlations are discussed later in this chapter.

The opera *Benvenuto Cellini* is based on *Vita* (Life), the autobiography by sixteenth-century Florentine sculptor and goldsmith Benvenuto Cellini (1500–1571). A new French translation had recently appeared, and Alfred de Vigny, a star of the Romantic movement and member of Berlioz's circle of literary friends, recommended Berlioz set it after completion of *Harold en Italie*. In real life Cellini made jewelry and sculptures, created dyes for metals, worked in the papal mint casting coins, and wrote treatises on the art of goldsmithing, sculpture, and design. Briefly he was a flute player in the pope's court in Rome. Known also for being a rogue adventurer caught up in jealousies and rivalries, he was imprisoned for avenging the death of his brother by murdering the killer. Eventually Cellini found favor with the pope through the influence of several cardinals.

Berlioz and Cellini were multitalented and had much in common: flute player, writer of treatises and an autobiography, intrepid traveler, adventurer, and passionate devotee to the highest artistic ideals. And they shared a deep love of Italy. Certainly, Cellini's extraordinary life inspired the comical antics and spectacular musical novelties in the opera. Among his most famous creations is the bronze sculpture of Perseus with the severed head of Medusa. In the opera, Cellini is required to finish it for the pope before nightfall or be handed over as a murderer. The finale dramatizes the sculpture being cast.

Why choose Cellini's statue of Perseus as the opera's centerpiece? In Greek mythology, King Polydectes sent away the demigod Perseus, who was the son of Danaë and Zeus, so that Polydectes could wed Danaë. Polydectes's charge to Perseus, deemed to be impossible, was to bring him the head of the gorgon Medusa, a hideous female creature made so by the goddess Athena. Her hair was turned into snakes, and anyone who looked at her became stone. To bring back Medusa's head, Perseus put on a cap that made him invisible. Using a mirrored shield to see only a reflection of her face, thereby avoiding being turned into stone, he beheaded her. The myth of Perseus's ingenuity and heroism was the inspiration for many artists since the Renaissance and particularly so in the early nineteenth century. In the opera, Perseus's statue is a metaphor for Cellini's ingenuity and heroism. Together the three, Berlioz, Perseus, and Cellini, are quintessential romantic heroes upholding the visual and musical arts.

Cellini's bronze sculpture of Perseus with the severed head of Medusa, cast in 1545, stands today in its original location, the Loggia dei Lanzi of the Piazza della Signoria in Florence. The detailed commission instructions required that it correlate with other sculptures already erected there, all of which were made of marble: Michelangelo's *David*, Bandinelli's *Hercules and Cacus*, and Donatello's *Judith and Holofernes*. Indeed, one can easily imagine Medusa having had her way with just a glance and turning these historical and mythological characters into stone. Berlioz probably saw all the statues while traveling through Florence on his way to Rome in February 1831. Arriving in Rome he could observe the carnival festivities firsthand.

The opera is a historical comedy with an unabashed mix of the heroic and farcical. Briefly, the plot proceeds as follows. Cellini (tenor) owes the Pope (bass) a bronze statue of Perseus, which the Pope had commissioned. From the outset and throughout the opera, Cellini loves Teresa (soprano), and she loves him. Balducci (bass), father of Teresa, is the Vatican treasurer and a buffoon who favors mediocrity; he intends for his daughter to marry another sculptor, Fieramosca (baritone). Cellini hoodwinks Balducci to gain his permission to marry Teresa, secures a pardon from the Pope for inadvertently stabbing a monk at a brawl, and against seemingly insurmountable odds and with significant personal sacrifice, fulfills the commission and casts the statue. Despite the comedy and intrigue woven in throughout, the message is serious: the highest artistic standards must be upheld, and not only art but also artists have earned a preeminent place of honor in society.

The journey from conception to production was a bumpy ride. It began in 1834 when Berlioz asked two well-regarded poets, Auguste Barbier and Léon de Wailly, to write a comedy for production at l'Opéra-comique in Paris. It was to be loosely based on events in Cellini's autobiography and include spoken dialogue, as required by the conventions of the *opéra-comique* genre. The love story of Teresa and Cellini was invented; the action moved from Florence to Rome; and the actual commissioner of the statue, Duke Cosimo I de' Medici, changed to Pope Clement VII. The proposed libretto was rejected by l'Opéra-comique, so after making revisions they approached l'Opéra even though it produced mostly noncomedic works and did not permit spoken dialogue. But l'Opéra was the top-tier house in Paris with significantly more resources. Berlioz and his librettists saw the opportunity to fill its larger stage and have use of lavish costumes and sets, so at this point they likely expanded the famous carnival scene. Compared to the original libretto, the opera as approved was significantly revised, longer, more opulent, and without spoken dialogue. Though still a comedy, it leaned toward the new style of French grand opera generally produced at the theater.

Fortunately, the historical topic—a Renaissance artist superhero—was in keeping with audience expectations. But "art as virtue" and "artist as hero" did not resonate as deeply with patrons as it did with the creators of *Benvenuto Cellini*, and the absence of themes such as unrequited love and religious or political conflict was a significant downside. Absence of themes such as unrequited love and religious or political conflict was a significant downside. Heavily weighted with comedy, unusually so for a production in the one Parisian house devoted mostly to serious themes, its prospects for success were a bit cloudy. No doubt some in the audience noticed the parallel between the character of Cellini and Berlioz himself. Perhaps there was a bit too much self-involvement and self-aggrandizement. But to Berlioz the opera was all about comedy, festivities, steadfast love, a terrific story line, great music, and, yes of course, the triumph of art.

Strategy for Listening, Versions, Roles, the Original Cast, and Ten Music Highlights

For newcomers, gaining a deeper understanding of an opera requires a strategy and time. So many features—plot, characters, scene locations, text in translation, music themes, and gestures—are impossible to process simultaneously. Keeping up with more than one or two threads inevitably leads to losing others! So, a suggested strategy is the following: (1) know who's who in the cast, and read a good plot synopsis in advance; (2) listen to highlighted segments; and (3) *then* listen to the opera. Familiar music will resurface, like finding an old friend in a crowd, and more will make sense.

Ten excerpts from *Benvenuto Cellini*, which are based on Paris 1 and 2 versions recorded and conducted by John Nelson (EMI Virgin Classics, 2004), are highlighted below. Tracks and durations are provided. Highlights are in opera order and include a variety of genres: recitatives and arias, a chorus, an aria (*ariette*, as Berlioz called it) not sung but played by an instrument, and a trio of vocal soloists. The two overtures containing music derived from the opera are discussed in the following section. But before all this comes three layers of groundwork: version clarification, roster of roles and their voice categories, and snapshots of the artists who sang in the first performance.

Three Versions: Paris 1, Paris 2, and Weimar

The story of *Benvenuto Cellini* versions is a peek into the trials and tribulations of opera production. But for the listener, knowing about versions is also important because some musical selections exist in one production but not another, so finding specific passages in recordings can be difficult. Here's a brief summary.

- First: Paris 1 corresponds to the full score delivered by Berlioz to copyists at l'Opéra in early 1838 to be used for preparation of performance parts and for rehearsals and performances. It contains Berlioz's freshest, most audacious, and technically challenging music, some of which was cut in deference to performer limitations or at the request of management.

- Second: Paris 2 corresponds to the full score made by l'Opéra's staff to document the opera according to its last complete performance in January 1839, an archival score. Modifications made during rehearsals and the four Paris performances included cutting Balducci's aria no. 1; raising the tessitura of passages for Teresa's Romance no. 3a; replacing the Romance with the flashy Cavatina no. 3b; adding no. 7 Cellini's Romance; and adding no. 24 Ascanio's aria, among others. The Nelson recording is based on Paris 1 and 2.

- Third: The Weimar version is a reallocation of music from the original two acts into three acts: tableaux 3 and 4 of act 2 became act 3 in Weimar. These and other changes and omissions made by Franz Liszt and Hans von Bülow in 1852–1853 were sanctioned by Berlioz, and performances were conducted in Weimar by Liszt. Additional minor changes were made for the second round of Weimar performances in 1856, and Berlioz conducted. Most present-day performances use the Weimar version, although some opera houses are reassessing.

Major roles, Voice Category, and Character

Balducci	bass; father of Teresa, treasurer for the Vatican
Teresa	soprano; daughter of Balducci and in love with Cellini
Cellini	tenor; artist-hero-romantic; in love with Teresa
Fieramosca	baritone; another sculptor; wants to marry Teresa
Ascanio	mezzo-soprano; apprentice to Cellini ("pants role")
Cardinal/ Pope[1]	bass; commissioner of the Perseus statue

Original Cast Snapshots

Oh, to have heard the 1838 premiere—Berlioz's first opera, the controversy, and the music! Snapshots of four artists who created their onstage character give us a glimpse into what that first audience saw and heard.

Voice categories are determined by range, tessitura, timbre, weight (size or volume of sound), and agility.

Teresa

Full lyric coloratura soprano: a high female voice of medium size and warm timbre. She specializes in long legato lines but also is adept at singing quick runs, leaps, and elaborate ornamentation.

Julie Dorus-Gras (1805–1896), from Belgium, made her operatic debut in 1825 at the Théâtre de la Monnaie in Brussels. There she performed in the 1830 production of Auber's *La muette de Portici* (The mute girl of Portici), an opera that helped ignite the Belgian Revolution of 1830–1831. From 1831, she worked at l'Opéra for the next fifteen years; by 1838 she was an established international star, having created roles and starred in operas by Auber, Rossini, Meyerbeer, Donizetti, and Halévy. She had enrolled in the Paris Conservatoire in 1821 and sang in the London 1847 production of Donizetti's *Lucia di Lammermoor* (The Bride of Lammermoor), which Berlioz conducted. An excellent singer with a high, flexible voice, Dorus-Gras also had firmness of tone and lyricism, traits especially welcome in French grand opera. She was not a particularly convincing actress, but the accuracy and brilliance of her voice ensured her success.

Cellini

Dramatic tenor (*tenore di forza*): a high male voice, weightier and more robust than a lyric tenor.

Gilbert Duprez (1806–1896), a Frenchman, debuted as a lyric tenor in 1825 at the Paris Odéon singing in Rossini's *Il barbiere di Siviglia* (The barber of Seville). In 1828, he went to Italy to retool his vocal technique and became among the first to sing a virtuosic high C in a ringing, powerful chest voice rather than using a mixture of head and chest registers. Considered the first great *tenore di forza*, he was also known for excellent declamation of text and the smoothness of his delivery. However, his acting was exaggerated. First successes as a dramatic tenor were in a Bellini opera in Turin, 1831, followed by important roles in bel canto era operas including Donizetti's *Lucia di Lammermoor* in 1835, and more by Rossini and Bellini. When he returned to Paris in

1837 to sing the lead in Rossini's *Guillaume Tell* (William Tell), Duprez was received with such tremendous enthusiasm that audiences attended the production only if he was performing. Rossini, resistant to change, compared his sound to "the squawk of a capon with its throat cut."[2] Duprez also created roles in premieres by composers of French grand opera Auber, Halévy, and Verdi. At the time of *Benvenuto Cellini*, though, his success thus far had not been in the French repertoire. The story of a famous tenor's rise and fall in Berlioz's "Sixth Evening" in his collection of essays *Les soirées de l'orchestre* (Evenings with the orchestra), is largely based on Duprez's career.

But Duprez was not the tenor Berlioz had in mind when writing the role of Cellini. Rather, it was Adolphe Nourrit (1802–1839), whose first important successes were singing the operas of Christoph Willibald Gluck, Berlioz's idol. In Berlioz's formative Paris years, Nourrit sang Berlioz's *romances* in a recital, and they became good friends. From 1826 until 1836, he was the principal tenor at l'Opéra, creating all the leading tenor roles for Rossini's French operas from 1826 to 1829, and singing leads in operas by Auber, Meyerbeer, and Halévy. His voice was described as mellow and powerful, and he was a master of the head voice (*falsetto*), although he must have used a mixture of head and chest voice to sing roles written for him by Rossini and Meyerbeer. In 1836, two years before *Benvenuto Cellini*'s premiere, Edmond Duponchel, director of l'Opéra, engaged Gilbert Duprez with his new and exciting chest voice high C, to share the "first tenor" position with Nourrit. Later that season Nourrit went hoarse and resigned. He went to Italy to retool his vocal technique but, suffering from depression, tragically took his own life.

In *Benvenuto Cellini*, much hinges on the dramatic and vocal integrity of the tenor. One wonders how different the work's fate would have been if Nourrit had sung the premiere and Berlioz had conducted.

Ascanio

Light, lyric mezzo-soprano radiating youthfulness; a slender, bright voice able to move quickly and flexibly through coloratura passages. Ascanio is a pants role sung by a female costumed and acting as a young male.

French mezzo-soprano Rosine Stoltz (1815–1903) was a prominent member of l'Opéra who, similarly to other leads in *Benvenuto Cellini*, created roles composed by Auber and Donizetti. She, like Duprez, received her early training at the École Royale de Chant et Déclamation (Royal School of Song and Declamation) in Paris.[3] Stoltz performed under different names as she burnished her image and vocal abilities in centers from Brussels, Antwerp, Amsterdam, and Lille to Paris. She sang secondary and principal roles in operas by Berlioz's contemporaries Auber, Meyerbeer, Halévy, Rossini, and Hérold. Praised for the remarkable timbre of her lower notes and her extraordinary range, she was criticized for her harsh upper register and lack of technical control. While in Lille, her versatility and broad spectrum of timbres and range rivaled soprano Julie Dorus-Gras, and in Paris she competed for roles with the famed mezzo-soprano Pauline Viardot. Hearing her in Brussels, Adolphe Nourrit was impressed with her talent and probably helped arrange her debut at the Opéra in 1837. The famous cabaletta composed for her by Donizetti in 1840, with its extended low passages, jagged contours, and abrupt shifts between extremes of range, had a forceful impact on the audience. Stoltz was well suited for action roles and celebrated for the intensity of her acting, but in the 1840s she was accused of competing unfairly with rivals and of profiting from her romantic liaison with Pillet, director of l'Opéra—he refused to produce any opera that lacked a role for her. Stoltz left in 1847 after having lost her temper in a performance.

Cardinal (Paris 1 and 2) or Pope Clement VII (Weimar)

Lyric bass: a deep, low male voice having a smooth, rich flow.

Jacques-Émile Serda (1804–1863) created numerous roles at l'Opéra, including Saint-Bris in Meyerbeer's *Les Huguenots* (1836), in which Julie Dorus-Gras also performed and François Habeneck conducted, and Monsieur de Morlaix in *La Esmeralda* by Louise Bertin (1836; adapted from Victor Hugo's novel *The Hunchback of Notre Dame*).[4] Berlioz had coached the soloists in *La Esmeralda* for its premiere during the same period he was composing *Benvenuto Cellini*. In 1844 Serda also created the role of the Baron in *Marie Stuart* by Donizetti at l'Opéra, with Rosine Stoltz in the title role. While the Cardinal/Pope appears onstage for only a short time as the commissioner of the Perseus statue, his brief but grand aria pardoning Cellini is the turning point of the opera; Berlioz placed the theme prominently in the overture.

Ten Music Highlights

Audio recordings of the ten highlights may be easily located online by searching the first line of text in French or by opera title and music number on the Nelson EMI Virgin Classics 2004 recording indicated below. Other recordings may be based on the Weimar version; if listening to the Weimar version, highlight 1 (no. 3a, only in Paris 1 and 2) will not be available. Translations by David Cairns and Liza Hobbs are excerpted from the Nelson CD liner notes.

1. Teresa, Récitative et romance

No. 3a in act 1, tableau 1, scene 2. Teresa, *Récitative et romance* (nine minutes): *Les belles fleurs! / Ah! Que l'amour une fois dans le coeur* (What lovely flowers / Oh, how hard it is for love, once in the heart; 0:48/3:52; CD 1, tracks 5–6). The *romance* has an orchestral introduction, two verses with a refrain, and an interlude between verses.

The opera is great fun right from the very start. Lyric bass Balducci's hilarious aria, *Ne regardez jamais la lune* no. 1 (Never look at the moon, CD 1, track 3; cut from Paris 2 and Weimar), employs a noodling-wiggly bassoon gesture that recurs often. It, along with strings crazily rolling up and down, set him up as a buffoon. Balducci warns his daughter that men are hideous and she must be suspicious, for instead of one mask they wear two! In the following chorus and solo ensemble scene (Chorus of the Maskers, track 4), Balducci declares he would rather hang himself than have Cellini as a son-in-law.

Then all silliness stops. On stage alone and in the first serious moment of the opera, Teresa declares she deeply loves Cellini. In the *romance*, the simple but quasi-turbulent accompaniment for the first several lines is reminiscent of the early versions of Berlioz's *romance*, *La captive*. The melody is lyrical and powerfully passionate. However, showstopping vocal coloratura and a flashy cadenza, rather odd concessions to the popular Italian vocal style of the day, ensue. It appears that Berlioz was never truly inspired by the coloratura/lyric soprano voice because he did not compose for it again, except one solo song (*Zaïde*), until 1860 in his comic opera *Béatrice et Bénédict*. Still, Teresa's character has wonderful gravitas, and her music at times is deeply expressive with poignant, subtle juxtaposition of harmonic contrasts and instrumental colors. Most of the beautiful lower passages in the original version (no. 3a) are preserved in the Nelson recording, but for the premiere Julie Dorus-Gras asked Berlioz to move them higher to better display her best vocal features. Unfortunately, after the premiere, no. 3a was never performed again during Berlioz's lifetime. Rather, Dorus-Gras once more prevailed upon Berlioz and his librettists to substitute no. 3b, which is in Paris 2 and Weimar and discussed next.

2. Teresa, Récitative et air

No. 3b. Teresa's Cavatina (or Cantabile) and Cabaletta: *Entre l'amour et le devoir / Quand j'aurai votre âge* (Torn between love and duty / When I'm as old as you; 3:22/3:43 CD 3, track 16–17 in recording appendix).

Conceding to Julie Dorus-Gras's request, Berlioz replaced the recitative and *romance*, no. 3a, with a showy two-part cavatina and cabaletta, no. 3b. So, instead of a deeply-in-love young woman, we encounter a flighty, fanciful adolescent. Longer by two minutes, the new version gave Dorus-Gras more stage time, a sought-after commodity for singers, of course. But the gravitas of a woman genuinely in love, heard previously in no. 3a, is gone.

The opening cavatina (in French, *cantabile*, meaning lyrical) of 3b begins simply, and soon an obbligato oboe and a few vocal pyrotechnics are added. The extended cadenza fireworks at the end of the second section (the cabaletta) are more characteristic of the in-vogue Italian vocal styles of Rossini and Donizetti than of Berlioz's French style, and it was a huge success with Parisians. The cabaletta proper is coquettish, and the words come from a defiant, shallow young girl: "When I am as old as you, dear parents, that will be the time to behave better! But not now when I'm seventeen." The "oom-pah-pah" underpinning is in keeping with the comic tone of the opening scene, and Teresa's display of vocal prowess and her showy cadenza seem to say, "So there, ha! No one in the audience (or onstage, for that matter) can sing like me!"

Perhaps today, trusting Berlioz's initial judgment, many might vote to hear no. 3a instead.

3. Trio for Soloists

No. 4 Trio (Teresa, Cellini, and Fieramosca) in act 1, tableau 1, scene 4: *O mon bonheur, vous que j'aime plus que ma vie* (O my happiness, you whom I love more than my life; 5:06 and 6:38; CD 1, track 9).

A great deal of action occurs when leads sing in ensembles of three or more. The quicksilver back-and-forth exchanges are extremely challenging to perform and great fun for the audience to hear. But pushback from overwhelmed, frustrated artists over the opera's difficulty was in part responsible for its subsequent neglect. Singers today are far more open and up to the challenge, and the rewards are substantial.

Cellos alone present the first phrase of the love theme; then Cellini sings it through completely. Fieramosca, also a sculptor wanting to marry Teresa and who, unlike Cellini, has Balducci's approval, creeps in on tiptoes accompanied by pizzicato strings. At first, he is unseen and unheard by all but the audience, thereby upending the passionate love duet and turning it into a hide-and-seek comic trio. Teresa responds in kind to Cellini by singing the theme to him but also teases him, saying his love is folly. All the while in a sideshow, Fieramosca interjects snippets of commentary to himself and the audience. In suddenly turbulent music, Cellini, still unaware that Fieramosca is hiding, sings that he will never release Teresa into the arms of Fieramosca; she replies she will die if she is promised to Fieramosca.

The music of the two lovers is dreamy as they sing the theme in a canon over light accompaniment. Magnifying the fragility of such a delicate moment, Cellini floats up into a sweet falsetto, and the lovers' voices entwine in a breathtaking cadenza. Hearing this and of their plans to secretly flee to Florence, Fieramosca, still unseen, declares his intention to foil their scheme. Never in the opera is there any question of Cellini's devotion to her, nor hers to him. If still in Rome, though, they need to persuade Teresa's father to give permission to marry.

The trio's second section is in a frenetic 9/8 meter like the chorus *Venez, venez peuple de Rome* in 6/8 (no. 12 Carnival scene; CD 2, track 2). The breathless, fast-paced, back-and-forth patter requires exquisitely solid musicianship from all artists. That later in the next scene Fieramosca is accused of being a bedroom prowler is totally hilarious; now he is trapped! How jarring to think that, had the opera been accepted by l'Opéra-comique, much of this splendid musical repartee might have been just spoken dialogue. How boring, what a letdown compared to this wonderful music!

4. Cellini, Récitative et romance

No. 7 in act 1, tableau 2, scene 8. *Récitative et romance* (in Nelson recording appendix). *Une heure encore / La gloire était ma seule idole* (One more hour / Fame was my only god; 1:54/4:13, CD 3, tracks 18–19 in recording appendix, from Paris 2 and Weimar).

No. 7 is a recitative and two-verse *romance* with refrain. Composed just a week before the premiere, quite likely at the request of Duprez, it was added at the last minute. This lyric, ardent love song is quite famous and frequently performed in orchestra concerts.

In the opening recitative, Cellini anticipates he will see Teresa in an hour. In the *romance* he ruminates, at first without accompaniment, that only Teresa rules his heart; he asks Love to protect them. The music is a serious, passionate counterbalance to Teresa's frothy and frivolous newly substituted cavatina-cabaletta, no. 3b. It also perfectly suits a *tenore di forza* singer such as Duprez: the lines are long and require rich vocal resonance to fit well in the surrounding orchestra textures. In the last two phrases of each verse, beginning with *Vois donc, amour* (Behold, love), Cellini floats into his uppermost register and then gently descends, joined by a simple, endearing accompaniment.

The inconsistency of characterization between the semicomic adolescent Teresa in no. 3b, the version most often heard today, and the fervent, mature Cellini of no. 7 just doesn't ring true. Teresa's original no. 3a recitative and *romance*, so genuinely expressed, portrays a deeper character; it is a far better match for a Cellini so unreservedly in love. Both new arias were accommodations by Berlioz to singer requests for music they believed better matched their voices and characters.

5. Chorus

No. 8 in act 1, tableau 2, scene 8b: *À boire, à boire! / Chant des ciseleurs* (Let's drink! / The goldsmith's hymn); *Si la terre aux beaux jours se couronne* (If the earth on fine days is crowned; 1:23/3:55; CD 1, tracks 14–15). Participants are the Goldsmiths, Cellini, two minor characters Bernardino and Francesco, friends, and apprentices. Location is the Piazza Colonna.

It is Mardi Gras, the last day for revelry before Ash Wednesday when Christians consider their wrongs, repent, and ask God's help for spiritual growth. The Goldsmiths sing "Let's drink!" (*À boire, à boire!*). Cellini declares absolutely not; there will be no tavern songs today. Instead "we will sing to the glory of goldsmiths and our divine art." Thus begin high-wire musical novelties and one of the most rhythmically acrobatic men's choruses ever composed. Berlioz wrote the Goldsmith's chorus first; like a motto, it encapsulates the spirit of the opera.

Berlioz toys with the 3/8 meter by beginning the men's first phrase on beat 2, the weakest of the three beats, rather than on beat 1, the strongest. Elsewhere accents and new entries are often on the third beat (also weak) rather than on the first. The wait for the second phrase to begin seems too long by a split second, as though Berlioz wanted to throw the listener off kilter a bit more. We are caught, arrested by the sparkling allure of gold! After feeling suspended, the next phrases begin either on beat 2 or the second half of 3, perpetuating the off-tilt feeling. At such a fast pace (*Allegro con fuoco e marcato assai*, pulse = 184; lively with fire and very accented), choristers must expertly articulate tongue-twisting syllables to deliver the desired razzle-dazzle.

In the contrasting next section, which begins with a unison rising line in the voices at the text *Quand naquit la lumière* (When light was first created), Berlioz shifts singers into lower registers, simpler rhythms, and richer sonorities for a conspiratorial effect. The new color and texture are like a passage in *Sara la baigneuse* composed about the same time (in 1834; see chapter 1). The Goldsmiths laud all materials used in the arts: the Creator gave stone to the architect, color to the painter, marble to the sculptor, and gold to the goldsmith. Metals are subterranean flowers that shine brightest on kings and popes. Hail to us, the master goldsmiths!

What great fun to be one of these male choristers! While the music is difficult to execute, it radiates sparkle and vivacity. High art is an indispensable virtue that must be draped in the robes of honor and heroism. The Goldsmiths' chorus returns twice in the opera: in the act 1, scene 10 finale and at the end.

6. Ascanio, Récitative et air and Chorus with Cellini

Within no. 8 in act 1, tableau 2, scene 10. *Récitative et air*: *Un instant, un instant/Cette somme t'était due* (Wait a minute/You are owed this money; 4:19; CD 1, track 17).

Soon following the Goldsmiths' chorus, Ascanio, Cellini's apprentice, enters the tavern with a large bag of money from the Pope; it is Cellini's advance payment to cast the Perseus statue. But there's a hitch: Cellini and his Goldsmiths have a standing wine bill to pay. Ascanio tells Cellini he can have the money only if he swears an oath to cast the statue tomorrow.

Ascanio's aria is in two verses of stentorian grandeur. He expansively sings the first verse; the Goldsmiths and Cellini sing the second. From the very beginning, three quite different gestures in the accompaniment happen in quick succession: (1) pulsing string chords; (2) an oddly nudging, rising two-note figure in bassoons, cellos, and basses; and (3) a low, walking pizzicato line in strings with descending notes roughly adjacent to one another. A map of the phrases is: *ab ab' a''b''' (extension) cdef.*[5]

For the second verse, Cellini and his apprentices sing the same material, but it is harmonized homophonically. From above, Ascanio decorates it with a coloratura countermelody. The form is only slightly varied: *ab ab' a'b'' a''b''' (extension) cdef*. New features include the following:

- instead of pizzicatos (gesture 3), the pitches are fully bowed (sustained) but still sound separately, lending a more monumental effect;
- woodwinds and brass instruments double the men's voices, giving the voices an even richer luster; and
- the burbling woodwind gesture from Balducci's aria, *Ne regardez jamais la lune* (Never look at the moon, act 1, scene 1, no. 1 in Paris 1; cut from Paris 2 and Weimar), returns.

7. Instrumental Aria

Within no. 12 of act 1, tableau 2, scene 12 (Carnival Scene): *Ariette d'Arlequin* (Harlequin's little aria; 1:37; CD 2, track 5).

A pantomimed comedic play within a play is staged at Cassandro's Theater during Carnival;[6] it is a singing competition entitled "King Midas or the Ass's Ears." After the revelers shush one another in rapt anticipation, an English horn in the orchestra pit represents the first competitor, a man dressed as a Harlequin and known to be the finest tenor in Rome; the character on stage mimes singing and playing a lyre, represented by a harp also heard from the orchestra pit. The English horn color is endearing and the tune poignant, but the textless *ariette* is heard only one time and leaves us wanting more. Balducci's actor clone, designated to select the winner, true to form falls asleep during it.

The second competitor, Pierrot, has entered wearing donkey's ears. He also mimes his selection, an absurd cavatina. The orchestra's ophicleide, a somewhat rough-sounding low brass instrument out of use today, plays Pierrot's melody, and he accompanies himself with a small drum hanging from his neck. The music is artless and crude. Not noticing, Balducci enthusiastically beats time, oblivious that he is doing so against the rhythm of the song. Who gets the prize? Balducci awards one gold coin to the Harlequin and a bagful to Pierrot. The chorus cries, "It's no surprise if Pierrot gets the prize; his judge has the same kind of ears!" They label Balducci "Midas."

Musically, the *Ariette* is slow and broad in 3/4 meter (Larghetto, pulse = 58). While the English horn plays over a solo cello bass line and triplet pattern in the harp, the chorus patters away in richly filled-out yet hushed chords singing phrases such as "Ah, what a divine voice!" The form is (a) two long phrases; (b) three short phrases all connected; and lastly (c) a closing single phrase by chorus and English horn resembling the opening. Such an exquisite melody! Like many of Berlioz's, it is long and like sticky paper—it becomes harder to shake off, more and more so as it moves from one phrase to the next.

Berlioz featured the *Ariette d'Arlequin* theme prominently in the *Overture to Benvenuto Cellini*. What could possibly make it that important? After all, it's from a play within a play, it's short, it doesn't have any words, and it certainly doesn't seem particularly relevant to the plot or main characters. But there is a backstory. In 1834, just before he began working on the opera, Berlioz composed a simple vocal *romance* with piano, *Je crois en vous*, "I believe in you." He found the melody compelling and later imported it for just this moment. Though brief, its fine musical qualities express the core message of the opera ever so simply: artistry, virtue, and humility. The message is so clear, in fact, that no words are needed for it to reach us deeply.

8. Pope's Air

No. 19 Sextuor in act 2, tableau 3, scene 6: *Le pape ici! / A tous péchés pleine indulgence* (The Pope is here! / For all sins full indulgence; 2:40; CD 2, track 19).

The Pope's *Air* is sung after his grand entrance and before he learns the bad news: Balducci and Fieramosca accuse Cellini of having ravished Balducci's daughter (untrue), killing Pompeo (true, perhaps an accident), and not yet casting the Perseus statue (true). Contrary to her wishes, Balducci still wants Teresa to marry Fieramosca.

Harp and scraped tam-tam (sounds like a "swish") and timpani together play a single note, letting it ring for an eerie aura of sanctity. The tempo is a regal *Larghetto sostenuto* (slow and sustained; pulse = 58), and the 3/4 meter denotes the Trinity. The *Air* melody is first played by cellos, basses, and bass clarinet while in a hushed patter Teresa, Ascanio, Cellini, Fieramosca, and Balducci sing in the background; they kneel before the Pope. He then sings his melody as cellos and contrabasses move into a rich supporting role; in later phrases violins enrich his line by doubling it from above. The harp, scraped tam-tam, and timpani gesture from the beginning recurs irregularly, usually when no other events are happening, adding mystery and awe. The luscious colors of violas and cellos combined with trombones and bass clarinet bestow majesty and dignity. A rising-falling scale played by violins between the two verses could easily signal a magnanimous Pope raising his arms in blessing. On the second time through, the accompaniment becomes more active and the solo bass clarinet more assertive.

The organization of the melody is easy to hear: section A (two phrases), section B (three shorter phrases), and section C (three phrases). Although in strophic form, the verses are varied: only verse 1 includes section C. The form is as follows:

Instrumental introduction: AB
First verse (sung): ABC
Second verse (sung): AB

The slow section near the beginning of the opera's overture starts with the Pope's *Air* music, a moving declaration of forgiveness "for all his children." By placing it there, Berlioz framed the opera with music signifying one of its most important messages.

9. Ascanio, Air

No. 22 at the beginning of act 2, tableau 4, scene 7. *Tra-la-la! Mais qu'ai-je donc?* (Tra-la-la! What's the matter with me? 5:14; CD 3, track 2).

The foundry for casting the statue has been set up in Rome's Colosseum (onstage the furnace and workers are concealed behind a curtain). Cellini's own artwork, items made of gold, silver, bronze, and pewter, are scattered on the floor ready to be thrown in the fire. The clock chimes four and the statue must be cast by midnight. In a fast 6/8 meter, Ascanio jubilantly bounds in to announce that tonight "our bronze child" is to receive its baptism of fire—the Colosseum will be the church; His Holiness, the godfather; and all the people of Rome, the witnesses. The form of the aria is ABA. In the middle section (after the second "tra-la-la"), Ascanio becomes a comedian, first imitating the Pope and then Cellini. Premiering mezzo-soprano Stoltz was destined to display her famous low register at just this moment. Yes, we are going to see the statue take form!

Ascanio's *Air* was a huge success. It is breezy, cheeky, and a welcome change after the tense Finale of tableau 3 where the audience learned Cellini's only remaining supporters are Teresa and Ascanio. It's easy to see why audiences found it so appealing, especially since the virtuosity required is like that of a standard "stand-and-sing" bel canto aria so familiar at the time. Berlioz composed it between Paris 1 and the premiere, another major adjustment along the road from approval to performance.

10. Cellini Récitative et air

No. 23 in act 2, tableau 4, scene 8. Récitative et air. *Seul pour lutter /*
Sur les monts les plus sauvages (Alone for the struggle / On the wildest
mountains; 2:48/5:39; CD 3, tracks 3–4).

Cellini bemoans his perilous predicament immediately after Ascanio's
aria, *Tra-la-la! Mais qu'ai-je donc?* (highlight 9, no. 22 above). Alone in
the cruel winds and furious waves of struggle; only courage can sustain
him. Beginning with a single unison note in low strings, then another
and another, the opening instrumental passage paints the backdrop for
a distraught, isolated artist-hero. Lines surge forward and withdraw in
the push and pull of struggle and uncertainty. The instruments want to
speak words: there is no melody; phrases fracture and dissipate. An
oboe, alone, eerily sustains yet another single note.

In the aria, woodwinds and strings play in radiant harmonies to de-
note a blissful pastoral location. While Cellini wishes he could be a
simple shepherd and sleep peacefully as if in his own mother's arms,
woodwinds shadow his phrases savoring every lingering, questioning
thought. They seem to hold, even touch his words just sung. Imagining
freedom from toil and escape from cities, Cellini's voice soars, and he
fantasizes singing like a lark.

How can Berlioz not have been writing about himself? He most
certainly experienced the listlessness and indecision that are part and
parcel of an artist's interior life, and he made Cellini's character utterly
transparent about it. Struggle and uncertainty are not character faults,
nor is honesty in revealing them. Cellini's new self-doubt and soulful-
ness humanizes him and adds depth to an opera that has plenty of
bravura and comedy elsewhere.

An Opera Begets Two Overtures

As indicated earlier, Berlioz wrote two overtures related to *Benvenuto*
Cellini: the overture by the same name played prior to the curtain's
rising, which introduces important thematic ideas and characterizes the
dramatic spirit; and several years later, *Le carnaval romain*, primarily an
instrumental elaboration of the carnival music. Both are often presented as independent concert works. With one exception Berlioz used

different themes and gestures in each. Well, which ones? Where in the opera do they come from? Why are those passages important? What should I listen for? Rather than listening to them as a wash of terrific but vaguely associative music, let's tie their easily recognizable themes to their source.

Overture to Benvenuto Cellini

Five standout musical themes/gestures from the opera, and one brief new one, are listed in table 5.1 as they first appear in the *Overture to Benvenuto Cellini*.[7] The music is in three sections: fast-slow-fast. Theme/gestures A, B^1, C, D, and E^1 are from the opera; B^2 is a new short motive. In quite a nice touch, theme/gesture E^1 is a portion of the love duet of Cellini and Teresa. Related portions of it are in *Le carnaval romain*.

Table 5.1.   Themes/gestures in Overture to Benvenuto Cellini

Section	Theme	Description
Fast	A	acrobatic twisty-twirlygig
	B^1	furiously intense, fast string figuration derived from no. 12 carnival chase-fight scene (CD 2, track 8)
	B^2	Beethoven-like tutti chords—stark, sudden, with punch
Slow	C	Pope's *Air*, no. 19 (opera highlight 8; CD 2, track 19)
	D	Harlequin's *Ariette*, no. 12 (opera highlight 7; CD 2, track 5)
Fast	A and B^2	
	E^1	Cellini and Teresa love theme, no. 4 Trio (opera highlight 3; CD 1, track 9)
	A then C	
Coda (fast)	C and B^1	combine

Listen first to opera highlights 8, 7, and 3 discussed previously, which correspond to overture theme/gestures C, D, and E in table 5.1. Then listen for them in the Overture.

Fast   Acrobatic twisty-twirlygigs, theme/gesture A, give the overture its rousing start. Our artist-hero-romantic—the irrepressible Cellini and surely Berlioz himself—is characterized by its quirkiness, vivacity, and charm. Theme/gesture A is played at an almost frenetic pace,

Allegro deciso con impeto (lively, decisive with impetuosity; pulse = 112) by tutti orchestra. But suddenly everything halts. After an abrupt silence, strings play a surface texture of fast-and-furious reiterated notes, B^1, in a *forte* dynamic. The submotive B^2, with strong, sturdy slashes of chords, harkens back to the famous "fate" motif in Beethoven's Symphony no. 5. While they are not tunes but rather gestures, B^1 and B^2 provide tremendous variety of texture, exciting forward momentum, and threads of continuity. The listener will want to remember them—they come back! In an amazing tour de force near the end of the overture, the fast-and-furious string idea B^1 is simultaneously superimposed with the Pope's stentorian *Air* melody (C, highlight 8) from the slow section. Their combination in both the overture and opera signals the Pope's blessing upon Cellini's impetuosity and valor.

Slow   The Pope's magnificent *Air* (C) from near the end of the opera begins the slow section. In the opera, he sings it upon entering Cellini's sculpture studio amidst bickering by the other characters; surprisingly, he absolves everyone's sins before even hearing their disputes. In the overture, by contrast, widely spaced pizzicatos played by cellos and contrabasses draw us in. At first the wait between notes seems eternal, luring us into guessing what will happen next. Gradually it becomes apparent that the low pizzicato figure is the Pope's *Air*. The hollow-sounding tam-tam and timpani add majesty and portent. By setting C near the beginning of the overture but disguising it in a hesitant, almost quizzical pizzicato, Berlioz draws attention to the importance of its message: forgiveness.

After C, high-unison woodwinds soon play a slow, sustained descending line that sounds aimless and, seemingly, of no particular interest. At the point when horns enter, flutes and oboes begin a new melody that is unhurried, searching, and expansive. To our surprise, it is the textless *Ariette d'Arlequin* theme (D; highlight 7) that Berlioz borrowed from an earlier *romance*; it emerges quite unexpectedly from nowhere. As previously discussed, D can be thought to stand for artistic integrity, an attribute not understood by Balducci or others of undiscerning taste.

The complete D theme is repeated by warm, unison strings; each phrase seems to inspire the next. Trombones play a reminiscence of the opening Pope's *Air* (C), which is repeated by low, sustained cellos with basses and decorated by woodwinds and wispy string patterns. The slow section ends with bits of D used as transition material; each phrase moves a step higher.

   Fast   The signature acrobatic/impetuous A theme from the beginning returns two more times in delightfully scattered-about snippets. Big crashes and quasi-Beethoven quotes (B^2) are again like "fate knocking at the door," but Berlioz uses two knocks rather than four. Instead of introducing E at its beginning (no. 4 love theme *O mon bonheur*; highlight 3) as one might expect, Berlioz begins it later, where Cellini sings *chère et tendre promesse* (dear and tender promise).[8] This is precisely the moment in the opera when the lovers promise unwavering fidelity to one another, pledge to confront their conflict with Balducci, and vow never to flee from happiness. The theme in the opera feels different from its appearance in the overture because Berlioz wrote them in different meters: 3/4 in the opera and 2/2 in the overture! The experience of hearing themes return but not identically is tantalizing and powerful. This kind of thematic transformation is one of Berlioz's most successfully expressive techniques.

   Berlioz recapitulates the opening Allegro's acrobatic/impetuous material (A) joined by a sumptuous timpani-roll crescendo. The Pope's theme (C) is hinted at and then fully decked out in glorious orchestral heft and splendor.

   Coda   The coda then comes on fast and furiously: the dazzling combination of the pope's *Air* theme (C) and the second theme B^1 played by strings is an even more decorated version. After a full stop, C is played solely by cellos and basses and for the last time.

   The Pope's *Air* functions like bookends for the Overture, and each presentation is enticingly different. The first is tentative, under cover, and waiting to emerge; for the second and third it is all decked out in resplendent glory. Its message of forgiveness is a thread linking together all the other dramatic themes in the story—love, artistic integrity, and heroism.

Le carnaval romain Overture

Listen first to opera highlight 3 and the Carnival scene following highlight 7 discussed above, which correspond to overture theme/gestures E^2, F^1, and F^2. Then listen for them in the Le carnaval romain.

   While both overtures prominently feature portions of the love song of Cellini and Teresa, no. 4 Trio (E; highlight 3), in *Le carnaval romain*

E^2 shares the center of attention with the fun of Carnival. Two theme/gestures, F^1 and F^2 in a saltarello rhythm bring that fun to the fore. A *saltarello*, from the Latin "to jump," is a lively Italian dance in 3/4 or 6/8 time characterized by a spritely hop or step beginning each measure. In both opera and overture it is in a fast and furious *Presto scherzando* (pulse = 152) and 6/8 meter.

As described above, in the opera's Carnival scene Cellini and his friends gather near Cassandro's Theater to hear the pantomime play "King Midas or the Ass's Ears." They call on everyone—harlequins, jokers, dancers, acrobats, and clowns (*saltimbanques*)—to join the festivities and see the play. Let the gay bagpipes and tambourines sound! Balducci, ridiculous treasurer for the Pope and father of Teresa, has agreed to watch the farce; he is unaware the play will ultimately mock him. Following a flashy brass fanfare, Cellini and friends sing the two-part saltarello theme. The first part, F^1, begins with an ascending interval followed by short notes capriciously skipping along to the text *Venez, venez, peuple de Rome* (Come, good people of Rome). The music is full of breathless, back-and-forth exchanges between instruments and voices. Second part, F^2, begins with a long-held note that descends a wide pitch interval and then quickly skitters upward. The text first sung is *Ah! Sonnez trompettes* (Oh, let the trumpets ring out).

Below is a snapshot of thematic/gesture events in *Le carnaval romain*. See table 5.2.

Table 5.2.   Theme/gestures from *Benvenuto Cellini* opera in *Le carnaval romain*

Section	Theme	Description
Fast intro	F^2	saltarello—long note, descending first interval (*Ah! Sonnez trompettes*) from near the beginning of no. 12 Carnival scene from act I (5:14; CD 2, track 2)
Slow	E^2	Cellini and Teresa love theme, no. 4 Trio (opera highlight 3; CD I, track 9)
Fast, w/coda	F^1	saltarello—short note, ascending first interval (*Venez, venez*; CD 2, track 2)
	F^2	(see above)

Fast (Brief Introduction)   A fantastic, bravura *Allegro vivace saltarello* opens; the music is the second theme group F^2 from the signature Carnival scene, no. 12, not the first. In a close canon, strings lead and winds follow in lightning-fast succession. The furious forward momentum is arrested by the elimination of all instruments save a long note held by a solo horn and then another by a solo clarinet.

Slow   The Cellini-Teresa duet melody (E^2) occurs twice. The first time it is played by an English horn with strings accompanying; strings then play it, and woodwinds respond phrase by phrase for the second time, as though in a reverie. It is then presented in canon, reminiscent of the way Cellini and Teresa sang it in the opera. Now lower strings and flute lead while upper strings answer; trumpets with percussion (particularly tambourine) punctuate. It is a luscious, ecstatically passionate passage followed by a quiet, tender close. More whirling scales in the woodwinds and a light touch of cymbals three times serve as transition.

Fast   Strings play the delightful *Venez, venez, peuple de Rome* melody, the first part of F^1 from the Carnival crowd scene. The tempo, *Allegro vivace* (lively, very fast), is more tame than the opera's original *Presto scherzando* (extremely fast, playfully), although it is often played faster. The grand saltarello theme F^2 that opened the overture follows with the addition of punctuating brass and cymbals.

After ample repetitions of snatches of F^2 and F^1 and plenty of delightful call-and-responds from strings to brass to winds over a long buildup, the music winds down to almost nothing. The saltarello rhythm disappears, but soon violas stubbornly reestablish it. Then a miracle happens: the *Andante* love theme (E^2) returns, played by bassoons in a rich color. Trombones echo it, and then flutes play it in canon. Following, it is played in swift succession by different groups of instruments, one on top of the other, over the saltarello rhythm. Then F^2 returns full blast, and another long buildup begins: F^2 phrases are heard one right after the next from bottom to uppermost strings, and trombones barrel through with the E^2 theme, all leading to a flashy, riotous coda.

Saltarello theme fragments persistently appear on expected and delightfully unexpected beats just as they do in the opera. They are impish and tricky. *Le carnaval romain* is pleasurably challenging for conductor and players and an exquisite experience for listeners. Surely Berlioz had an incredibly good time composing it.

An Opera's Rocky Journey

Benvenuto Cellini may seem an unlikely focus for a chapter on Berlioz's operas. At the premiere it was considered a failure and only later was it resuscitated. Its novel design involving a dual dramatic thrust of both serious and comic themes possibly could have been its near-fatal blow, but other problems also wreaked havoc. Yet we know the music is fantastic! A look into the opera's rocky journey gives us behind-the-scenes insight into contemporary institutions and attitudes, his music, and Berlioz. In a sense, *Benvenuto Cellini* is a metaphor for his lifelong struggle to find success. Here is a quickstep march through what happened.[9]

Prepremiere

- Proposal of the *Benvenuto Cellini* libretto is declined by the Opéra-Comique in 1834; l'Opéra accepts it in 1835 as an *opera semi-seria* even though its audiences expect and prefer serious grand opera.
- The director of l'Opéra, Louis-Désiré Véron (1831–1835), who opposed the prospect of a Berlioz production, is replaced by the devious impresario Edmond Duponchel, a stage designer with whom Berlioz has a precarious relationship.
- Operas already in the production pipeline by lesser-known composers today (Niedermeyer, Halévy, and Auber) delay *Benvenuto Cellini* for two years. During this time, Adolphe Nourrit, the tenor Berlioz had in mind while writing the Cellini role, loses his voice; Duprez, the other "first tenor," who has a very different type of voice, takes his place as Cellini.
- Also during the delay, Berlioz applies for two positions to bolster his standing and income: director of Théâtre-Italien and instructor of harmony at the Conservatoire. He is turned down for both. Running out of money, he asks his friend Ernest Legouvé to extend the due date for his thousand-franc loan.
- Even though Berlioz has taken a sabbatical from writing reviews of operas and concerts, his prior articles have angered the music establishment. He fears retribution on opening night.
- Success of the *Requiem* in 1837 bolsters Berlioz's status at l'Opéra and helps move production plans forward. But he makes a scene in front of a government official about unresolved payment of the *Re-*

quiem commission, consequently tarnishing his image with the same government bureaucracy that funds l'Opéra.

- The government censor requires libretto changes, some relating to racy lines delivered by the pope. To avoid controversy, the rank of pope is downgraded to cardinal.

Rehearsal Issues

- Rehearsals begin in March 1838 with performances scheduled for June. Then production delays cause scheduling conflicts with the lead soprano's vacation, so rehearsals are postponed until her return. The first performance is rescheduled for August, but more delays ensue.
- In rehearsals Habeneck, l'Opéra's primary conductor, is ill humored about having to conduct such difficult music. He resists Berlioz's repeated insistence on faster tempos and considers Berlioz arrogant for tampering. Habeneck is underprepared, just as he was when conducting the premiere of Berlioz's *Requiem* (see chapter 4), and rehearsals are going badly.
- Berlioz, who coached the soloists for months, requests that he conduct but is refused. Whereas Meyerbeer closely supervised every aspect of his operas, Berlioz is not permitted similar access.
- The orchestra is playing hundreds of wrong notes due to the rhythmic complexity, and players become recalcitrant. Habeneck is no help.
- Chorus members are in near revolt over the difficulty of their parts, asserting the music is unperformable. Their obvious resentment leads to malicious backstage gossip; they predict the opera will fail.
- Just before the premiere and in response to complaints and requests from singers and management, Berlioz makes numerous changes. He eliminates passages and composes new arias for Teresa and Ascanio, modifies Fieramosca's role, eliminates Balducci's *Ne regardez jamais la lune* (the terrific *buffo* piece near the beginning), and shortens the overture.
- Just before the opening, the lead tenor, Gilbert Duprez, alleges an indisposition that delays the opening by a week. During it Berlioz composes a new *romance* for him at his request (no. 7 *Une heure encore . . . La gloire était ma seule idole*).

178

CHAPTER 5

Performance and Reception in Paris

- Only four performances are given: September 10, 12, and 14 in 1838, and January 11 in 1839. They are viewed by many as a disaster. Later in February, act 1 is performed twice, sharing the program with opera excerpts composed by others, an indignity for Berlioz.
- Gilbert Duprez never wholeheartedly committed himself to the role because it was too hard for him, and others were discontented, too. His wife delivered their first son during the third performance; when the doctor entered the stage wings to bring the good news, Duprez lost his place in the music and never recovered. Duprez resigned and took a holiday, requiring that a substitute tenor be engaged for the final performance.
- Changes continued to be made during the four-performance run, including cutting the innkeeper's scene and the pantomime in the second tableau. They were made in a rush, and no two performances were the same.
- The impact of the music was marred by slowing down fast tempos, which was done to placate the orchestra. Still, musicians continued to bristle at the difficulty.
- The stage action was so frenzied at times that the dialogue could not be followed.
- Audiences were unaccustomed to the musical intensity and believed the work was overloaded with novelties.
- Having arrived late, as was fashionable in Paris, many in the audience missed some of the best parts, most importantly Teresa's air (no. 3b), the Trio with love duet (no. 4), and the Goldsmiths' chorus (no. 8). The audience's lack of enthusiasm spread to friends and acquaintances, and poor attendance led to cancellation.
- Not surprisingly, the reviews were bad. One critic quipped the music was clever to the point of unintelligibility and criticized Berlioz for his arrogant ambitions as an innovator. According to some, the music was detestable and the libretto absurd. Others objected to the provocation of using contemporary colloquial language instead of the conventional heroic style used by Eugène Scribe, the most popular librettist at the time. While other reviews were generally positive, the negativity took a toll. Ironic pamphleteers cartooned the opera in the press as *Malvenuto Cellini* ("Unwelcome Cellini" rather than "Wel-

come Cellini"). Berlioz had vastly underestimated the offenses caused by his prior reviews, and those offended took retribution.

Comeback in Weimar, Disappointment in London

Amidst the landslide of negatives, not all was bad. Many influential people supported Berlioz, particularly the Bertins, who owned the *Journal des débats* for which he wrote reviews. Paganini said he would commission four more operas from Berlioz if he could. When Liszt heard the production was canceled, he wrote an article defending it, "The Perseus of *Benvenuto Cellini*," and twelve years later as kapellmeister (musical director) in Weimar, he worked with conductor Hans von Bülow to make changes. They sent Berlioz suggestions by letter, which he accepted for the most part, and he replied with recommendations for how it should be conducted. Berlioz insisted on retaining music from arias that had been cut, though, which necessitated awkward changing of words elsewhere and undermined dramatic coherence.

The new opera was received with acclaim—a comeback! Two runs were staged in March–April 1852 and the following November; the latter Berlioz attended. He conducted the second set of Weimar performances in 1856. Par for the course, changes of detail were still being made. Little more than a year later Berlioz conducted a full-scale production of *Benvenuto Cellini* in London in June 1853, during his fourth extended visit there. To adhere to the Italian-opera-only policy of the Royal Opera House at Covent Garden, the libretto was translated into Italian, and for the first time the highly popular *Le carnaval romain* opened the second half.

But the evening marked yet another devastating failure for Berlioz, and sadly, Queen Victoria and Prince Albert were in attendance. Despite all its obvious strengths—the high quality of staging, sets, and costumes, an excellent international cast of singers, a fine orchestra, and the expert Berlioz on the podium—the performance was hissed and whistled down solely for political reasons. A faction of the audience believed that only Italian composers and Italian lead singers should be allowed to perform in the Covent Garden opera house. So, despite its Italian subject, its location in Italy, and being sung in Italian, the opera was shouted down. The cabal of dissenters prohibited the rest of the audience from enjoying the performance, and so Berlioz withdrew the opera that same night. He later wrote that the experience was the worst in his life as a conductor.

Over the next week no less than twenty-six reviews of *Benvenuto Cellini* came out in the London press, quite remarkable for an opera performed only once, and that while being shouted down.[10] Reviews were mixed. Oft-repeated characterizations included "freshness and vigor" and "brilliant instrumental combinations." But then critics dug in for the kill: "Music was more fatal in an opera-house than a concert room"; "confusion and disorder"; "all form is perversely obliterated"; "barrenness and laborious buffoonery of the libretto"; and "unnecessarily noisy." References to Berlioz as "musically defective" and to his "disdain for known rules" strike many today as oddly out of character in an era known for innovation. We are reminded of how progressive Berlioz was for his time and that change can be slow. Indeed, what annoyed some listeners in the past may be just what tantalizes us today.

The complete *Benvenuto Cellini* was performed only fourteen times in Berlioz's lifetime and almost every time with changes. Accolades are owed to Liszt and von Bülow for their wisdom and industry in not letting the opera be forgotten. Berlioz could have burned it, as he did other scores, but he believed in it, and rightly so.

Reception Since

Few productions of *Benvenuto Cellini* were given between the mid- and late nineteenth century; only excerpts popped up here and there. Recently it has been performed more often and with panache, but in reviews stage directors have been criticized for too much happening onstage at once. The music inspires them to replicate its brilliance with hyperactive stage action; in effect they are tempted to go toe-to-toe with Berlioz as if to match or even outdo him! The result is sensory overload. In 1983 Eve Queler conducted a concert version (unstaged) in New York's Carnegie Hall, which was enthusiastically received. For an interesting twist, spoken dialogue was substituted for recitatives, similar to how *Benvenuto Cellini* might have been produced when it was first conceived as an *opéra-comique*. The reviewer wrote that the music was more than sufficient to satisfy any audience, and the overall effect did not suffer for lack of staging.

What's good about *Benvenuto Cellini*? Everything! The opera is witty, swiftly paced, and has a light touch. It is a somewhat serious historical comedy with a four-pronged happy ending: Cellini casts the Perseus statue, the Pope pardons Cellini for killing Pompeo, Balducci and Fieramosca are won over by Cellini's success, and Cellini and Teresa will be married. All the while the prevailing messages are kept clearly in sight: art is serious business, artists are heroes, forgiveness is the right thing to do, and love will prevail. Particularly unique traits are its vivacity and phenomenal ensemble writing. Berlioz made few musical concessions as he challenged performers' skills to the hilt for the effects he desired. Other composers did not have his imagination and were not willing to take such risks. But today the requisite performer expertise is at hand, and artists are more than ready and willing to take it on.

LES TROYENS

Considering all the difficulties he encountered with *Benvenuto Cellini*, it makes perfect sense that Berlioz would take more control of the composition process: for his last two operas, *Les Troyens* and *Béatrice et Bénédict*, he wrote his own libretti. In the case of *Les Troyens*, his passion for Virgil's *Aeneid* had never subsided: the characters were his companions since childhood, and he knew the story inside and out. His friend Princess Caroline von Sayn-Wittgenstein urged him to realize his lifelong vision. After all, twenty years had elapsed since his composing *Benvenuto Cellini*, and now at fifty-three, his final years seemed to be at hand. Sadly, he was dealing with what was probably the onset of Crohn's disease. So, despite feeling more appreciated abroad than at home, Berlioz ventured yet again into the risky business of composing an opera and getting it produced in Paris.

Once more he was drawn to Italy. The *Aeneid* by Virgil is a Latin epic poem relating the legendary flight of Aeneas (*Énée* in French) from Troy to Italy. The central character is the commander of the Trojan army whose descendants will go on to found Rome. Virgil (70–19 BC) lived in the first age of the Roman Empire prior to and during the reign of Emperor Augustus. By weaving interventions of gods, ghosts, and decrees of fate into the story, Virgil sought to legitimize the brutal rise to power and current reign of his patron, Augustus.

Berlioz freely adapted Virgil's poetry from selected books in the *Aeneid* and, in 1856–1858, composed what many consider his crowning masterpiece. It is a true French grand opera in five acts. By the premiere at the Paris Théâtre-lyrique in 1863, though, he had been forced by management to divide it into two operas. Acts 1 and 2 became *La prise de Troie* (The sack of Troy; drawn from *Aeneid* book 2), which was not performed in Paris until 1879, after his death. Acts 3–5, mutilated by cuts and alterations, became *Les Troyens à Carthage* (Trojans in Carthage; drawn from *Aeneid* books 1 and 4). Performances today range from staging part or all of one of the halves or the entire *Les Troyens*, which lasts anywhere from four and a half to six hours depending upon the production.

As was requisite for the genre, choral singing is prominent and choristers play an essential role in advancing the plot. Berlioz calls for a large orchestra including, unusually, antique instruments appearing onstage. The multiple leading roles and many dancers and supernumeraries in the huge cast require the largest of stages. The fantastic spectacle of costumes, sets, processionals, and ballets is magical, and Virgil's story could not be any more epic. There is no overture; instead, Berlioz drops the audience right into staged action.

During Berlioz's life, acts 3–5, *Les Troyens à Carthage*, had only one run. Those twenty-two performances, in 1863 at the Théâtre-lyrique, were over a two-month period and received generally good press. In 1890, the first complete performance of all five acts was given in Karlsruhe, but it was split between two nights and still had cuts and alterations. The first complete and uncut performance given in one evening was produced by the Scottish Opera in Glasgow, May 1969, using the soon-to-be published *Hector Berlioz: New Edition of the Complete Works* (*NBE*), volume 2a–c, edited by Hugh Macdonald.

After the successful but relatively short Paris run, Berlioz arranged the popular *Marche troyenne* (Trojan's march, from the act 1 finale) for performance in concerts. It is believed to be the last composition he undertook, and he never heard it. In the same year, since the full score and orchestra part manuscripts of the opera had been extensively altered for use in performances, Berlioz prepared and published a piano-vocal score. It is the lone, definitive source for the opera's complete contents, the order of movements, and his metronome markings. Unfortunately, Berlioz never oversaw publication of the full score.

By way of introduction, the plot of the opera in a nutshell is as follows. In acts 1 and 2 Énée escapes from the city of Troy, which has been sacked by insidious Greek invaders, and is called to found Rome. Led by Cassandre, the women of Troy commit suicide rather than be captured, raped, and killed by the Greeks. In acts 3–5, the drama includes the ecstatic romance between Énée and Didon, the sacrifice of love by Énée to obey destiny, the crushing blow to Didon of her lover's abandonment, and the Carthaginian's cry for vengeance. The geographical reach of the opera is immense, spanning all the Mediterranean, from Troy to Carthage and an imagined Rome. Not every French grand opera is tragic, but *Les Troyens* more than fits the bill. It ends with the suicide of Didon, the Carthaginians' condemnation of the Trojans, and predictions of the end of Carthaginian society. The only winners are the departing Énée and his Trojans who, having enjoyed a luxuriously pleasant sojourn while in Carthage, set sail to found Rome.

Snapshot Character Guide

The challenge of staying on top of who's who in *Les Troyens* is daunting. Events and characters (persons and gods) referred to in the opera are many, and most of us are not well versed in historical-mythological antiquity. Nor have we necessarily read the *Aeneid* as all in the French-educated classes would have in Berlioz's day. Rather than listing characters in order of appearance, as is usually done, I have listed them below by affiliation and prominence in the story. (English translations of names are in parentheses.) Trojans are primarily in acts 1 and 2; Carthaginians are only in acts 3–5. An asterisk indicates Trojans who also are in acts 3–5 along with the Trojan sailor-soldiers. Numerous references to mythological gods are easily clarified by referring to a Greek/Roman mythology glossary available in hard copy and online.[11]

Trojans (primarily in Acts 1 and 2)

*Énée (Aeneas; tenor), fearless hero and commander of the Trojan army; has deep respect for the will of the gods. His journey from Troy to Italy is motivated by the call of destiny. Convinced Laocoön angered the Greek goddess Pallas (also known as Athena or Athené), he and King Priam (Énée's uncle) decide that the wooden horse, seemingly a gift from the apparently departed Greeks, must be brought into the city.

*Ascagne (usually sung by a mezzo-soprano), fifteen-year-old son of Énée; a reminder of Énée's destiny

Priam, king of Troy (bass), father of Cassandre and Hector, is slain during the fall of Troy

Hécube, queen of Troy (Hecuba; soprano) and married to King Priam

Cassandre (Cassandra; mezzo-soprano), daughter of King Priam and Queen Hécube, cousin of Énée. She was given the gift of prophesy by Apollo but is condemned never to be believed. Convinced the wooden horse left behind by the Greeks is evil, she predicts her cousin Énée will escape during the fall of Troy and found Rome. (Her mad scene in *Agamemnon*, a play by Aeschylus, may have inspired Berlioz to invent her torment scene in act 1, which includes her aria *Malheureux roi*; highlight 1 below).

Chorèbe (Chorebus; baritone), Cassandre's fiancé, an Asian prince; he is killed in the fall of Troy.

Laocoön (not onstage), priest who pierced the wooden horse with his spear and urged the Trojan people to set it on fire. In so doing he was killed by two mysterious sea serpents.

*L'Ombre d'Hector (ghost of Hector; bass). Hector was the greatest warrior of the Trojan Wars; deceased brother of Cassandre. He was slain by Achilles, the greatest of Greek warriors.

Pallas (referred to, not present; also known as Athena or Athené), goddess of the Greeks

*Panthée (Pantheus; bass), Trojan priest, friend of Énée

*Hylas (tenor), a young Phrygian sailor; his song of homesickness for Troy is frequently excerpted (highlight 6 below).

Helenus (tenor), a Trojan priest, Priam's son

Andromaque (Andromache; silent), Hector's widow. Énée tells Didon the story of Andromaque's enslavement and marriage to her Greek captor who was also her father's killer and son of her husband's killer.

Astyanax (silent), eight-year-old son of Andromaque

Polyxène (Polyxena; soprano), Cassandre's sister

*Two Trojan soldiers (basses)

A Greek Chieftain (bass)

A Priest of Pluto (bass)

Carthaginians (only in Acts 3–5)

Didon (Dido; mezzo-soprano), queen of Carthage in northern Africa (now in modern Tunisia); widow of Sichée (Sychaeus) who was prince of Tyre (now in Lebanon). She left Tyre to found Carthage. As Énée's consort she has become the pawn of the gods.

Anna (alto), Didon's sister

Narbal (bass), trusted minister to Didon

Iopas (tenor), Tyrian poet to Didon's court. His aria, like Hylas's aria, is frequently excerpted.

Mercure (Mercury; baritone/bass), messenger of the gods

The chorus is comprised of Trojans, Greeks, Tyrians/Carthaginians, nymphs, satyrs, fauns, sylvans, and invisible spirits.

Plot Overview by Act

First, here's a little background. In Greek mythology, the Trojan War began after Paris, a Trojan prince, fell in love with and abducted the beautiful Helen of Sparta. When her husband, Menelaus, demanded her return, the Trojans refused. For nine years the Greeks destroyed Troy's surrounding cities, temples, and countryside. However, the city itself, commanded by Hector and other sons of the royal household of King Priam, was well fortified. Four days in the final decade-long siege of Troy are recorded in Homer's *Iliad*. Such a war possibly occurred in the eleventh or twelfth centuries BC.

Musical highlights 1–8, discussed later in this chapter, are noted in the following plot overview.

Act I

Near the ancient city of Troy (today the Anatolia region of northwest Turkey) at the site of an abandoned Greek camp. The Trojans are rejoicing now that the Greeks have departed after ten years of war. But someone has left an enormous wooden horse outside the city wall. Cassandre, daughter of King Priam, can see into the future but is cursed with not being believed. She foretells disaster (highlight 1). Her lover Chorèbe and the others doubt her assertions. Priest Laocoön, suspecting the Greeks are up to a trick, throws a javelin against the horse's flank and urges the crowd to set it on fire; he is immediately and brutally killed by two sea serpents. To appease the goddess Pallas (Athena), the wooden horse is brought into the city at Énée's command (highlight 2).

Act 2

In Énée's palace in Troy. Énée is visited by the ghost of the slain Hector, Cassandre's brother, and urged to flee to carry out the Trojans' destiny in Italy. Greek soldiers have burst out of the horse to destroy the city, and Troy is in flames. Terrified, the women huddle in the Temple of Vesta, and Cassandre leads them to mass suicide rather than let them be captured and raped. They die with *Italie!* on their lips.

Intermission

Act 3

Years later in Carthage, North Africa, a hall in the palace of Queen Didon. Didon's sister, Anna, suggests a new marriage; Didon, though, asks to be cursed if she ever betrays her husband's memory; she still wears his ring. A strange fleet of ships is reported to have been driven ashore by a storm; it is the remnants of the Trojan army. Énée enters disguised as a sailor. Ascagne, Énée's young son, asks Didon for asylum and offers riches from Troy in return; they are welcomed into Carthage. Numidian soldiers (native to the area of present-day Algeria) invade, led by a suitor whom Didon had refused. Énée throws off his disguise and offers the help of his sailor-soldiers; the Numidians are defeated.

Act 4

In a forest outside Carthage, Énée and Didon are hunting (highlight 3). The gods conspire to bring them together by sending a storm. Énée and Didon enter a cave for refuge and lovemaking; the word *Italie!* is intermittently sung by spirits. In scene 2 back in Carthage, festivities deepen their bond. However, Mercure warns Énée of his destiny and commands him to sail to Italy (highlights 4 and 5).

Act 5

At the seashore by Carthage, Hylas, a young Trojan sailor, sings of his lost homeland as he falls asleep (highlight 6). Some soldiers have seen ghosts warning them to be on their way; others are perfectly happy to continue enjoying the pleasures of Carthage. Énée is deeply torn but concludes he must leave; he, too, has seen the ghosts (highlight 7). Upon telling Didon his decision, she curses him. Distraught, she decides to offer Énée's gifts to the gods of the dead and tells her sister she will kill herself. A funeral pyre is built and lit; she climbs onto it and stabs herself. As she dies, she predicts eternal strife between Énée's people and her own, saying, "Rise up from my bones, avenging spirit." Much later in history the same well-known call to war was invoked against the Romans by Hannibal, considered to be the greatest Carthaginian military strategist in history. Didon's people cry out their own curse on the race of Énée (highlight 8), whose descendants will found Rome centuries later and defeat the Carthaginians in multiple Punic Wars.

Music Highlights

Consider enjoying the following eight highlights before attending or listening to the opera in its entirety.

1. No. 2 Récitatif et air: Les Grecs ont disparu / Maleureux roi! (The Greeks Have Vanished / Ill-Fated King!)

Sung by Cassandre in act 1 (8:31)

Apparently the Greeks have retreated, so the Trojans run out to see the wooden horse and drag it inside the city walls. At the beginning of the recitative, a dark, slithery, and unmelodic line alternately writhes upward and falls in fits and spurts; it signals disorientation and fear. Alone, pale, and troubled, Cassandre paces as she questions the Greeks' sudden departure. Her lament evolves into an impassioned prediction of the Trojans' impending demise. Note the turbulent bass lines, the gnarled and dissonant harmonies, and the rapid shifts from angst to sadness and then sweetness when she thinks of her lover, Chorèbe. As always with Berlioz's music, listen not only to the singer but also to the role of the instruments, which anticipate, frame, and comment on the message. Listen particularly to single lines as they move forward and to the arresting colors of such remarkable harmonies. Enjoy how Berlioz energizes culminating moments by adding rhythmic layers and to his enrichment of textures and dynamics by adding instruments.

2. No. 11 Final: Marche Troyenne (Trojan March)

Sung by Cassandre and chorus at the end of act 1 (7:09)

Mistakenly thinking the wooden horse is a holy object wrongly attacked by Laocoön, King Priam orders Énée and his warriors, women, and children to escort it into the city. Heard first from a distance, their robust and confident *Marche troyenne* is a supplication to the goddess Pallas asking forgiveness for Laocoön's attack on the horse. Cassandre, incredulous at their error, is frantic. As the procession moves closer, the crowd is oblivious to their danger—they sing of smiling garlands, spring lily of the valleys and flames of triumph. But when they arrive onstage, a clash of armor is heard from inside the horse; panic spreads, the music abruptly stops and begins again. As the procession exits the stage, Cassandre cries that fate has seized its victim and Troy is now ruined.

Berlioz brings back the *Marche troyenne* twice. Upon the arrival of Énée and his soldiers at Didon's court in Carthage, the music is rendered in a more foreboding, plaintive minor key (no. 26, act 3) rather than the original jubilant rendition in major. At the close of the opera, during the visual glorification of Rome in the background, the *Marche* is heard again in major, this time simultaneous to the opposing music sung by the Carthaginians cursing all things Trojan and Roman (no. 52, act 5). The bitter conflict will continue between the two civilizations for centuries; ultimately descendants of the Trojans win.

Berlioz's concert version of the *Marche troyenne* (4.5 minutes) is enormously popular despite its glorification of Trojan errors, their massacre by the Greeks, Énée's abandonment of Didon, and her suicide. Grandly stirring, it is among his most tuneful and compelling marches. Today, it reminds us of Berlioz's most important opera, still rarely heard, and of the Trojans' path from delusion and defeat to victory.

3. No. 29 Chasse royale et orage—Pantomime (Royal Hunt and Storm—Pantomime)

At the opening of act 4 (9:37); sung (often from backstage) by a chorus of nymphs, sylvans, and fauns. Note: Berlioz wrote lengthy stage directions in the score, which may or may not be evident in performances or provided with recordings. In a staged production, the pantomime usually includes dance; in concert performances, a more generous unleashing of the imagination is required. Rather than attempting to match Berlioz's stated events to the music, free-fall immersion and imagination are recommended.

It is a calm morning in an African forest. A leisurely descending melody is heard first in the violins. For each of its three repetitions (by violas, violins, and finally cellos), the sonic palette gradually becomes more lush. On stage we see a mountain crag, a small stream, the opening of a cave, and rushes and weeds. Two naiads bathe in a pool, but at the horn call they hide in the reeds, fearful of discovery. In a tumult of sonic weather elements, nymphs and sylvans dance, the sky darkens, a storm arises, and hunters pass by with their dogs. Didon and Énée appear, she as a huntress and he in semi-military garb; they enter the cave for shelter. Nymphs gesticulate wildly from the crag above, and amid their calls we hear *Italie!* Grotesque dancing visually magnifies the musical torrent of swirls, surges, and lunges. A tree is struck by lightning and catches fire; dancers take up the flaming branches and disappear. The storm passes, clouds lift. Serene music from the opening, joined by fading calls of horns, returns.

4. No. 36 Récitatif et septuor (Recitative and Septet)

Mais bannissons ces tristes souvenirs / Tout n'est que paix et charme autour de nous! (But no more of these sad memories / Peace and enchantment are all around us); sung by Didon, Énée, Ascagne, Anna, Iopas, Narbal, Panthée, and chorus near the end of act 4 (5:18).

In the previous passage and at her request, Énée tells Didon the story of Andromache, the widow of the renowned warrior Hector. After persistently refusing, Andromache fell in love with and married her enslaver Pyrrhus, the Greek who murdered her father and son of the man who killed her husband. The story affects Didon deeply, and she realizes that she too can overcome the loss of her husband. Didon tells Énée, "Everything conspires to overcome my remorse, and my heart is absolved." Distracted, she allows Astyanax, who is dressed as Cupid, to remove her wedding band.

In the no. 36 recitative, Énée changes the subject, asking Didon to breathe in the sighing whispers and caresses of the breeze around them. Time and reality are suspended. The nocturne septet, for seven Trojan and Carthaginian soloists and chorus, is in a gently rocking 6/8 meter, and the voices are in a homophonic, hymnlike texture. Sounding like depth charges plumbing Didon's deepest emotions, a group of horns, bassoons, bass drum, cellos, and basses enter intermittently and magisterially playing long notes. Persistently repeated short notes by woodwinds and single-pitch tremolos by strings are a consistent backdrop, like a transfixing far-off horizon. All seems radiantly transparent. Soloists sing the opening section; when the chorus enters for the second section, the soloists and Didon sing ancillary, more decorative phrases with them. "Night spreads its veil and the sleeping sea murmurs the softest harmonies in its slumbers." The onomatopoeic sounds of the French words *murmure en sommeillant* (murmur in slumber) are soothing, yet the sad tone forebodes Didon's fateful succumbing to despair. The gentle back-and-forth shifting by half step of flute and clarinet simulates light refracting on the water and leads into the opera's hallmark duet that follows.

5. No. 37 Duet: Nuit d'ivresse et d'extase infinie! (Night of Rapture and Infinite Ecstasy)

Sung by Énée and Didon at the end of act 4 (10:06)

Radiant and utterly transporting, the duet is at the pinnacle of romantic vocal music. Like the septet just before, it is in a pastoral 6/8 meter but a little faster. The text references loving relationships of mythological gods and Trojan characters: Venus and Anchises, Troilus and Cressida, and Diana and Endymion. So, this too is a love for the ages. While still singing, Didon and Énée leave stage arm in arm. But Mercury, god of messages and commerce, suddenly appears accompanied by diabolic brass; he strikes Énée's armor, which is hanging on a column, and gestures toward the sea declaring *Italie!*

Berlioz marks the duet *Andantino non troppo lento* (interior pulse in 6/8 = 126)—not too slow. Performers will do well not to take a slower tempo than Berlioz specified and not to overromanticize moments by adding rubatos he did not call for. If the duet slows to the point of tedium, luminescence and coherence of phrasing and structure are lost!

Listening to the changes in accompaniments from section to section and the exquisite intertwining of voices is pure joy. Enjoy.

6. No. 38 Chanson d'Hylas: Vallon sonore (Song of Hylas: Echoing Vale)

Hylas and two sentinels sing at the opening of act 5 (5:13).

The song performed by Hylas, a young Trojan sailor, is one of the most endearing moments in the opera. It is a simple strophic *romance* for a sweet-voiced tenor comfortable in a high tessitura. In one effective staging, Hylas is in a hammock high up in the rigging of a ship's mast. He reminisces about his long-lost home in Troy: will he ever again wander in a forested vale, rock gently on the breast of the eternal sea, or be cooled by scented green branches in his homeland? The two sentinels on the deck below know he will never go back. In simple duple time, waves gently rock the boat. Listen for the cello in dialogue with the tenor and to the instrumental sigh each time he sings *hélas* (alas). Each of the three verses is slightly varied; they are separated by a refrain in compound duple 6/8 (Rock gently on your mighty breast) that calmly contrasts with the duple before and after. The second refrain includes a storm squall; in the third, the voice falls away and clarinets finish his last phrase. Their entry reminds us of their startlingly cool, clear timbre in the introduction.

7. No. 41 Récitatif mesuré et air

Inutiles regrets! Je dois quitter Carthage! / Ah! quand viendra l'instant des suprêmes adieux (Futile regrets! I must leave Carthage / Ah! When the moment comes for the last farewell); sung by Énée in act 5 (6:37)

The time for a decision is at hand: will Énée leave Didon or stay? He examines every aspect of the argument in a tour de force recitative-aria sequence. Didon knows Énée must leave, but he is rattled by her disillusionment and cannot withstand the terrible power in her look. However, his mission is sacred, it is the gods' command, and they have given him many warnings. His son Ascagne's future and that of the Trojans hang in the balance.

In the recitative, an agitated marchlike but offbeat string accompaniment signals Énée's distress; he must make the right decision. Brass or winds, when imitating a previous phrase or anticipating the next, represent thoughts he cannot shake off. At times fragments of themes that the lovers previously shared are heard. The gods either chide or agree with him.

In his aria, Énée imagines his farewell to Didon. At the beginning, in a gently floating 6/8 *Andante*, woodwinds play a halting, mournful anticipation of his first phrase. In duet with a French horn, he asks how he can bear the anguish of her indignant grief. He weighs the possibility of not seeing her before leaving and argues he cannot ask forgiveness while at the same time breaking her heart. In the swirl of a faster *molto agitato*, Énée sings of his despair and resolve in his highest, most ringing *tenore di forza* register. Will he be a coward and avoid an in-person farewell; can he risk breaking the sacred laws of hospitality? No, he adores the Queen and will see her again, even though he knows her despair will break him.

8. Nos. 51 and 52 Ah! Au secours / Imprécation (Ah! Help! / Curse!)

Sung by Didon, Anna, Narbal, and chorus at the end of act 5 (2:36)

Standing on the funeral pyre where she placed all of Énée's gifts to be burned, Didon stabs herself. While dying she declares that fate is against the people of Carthage and they will perish. The Trojan fanfare is heard in the distance just as an image appears (Berlioz called it a distant radiance, an apotheosis). It is a capitol building labeled ROMA, and an emperor is surrounded by poets and artists; legions of soldiers are parading in front of it. As though prescient and the only one to see it, Didon cries bitterly, "Rome . . . Rome . . . eternal!" Witnessing her die, her people sing their furious curse: "Undying hatred for the race of Énée!" Their dissonant entry pitch is jarring and vehement. Simultaneously the orchestra, dominated by brass, plays the triumphant *Marche troyenne* again. As history will bear out centuries later and the audience already knows, the Trojans will prevail.

The Ending

Some say the ending is strange and doesn't really work. Like the final moments of *Benvenuto Cellini*, it wraps up so quickly that perhaps Berlioz ran out of time when writing it. Maybe for him all the fun was in getting there, so ending with an abrupt, rushed finale was acceptable.

Actually, though, Berlioz initially wanted a different conclusion. Clio, the muse of history, was to escort future great leaders and artists across the stage in an epilogue. There were to be individuals from both sides of the centuries-long conflict: Hannibal (the greatest Carthaginian warrior), Scipio (African Roman general in the Second Punic War), Caesar (general and emperor of Rome), and then the poet Virgil himself. Berlioz's friend Pauline Viardot, though, convinced him not to introduce new characters at the end of the opera, understandably so. But some argue the ending we now have is worse. The cry by the Carthaginians for revenge is subsumed by the Trojan's victory march, as though the people of Carthage will inevitably be defeated, no matter how many battles are yet to come. It's a cruel, ugly finale. By respectfully honoring Virgil and important heroes from both sides in his first version, Berlioz would have brought a wider lens to this monumental story and an element of reconciliation.

In effect, the bitterly confrontational conclusion of *Les Troyens* is diametrically opposite to endings of his other dramatic works and is quite unlike him. In *Roméo et Juliette*, the two warring Italian families are reconciled, thanks to the intervention of Le Père Laurence. In *La damnation de Faust*, seraphic spirits gather Marguerite up into the heavens instead of leaving her in prison, thanks to Faust having signed his life away to Méphistophélès. In *L'enfance du Christ*, the Ishmaelite family in Egypt provides safe harbor for the persecuted Jewish Holy Family, and the narrator and chorus reflect on the mystery of sacrifice and love in a stunning a cappella close. True, *Symphonie fantastique* ends badly: the artist-hero-lover witnesses his own beheading and macabre funeral. Not leaving it there, though, Berlioz wrote a sequel, *Lélio*, in which the artist-hero awakens, recovers his happiness, and immerses himself in music.

But in *Les Troyens*, the ending is truly tragic. From their spoiled relationship and Carthaginian suspicion that he had been disingenuous all along, centuries of hatred and war between the two races ensue. While the ending of *Les Troyens* is uncharacteristic of Berlioz, it is true to history and, also for many, excellent theater.

A SURPRISE BONUS AND CLOSURE:
BÉATRICE ET BÉNÉDICT

For his last opera, Berlioz pivoted again. Composed after *Les Troyens* but premiered before it, the high-spirited *Béatrice et Bénédict* is a true *opéra-comique*. Based on *Much Ado About Nothing* by Shakespeare, it is brimming with pure joy and fun. The idea had been on Berlioz's mind since 1833, when he came back from Italy. Like *L'enfance du Christ* and *Les Troyens*, he wrote the entire libretto, and like *Roméo et Juliette*, he returned to his favorite dramatist, Shakespeare, and to his favorite country, Italy.

The overture is one of his best and most often performed in concerts. Later in the opera, Berlioz used an early *romance*, *Le dépit de la bergère* (The spite of the shepherdess; composed about 1819), as the basis for a dance theme. By using a quite youthful composition at this late date in his life and having come full circle, perhaps Berlioz had already decided the opera would be his last. Or, more likely, he simply believed that a good tune, even if composed when he was an adolescent, could not be left an orphan.

The opera has other strategies we now expect from Berlioz. The Duo-Nocturne *Nuit paisible et sereine!* (Serene and peaceful night!) sung by Héro (soprano) and Ursule (mezzo-soprano), with its murmuring breeze, chirping cricket in the feathery grass (oboe), and images of a nightingale mingling her song with rustling woods, is reminiscent of the sublime duet *Nuit d'ivresse* (no. 37, highlight 5) in *Les Troyens*. The music for an invented buffo character not in the play, Somarone, master of the chapel, recalls the same concept as the "Amen" student-soldier fugue in *La damnation de Faust*. Here Somarone rehearses to his dissatisfaction a not-so-great-sounding Handelian-like fugue both with and without added ornaments. The music and comedic action are hilarious.

All ten complete performances of *Béatrice et Bénédict* during Berlioz's life were in Germany (Baden-Baden, Weimar, and Stuttgart), not in Paris, and several were sung in German. Sadly, it was the only opera Berlioz was commissioned to write. By now unquestionably the most formidable conductor of his time, Berlioz conducted six performances of it, thus setting traditions for how it would be performed in the future.

Composing *Béatrice et Bénédict* was a wonderful way to end his compositional career. After long immersion in *Les Troyens*, rebalancing back to his natural ebullience of spirit and good-natured humor was just the right step. And there were all the plusses: finally, he was commissioned to write an opera, he had full control of the libretto, it was set in Italy, the drama was Shakespeare's, he conducted it multiple times, and it was performed in Germany where he had always been most welcome. There was much for Berlioz to celebrate in his final years.

EPILOGUE

Just before a performance of *Grande messe des morts*, a group of amateur music lovers gathers for the preconcert discussion. Many are already Berlioz devotees, and others are there to figure out what all the excitement is about. A Berlioz admirer poses the question, "What is it, exactly, that attracts us? What about his music is so gratifying?" She loves his music but has never explored or articulated the reasons why. Somehow, mysteriously, she just knew. But *how* did she know?

Pinpointing the allure of Berlioz's music may be as elusive as trying to paint a fragrance. Knowing something is "just right" may be caused by any one or a combination of events, from a small change of harmony, turn of melody, or a sustained syllable in a word. The objective in this journey has been to offer the listener a starting point, a hook, a platform, a lifeline for how to listen to this remarkable music. No doubt we have discovered that we cannot be passive. Rather, for the music to be meaningful we must actively engage with it and bring our own imagination into play.

Berlioz was a groundbreaking composer in his time, and amazingly, he still seems so today. The freshness of his music is ever palpable and enticing. He wrote long themes with multiple and uneven phrases, and he used gestures—brief nudgings and callouts that seem to express a feeling, a word, or a landscape. With his themes, gestures, and discreet use of harmonies, he cooked up recipes for combining disparate materials, assembling them in different orders and timings, and using a tantalizing variety of instruments and registers. It is as though his music is made up of bits of a puzzle or a toy that can be fitted together in any layer, order, or space in time and move in any direction. Even today his mastery of special orchestral effects is extraordinary, from the extreme of stratospheric flutes paired with subterranean trombones to the tinkle of antique cymbals. While he did not invent the *style énorme*—huge orchestras and choruses used for his monumental architectural music—his ability to exploit the acoustical properties of a space and create a full spectrum of effects, from delicacy to somber introspection and cataclysmic tumult, is unmatched.

Though operating within confirmed genres, Berlioz was a genre buster. His early approach to songs, based on simple folk-song-like *romances*, evolved into forms that at times resemble an opera scene (*Élégie en prose*) or a miniature symphonic poem (*La captive* last version). He wrote a symphony that has traits of an oratorio (*Roméo et Juliette*), his oratorios behave in part like operas (*La damnation de Faust* and *L'enfance du Christ*); and one of his operas is a hybrid of the traditional *opéra-comique* and French grand opera (*Benvenuto Cellini*).

Although he was a masterful composer of orchestral music—he understood the limitations and possibilities of instruments better than anyone else of his generation—Berlioz wrote first and most often for voices. Materials from his earlier tune-smithing in songs and choruses reappear, repurposed and newly framed, in later extended works with instruments. In effect, Berlioz took a simple, compelling passage for voice and, using his remarkable skills, elevated it and its surroundings into something more far-reaching. In addition, many vocal works that were composed first with piano accompaniment were later more colorfully partnered by orchestra, and some vice versa. Simply put, he continued to write and revise songs and choruses because he believed in their veracity and accessibility, and they continued to be an important expressive vehicle for him throughout his career. Songs overlooked today, such as *La captive*, *Le trébuchet*, and *La belle Isabeau*, invite more frequent performance, as do numerous choruses such as the triple chorus *Sara la baigneuse*. Indeed, when compared to his instrument-only compositions, music for voices and orchestra comprise the greatest proportion of his works by far.

Berlioz inherited not only the French tradition of male-dominated choral voicing (three or six parts: soprano-tenor-bass or *divisi* soprano-tenor-bass) but also the calling to compose music for outdoor processionals and large open-air festivals. Living through the political upheavals of five different government regimes in France, along with his knowledge of conflicts in Ireland and Greece, Berlioz wrote numerous thrilling choruses, choral-orchestral cantatas, and marches on patriotic themes. The influence of the Choron and Orphéon movements in music education and the professional singer training in the Conservatoire and schools for church cantors and choristers afforded him a pool of committed amateurs and well-trained singers. As a consequence, the overwhelming sound of hundreds of choristers singing with large military bands or orchestras in pavilions, exhibition halls, cathedrals, streets, and plazas deeply influenced Berlioz's concept of how musical sound touches the emotions of listeners.

And what of Berlioz as a person? As was conventional for a well-educated doctor's son, his grounding was in literature. He had developed a deep love for the written word while reading the classics at an early age, and upon his arrival in Paris late in 1821 at age seventeen, his range expanded to contemporary and historical plays, novels, and poetry. All led to the defining ingredient of Berlioz's music: telling a story. With the exception of only one or two, all his works, with or without text, are based on a written narrative. Not only did he compose stories in music, but also Berlioz was a prolific and talented author in his own right. A smart, witty critic, he wrote reviews of concerts and operas in Paris, travelogues of his concert tours, letters, memoirs, and a treatise on the orchestra—how to write for it and how to rehearse and conduct instruments and voices. In late career he authored his own librettos.

As for Berlioz's music education, he studied guitar and flute as a youth in La Côte-St-André; he probably sang the *romances* he arranged from comic operas and his own *romances*, too. In his early twenties and overlapping in part with completing first steps toward a medical career, he sang in an opera chorus, taught guitar at a girls' school, sat in the pit with the opera orchestra musicians, studied scores in the Conservatoire library, took composition lessons privately, and enrolled in Conservatoire music courses. His basic keyboard skills were self-taught, but he was able to write accompaniments; perhaps they were conceived with guitar in hand as was the case when he composed *La captive*. Some believe that his novel way of thinking about orchestra textures and forms was in large part because he was not a pianist from childhood. In this he was quite unlike so many of his nineteenth-century composer colleagues.

The greatest disappointments in his life—initial reception of *La damnation de Faust* and *Benvenuto Cellini* and the brutalization of *Les Troyens*—reflect a quite bumpy career in Paris. Furthermore, he was not diplomatic. His vivid, impolitic, and overly clever reviews of productions and concerts caused resentment that contributed to politically motivated, negative reviews of his own music. So, while lauded abroad, Berlioz was never fully embraced in his homeland. The establishment blocked his entry into the opera inner circle, artistic director appointments, and teaching positions at the Conservatoire.

When we listen to Berlioz's music, though, we are hearing creations by a man who knew his ideas were durable and true. He rarely repeated them exactly, always revising and reframing them to new levels of expressive clarity. Finding it necessary to protect his music from disfigurement, he conducted nearly all his works in Paris and on tour, seeking to refine them and establish their performance traditions. Initial failures such as *Benvenuto Cellini* were given second chances outside of France. Despite criticism of it, he wrote that he had no regrets about having composed it. Its later success, along with that of *La damnation de Faust*, *L'enfance du Christ*, and numerous others, proved that he had been right all along, if only his music had been given a fair chance in Paris.

From the outset, Berlioz showed empathy for the defeated and outcast. Songs such as *Élégie en prose* and *Chanson à boire* are early examples. Surely his own disappointments worked to deepen his empathy for others' predicaments: his rejection in love by Estelle, Harriet, and Camille; rejection by his father, who never came to Paris to hear his music or see him conduct; and rejection artistically by the establishment in Paris. In this light, his choice of heroes and heroines is revealing: the outcast Jewish Holy Family in *L'enfance du Christ*; the discarded lover Didon in *Les Troyens*; the artist-hero-lover in *Symphonie fantastique*; and the flawed and defeated military hero Napoléon Bonaparte in *Le cinq mai*. Berlioz even had empathy for Faust, the lost seeker of truth who, by signing his fate over to Méphistophélès, enabled Marguerite to be lifted into heaven.

With the single exception of *Les Troyens*, reconciliation and redemption are the ultimate consequences of Berlioz's remarkable empathy for his characters. In *Roméo et Juliette*, Berlioz changed the ending of Shakespeare's drama to allow the lovers to say goodbye, and in the grand finale Le Père Laurence intervenes to bring the two warring families together. In *L'enfance du Christ*, Berlioz chose the portion of Christ's narrative where the family is saved by humble outcasts; we see not only common decency but also how love prompts sacrifice and humility. In *Benvenuto Cellini*, all the multifarious threads are resolved: Cellini's murder charges are forgiven; Cellini and Teresa may marry; the commissioned statue of Perseus is successfully cast; and, most importantly, art, the essence of humanity, is victorious.

While storytelling, empathy, and reconciliation inspired his music, Berlioz wrote that he hoped his audiences would, first and foremost, be moved by its sound: melodies and gestures, textures, compositional strategies, special orchestral effects, and much more. But perhaps the elusive attraction—why we at times know it's "just right"—is the ineffable intermingling of his amazing imagination, stories, and sound, and his incredible transparency of heart.

APPENDIX A

Song Inventory

Individual songs
Songs and arias often excerpted in concert from major choral-
    orchestral works
Songs and arias often excerpted in concert from operas
Collections assembled by Berlioz

This appendix documents the scope of Hector Berlioz's song compositions in the above four categories and provides titles the listener may
encounter (several early songs are not included). Works are listed
chronologically in each category by year of composition; Berlioz made
later versions of many of them. Solos, duets, and trios are included. For
a complete listing by title and more information, including Holoman
catalog numbers, refer to appendix B in *Berlioz* by Hugh Macdonald
(2000) and the *Catalogue of the Works of Hector Berlioz* by D. Kern
Holoman, volume 25, in *Hector Berlioz: New Edition of the Complete
Works* (*NBE*).

INDIVIDUAL SONGS (38)

Youthful Songs (10)

Youthful songs were composed from 1819 to 1828, prior to *Neuf mélodies*. There are five for one voice, four for two voices, and one for three voices. Notable works include the following:

- *Amitié reprends ton empire*, ca. 1819–1821, trio of two sopranos and bass
- *Le pêcheur*, 1827, incorporated into *Lélio*, tenor
- *Le roi de Thulé*, 1828, incorporated into *Huit scènes de Faust* and recast for *La damnation de Faust*, mezzo-soprano and soprano, respectively

Songs in *Neuf mélodies* (6)

A collection of songs composed in 1829: five songs for one voice, and one duet; three remaining titles are choruses (not listed), two of which have solos.

- *Le coucher du soleil*, tenor
- *Hélène*, duet (two versions)
- *La belle voyageuse*, (four versions)
- *L'origine de la harpe*, voice (often sung by soprano)
- *Adieu Bessy*, tenor
- *Élégie en prose*, tenor

Individual Songs (8)

Individual songs spanning 1832–1839:

- *La captive*, 1832 (six versions plus a reduction of the last orchestra score in 1863), mezzo-soprano
- *Le jeune pâtre breton* (*Le jeune paysan breton*), 1833 (four versions)
- *Les champs*, 1834 (two versions), tenor

- *Sara la baigneuse* in *32/33 mélodies*, 1863/1864 (the fourth version is a duet for soprano and contralto or tenor and bass; earliest version from 1834 for male quartet is lost)
- *Je crois en vous*, 1834
- *Le chant des Bretons*, 1835 (two versions), tenor solo or men's chorus
- *Chansonette de M. Léon de Wailly*, 1835, tenor or soprano (melody and text only)
- *Aubade*, 1839 (two versions), voice and two horns

Les nuits d'été (6)

The original six songs with piano are all for mezzo-soprano or tenor:

- *Villanelle*, 1840 (two versions)
- *Le spectre de la rose*, 1840 (two versions)
- *Sur les lagunes*, 1841 (two versions)
- *Absence*, 1840 (two versions)
- *Au cimetière*, 1841 (two versions)
- *L'île inconnue*, 1841 (two versions)

Individual songs (8)

Eight individual songs spanning 1842–1850:

- *La mort d'Ophélie*, 1842 (two versions)
- *La belle Isabeau*, 1843 (two versions)
- *Le chasseur danois*, 1844 (two versions)
- *Zaïde*, 1845 (two versions)
- *Le trébuchet*, 1846, duet for two sopranos or tenor and bass
- *Nessun maggior piacere*, 1847 (not published by Berlioz)
- *Le matin*, 1850, mezzo-soprano or tenor
- *Petit oiseau*, 1850 (same text as *Le matin*), tenor or mezzo-soprano or baritone

Total: thirty-eight individual songs; twenty-four titles were revised or orchestrated, some multiple times.

Songs Later Revised to Other Voicings

Solos Revised into Choruses

- *Hélène* was originally a ballade for two voices, 1829; revised in 1844 for men's chorus and orchestra.
- *La belle voyageuse* was a solo, 1829; arranged in 1851 for two-part women's chorus and orchestra.
- *La mort d' Ophélie*, composed for soprano or tenor voice in B ♭ major, 1842; revised in 1848 for soprano and contralto chorus with orchestra in A ♭ major. It was printed in *32/33 mélodies* in 1863/1864 for soprano and contralto chorus with the original piano accompaniment of the first version in A ♭ major.

Quartet Revised into Triple Chorus and Then Duet

- *Sara la baigneuse* was scored first for male quartet and orchestra (1834, lost), then STTB solo quartet, chorus, and orchestra (1838, lost), and then for three choruses, STB, SC, and TTBB, and orchestra (1849). In *32/33 mélodies* (1863/1864), it appears as a duet for solo voices, either soprano-contralto or tenor-bass.
- Originally for chorus or solo: *Le chant des Bretons*.

SONGS AND ARIAS OFTEN EXCERPTED IN CONCERT FROM MAJOR CHORAL-ORCHESTRAL WORKS (18)

Solos from major choral-orchestral works are often excerpted in concerts and recitals as "stand-alone" *romances* or arias. Some titles require choral participation. Berlioz did not write any roles for soprano soloists in his choral-orchestral works. Note: *Roméo et Juliette* is considered both a choral-orchestral work and a symphony.

From *Le retour à la vie: mélologue en six parties* (3)

Later called *Lélio, ou le retour à la vie*, 1831

   Le pêcheur (tenor)
   Chant de bonheur (tenor)

Scène de brigands (baritone)

From *Roméo et Juliette* (3)

Strophes: Premiers transports (contralto)
Bientôt de Roméo . . . Mab, la messagère (tenor)
Air (Pauvres enfants), Serment (bass)

From *La damnation de Faust* (8)

Le roi de Thulé (mezzo-soprano)
D'amour, l'ardente flamme (mezzo-soprano)
L'invocation à la nature (tenor)
Merci, doux crépuscule (tenor)
Certain rat, dans une cuisine (baritone)
Voici des roses (bass)
Une puce gentille (bass)
Devant la maison (bass)

From *L'enfance du Christ* (4)

O mon cher fils (mezzo-soprano and baritone)
Dans cette ville immense (mezzo-soprano and baritone)
Le repos de la sainte famille (tenor)
Air d'Hérode (bass)

Total: eighteen romances, arias, or duets from extended works (nonopera)

SONGS AND ARIAS OFTEN EXCERPTED IN CONCERT FROM OPERAS (19)

Some require choral participation.

From *Benvenuto Cellini* (5)

Entre l'amour et le devoir (soprano)

La gloire était ma seule idole (tenor)
Sur les monts les plus sauvages (tenor)
Une heure encore (tenor)
Seul pour lutter (tenor)

From *Les Troyens* (8)

Errante sur les mers (soprano)
Je vais mourir (soprano)
Chers Tyriens (soprano)
Les Grecs ont disparu . . . Malheureux roi! (dramatic soprano)
Non, je ne verrai pas (dramatic soprano)
Inutiles regrets (tenor)
O blonde Cérès (tenor)
Vallon sonore (tenor)

From *Béatrice et Bénédict* (6)

Je vais le voir (soprano)
Il m'en souvient (mezzo-soprano)
Mais qu'ai-je donc (mezzo-soprano)
Cette somme t'est due (mezzo-soprano)
Ah! qui pourrait me résister? (baritone)
Le vin de Syracuse (bass)

Total: nineteen opera songs and arias

Grand total: thirty-seven solos often excerpted from major works (opera, symphony, and choral-orchestral) in recital or on concert stage with orchestra and chorus.

Voice distribution is five for soprano; two for dramatic soprano; eight for mezzo-soprano or contralto (including two duets); thirteen for tenor; five for baritone (including two duets); and six for bass.

COLLECTIONS ASSEMBLED BY BERLIOZ (7)

Berlioz published individual songs and choruses with piano accompaniments, of which many were also orchestrated, in collections under one cover and a new title:

1. *Neuf mélodies*, 1830, retitled *Irlande* in 1849 (see above)
2. *Les nuits d'été*, 1841 (see above)
3. *Tristia*, 1849, revised 1851

   Méditation religieuse (chorus)
   La mort d'Ophélie (see above)
   Marche funèbre pour la dernière scène d'Hamlet (chorus sings "Ah"; no piano version available)

4. *Vox populi*, 1849

   La menace des Francs (chorus)
   Hymne à la France (chorus)

5. *Feuillets d'album*, 1850

   Zaïde
   Les champs
   Chant des chemins de fer (chorus)

6. *Fleurs des landes*, 1850

   Le matin
   Petit oiseau
   Le trébuchet
   Le jeune pâtre breton (Le jeune paysan breton)
   Le chant des Bretons (chorus)

7. *Collection de 32/33 mélodies*, 1863/1864 (see chapter 1). Includes twenty-three solos and duets, nine choruses, and one cantata. All titles were published previously. Information of note:

- *La mort d'Ophélie* is a two-part chorus often performed as a soprano-contralto duet.
- *Sara la baigneuse* appears as a duet for either soprano-alto or tenor-bass.

- The six *Les nuits d'été* are piano reductions of their last orchestral versions.
- Four titles are not included in any prior collections:

  - *Chœur d'enfants* (*Prière du matin*) for children's chorus, composed before 1846
  - *La belle Isabeau*, before 1843
  - *Le chasseur danois*, 1844
  - *Le cinq mai*, 1831–1835, cantata added for second edition

- *Marche funèbre pour la dernière scène d'Hamlet* is the only work excluded from *32/33 mélodies* that was previously published in a collection (*Tristia*).

APPENDIX B

Choral Music

Appendix B is an aid for locating Hector Berlioz's choral music according to genre, voicing, and topic of secular, sacred, or patriotic. In the first section, Choruses, titles are organized into five categories: brief, independent choruses; cantatas; symphonies with choruses; extended choral-orchestral works; and operas. The second section is a chronological listing of patriotic choruses correlated with the governing regime at the time and Berlioz's age.

Notes:

- Each title entry includes the composition date whether the first version is a song or a chorus.
- Due to the existence of multiple versions of some titles, Holoman catalog numbers (H.) and version letters (e.g., H.42D) are provided.
- Voicing is for a mixed ensemble of either STB, SSTTBB, or SATB unless described as for men's chorus, women's chorus, treble chorus (women or children), or double chorus.
- Many choruses feature one or more soloists.
- ∞ Indicates the title is also in a solo or duet version.

CHORUSES

Brief, Independent Choruses (24)

Choruses in this category are not part of a longer work, are ten minutes or less in duration, and may be a cappella or accompanied by piano or orchestra. Many include portions for soloists. Berlioz composed them from 1829 to circa 1860–1868.

Le ballet des ombres: ronde nocturne, 1829, H.37
from *Neuf mélodies*, 1829:

Hélène ∞, arr 1844, H.40B, men's chorus
Chant guerrier, H.41, men's chorus
La belle voyageuse, arr 1851, H.42D, women's chorus ∞
Chanson à boire, H.43, men's chorus
Chant sacré, H.44A (two versions)

Hymne des Marseillais, arr 1830, H.51A (TB-STB double chorus, orchestra); rev 1848 (SSTTBB, piano), H.51B
Chant du neuf Thermidor, 1830, H.51bis
Méditation religieuse, 1831, rev by 1849, H.56B; in *Tristia* compiled 1851, H.119B
Quartetto e coro dei maggi, 1832, H.59
Sara la baigneuse ∞, 1834; arr 1850 (triple chorus), H.69C
Le chant des Bretons, 1835, H.71A; rev 1850, H.71B, men's chorus
L'apothéose, arr 1848; from *Grande symphonie funèbre et triomphale*, H.80C
La mort d'Ophélie ∞, 1842, arr 1848, H.92B; in *Tristia* compiled 1851, H.119B, women's chorus
La belle Isabeau (*ad libitum* SSTBB brief chorus refrain), 1843, H.94
Hymne à la France, 1844, H.97, in *Vox populi*, H.120
Marche funèbre pour la dernière scène d'Hamlet (chorus sings "Ah"), 1844, H.103; in *Tristia* compiled 1851, H.119B
Prière du matin: chœur d'enfants, ca. 1846, H.112, children's chorus
La menace des Francs: marche et chœur, 1848, H.117; in *Vox populi*, H.120

Hymne pour la consécration du nouveau tabernacle, 1859, H.135
Le temple universel, 1861, H.137, two men's choruses (with organ);
    rev 1868, H.137B men's chorus (a cappella)
Veni creator: motet, ca. 1860–1868, H.141, treble voices
Tantum ergo, ca. 1860–1868, H.142, treble voices
Invitation à louer Dieu, ca. 1860–1868, H.143 (arr on a theme by
    Couperin), three equal treble voices

Cantatas for Soloists, Chorus, and Orchestra (6)

Composed from 1825 to 1854, Berlioz's cantatas are independent vocal works with orchestra of ten to thirty minutes in duration. Two of his four Prix de Rome cantatas include chorus; he won the prize on his fifth attempt with *Sardanapale*.

Youthful

Scène héroïque: la révolution grecque; composed 1825–1826, H.21A;
    in 1833 arr for chorus and military band, H.21B
La mort d'Orphée, 1827 (Prix de Rome), H.25
Sardanapale, 1830 (Prix de Rome), H.50

Mature

Le cinq mai, 1831–1835, H.74
Chant des chemins de fer, 1846, H.110
L'impériale, 1854, H.129, double chorus

Symphonies with Choruses (2)

Of Berlioz's four symphonies, his last two include chorus.
Roméo et Juliette, 1839, H.79
Grande symphonie funèbre et triomphale, rev 1842, strings and
    chorus added (mvt 3: *L'apothéose*; H.80B). *L'apothéose* was re-
    composed for solo, chorus, and piano, H.80C; also listed above
    under "Brief, Independent Choruses."

Extended Choral-Orchestral Works (7)

Works in multiple movements for soloists, chorus, and orchestra over thirty minutes, composed from 1828 to 1854.

Youthful

Messe solennelle, 1824; rev 1828–1829, H.20
  from *Huit scènes de Faust*, 1828–1829, H.33:

  Chant de la fête de Pâques
  Concert de sylphes
  Romance de Marguerite; Chœur de soldats

from *Le retour à la vie: mélologue en six parties (Lélio)*, 1831, H.55A; rev 1855 (H.55B) and renamed *Lélio, ou le retour à la vie*:

  Choeur des ombres irritées
  Chanson de brigands, men's chorus
  Fantaisie sur la Tempête de Shakespeare for SSATT chorus (*Miranda*, H.52)

Mature

  Grande messe des morts (Requiem), 1837, rev 1852, 1867 (H.75)
  La damnation de Faust, 1845–1846 (derived from *Huit scènes de Faust*; H.111)
  Te Deum, 1849, H.118, double chorus
  L'enfance du Christ, 1850–1854, H.130

Operas (3)

  Benvenuto Cellini, 1836–1838, rev 1852, H.76
  Les Troyens, 1856–1858, H.133
  Béatrice et Bénédict, 1860–1862, H.138

POLITICAL REGIMES DURING BERLIOZ'S LIFE AND PATRIOTIC CHORUSES

1804–1814

Napoléon Bonaparte I, first empire; Berlioz age one to eleven

1814–1830

First Bourbon restoration (monarchy); Napoléon's return and defeat at Waterloo; second Bourbon restoration (monarchy); Berlioz age eleven to twenty-seven

- *Scène heroïque: la révolution grecque*, 1825–1826, H.21A; BB solos, mixed chorus, orch; arr in 1833 for chorus and military band, H.21B
- *Chant guerrier*, 1829, H.41; TB solos, men's chorus, pv

1830–1848

July Revolution of 1830 and monarchy of King Louis-Philippe (Orléans lineage; constitutional monarchy); Berlioz age twenty-seven to forty-five

- *Hymne des Marseillais*, arr from Rouget de Lisle, 1830, H.51A; double chorus of TB-STB, orch; rev 1848, H.51B for T solo, mixed chorus, pv
- *Chant du neuf Thermidor*, arr from Rouget de Lisle, 1830, H.51bis (relating to events in 1794); T solo, mixed chorus, orch
- *Le chant des Bretons*, 1835, H.71A; rev 1850, H.71B; men's chorus or T solo, pv
- *Le cinq mai*, 1831–1835, H.74; B solo, mixed chorus, orch
- *Grande messe des morts (Requiem)*, 1837, rev 1852 and 1867, H.75; T solo, mixed chorus, orch
- *L'apothéose*, mvt 3 of *Grande symphonie funèbre et triomphale*, rev 1842 by adding strings, chorus, H.80B; M-S or T solo, mixed chorus, orch
- *Hymne à la France*, 1844, H.97; mixed chorus, orch
- *Chant des chemins de fer*, 1846, H.110; T solo, mixed chorus, orch

1848–1852

Revolution of 1848 and 1850–1852, Second Republic; Louis-Napoléon, president; Berlioz age forty-five to forty-nine

- *La menace des Francs* for piano, 1848, H.117; four-part men soloists or semichorus, mixed chorus, orch
- *Hymne des Marseillais*, arr from Rouget de Lisle, rev for piano 1848, H.51B; T solo, mixed chorus, pv
- *L'apothéose* (from *Grande symphonie funèbre et triomphale* of 1842, mvt 3), recomposed for piano 1848, H.80C; mixed chorus, pv
- *Te Deum*, 1849, H.118; T solo, mixed double chorus, two-part children's chorus, organ, orch
- *Hymne à la France* mixed chorus, 1849, H.97; pv reduction of orchestra version
- *Vox populi*, 1849, H.120 includes two works also listed above: *La menace des Francs*, H.117, and *Hymne à la France*, H.97, both piano-vocal reductions of orchestra versions

1852–1870

Second Empire, Louis-Napoléon becomes Emperor Napoléon III; Berlioz age forty-nine to sixty-six (Berlioz died in Paris on March 8, 1869)

- *L'impériale*, 1854, H.129; double chorus, orch
- *Hymne pour la consécration du nouveau tabernacle*, 1859, H.135; mixed chorus with organ or piano
- *Le temple universel*, 1861, H.137A; men's double chorus with organ; rev 1868, H.137B, for men's a cappella chorus

APPENDIX C

Program of *Symphonie fantastique*

1855 VERSION OF THE PROGRAM OF *SYMPHONIE FANTASTIQUE* BY HECTOR BERLIOZ

Note

The following program should be distributed to the audience every time the *Symphonie fantastique* is performed dramatically and thus followed by the monodrama of *Lélio*, which concludes and completes the episode in the life of an artist. In this case the invisible orchestra is placed on the stage of a theatre behind the lowered curtain.

If the symphony is performed on its own as a concert piece, this arrangement is no longer necessary: one may even dispense with distributing the program and keep only the title of the five movements. The author hopes that the symphony provides on its own sufficient musical interest independently of any dramatic intention.

Program of the Symphony

A young musician of morbid sensitivity and ardent imagination poisons himself with opium in a moment of despair caused by frustrated love. The dose of narcotic, while too weak to cause his death, plunges him into a heavy sleep accompanied by the strangest of visions, in which his experiences, feelings, and memories are translated in his feverish brain into musical thoughts and images. His beloved becomes for him a melody and like an *idée fixe* which he meets and hears everywhere.

Part One: Daydreams, Passions

He remembers first the uneasiness of spirit, the indefinable passion,[1] the melancholy, the aimless joys he felt even before seeing his beloved; then the explosive love she suddenly inspired in him, his delirious anguish, his fits of jealous fury, his returns of tenderness, his religious consolations.

Part Two: A Ball

He meets again his beloved in a ball during a glittering fête.

Part Three: Scene in the Countryside

One summer evening in the countryside he hears two shepherds dialoguing with their "Ranz des vaches"; this pastoral duet, the setting, the gentle rustling of the trees in the light wind, some causes for hope that he has recently conceived, all conspire to restore to his heart an unaccustomed feeling of calm and to give to his thoughts a happier coloring; but she reappears, he feels a pang of anguish, and painful thoughts disturb him: what if she betrayed him . . . . One of the shepherds resumes his simple melody, the other one no longer answers. The sun sets . . . distant sound of thunder . . . solitude . . . silence . . . .

Part Four: March to the Scaffold

He dreams that he has killed his beloved, that he is condemned to death and led to execution. The procession advances to the sound of a march that is sometimes sombre and wild, and sometimes brilliant and solemn, in which a dull sound of heavy footsteps follows without transition the loudest outbursts. At the end, the *idée fixe* reappears for a moment like a final thought of love interrupted by the fatal blow.

Part Five: Dream of a Witches' Sabbath

He sees himself at a witches' sabbath, in the midst of a hideous gathering of shades, sorcerers, and monsters of every kind who have come together for his funeral. Strange sounds, groans, outbursts of laughter;

distant shouts which seem to be answered by more shouts. The beloved melody appears once more, but has now lost its noble and shy character; it is now no more than a vulgar dance tune, trivial and grotesque: it is she who is coming to the sabbath . . . roars of delight at her arrival . . . . She joins the diabolical orgy. . . . The funeral knell tolls, [a] burlesque parody of the *Dies Irae*. The dance of the witches. The dance of the witches combined with the *Dies Irae*.

Reproduced with permission from Monir Tayeb and Michel Austin (http://www.hberlioz.com).

APPENDIX D

Mémoires References

The selected readings from Hector Berlioz's *Mémoires* provided below refer to individual works discussed in this book. All references are to the edition translated and edited by David Cairns: *The Memoirs of Hector Berlioz* (1969; New York: Knopf, 2002). The "Editor's Introduction" (pp. xi–xxi) and "Berlioz Described by His Contemporaries" in appendix I (pp. 574–79) are highly recommended, as is, of course, the entire volume.

Berlioz began compiling his *Mémoires* while in London in 1848. Portions were serialized in contemporary journals over many years. It was completed in 1865 and published posthumously in 1870, as per his direction.

Songs (Chapter 1)

Élégie en prose, 71–72
La captive, 172–73

Music for Chorus (Chapter 2)

Le cinq mai, 310, 367
L'apothéose (from *Grande symphonie funèbre et triomphale*),
    246–49

NOTES

INTRODUCTION

1. An early twentieth-century Berlioz collected works edition, edited by Charles Malherbe and Felix Weingartner and published by Breitkopf & Härtel, was a great first step but is unreliable. In the case of songs and choruses, the editors changed accompaniments. Other similarly unannounced changes were made in the extended works. Consequently, performers using scores from the series, many of which have been reprinted by other publishers and are available online, do so at their own risk.

I. SONGS

1. Berlioz reissued the collection a year later as *33 mélodies* to include one more choral work, the cantata *Le cinq mai*. The collection will be referred to as *32/33 mélodies*.

2. Berlioz destroyed some scores that he found unsuitable; we know of them through accounts of performances, his *Mémoires*, and correspondence.

3. The convention at the time was to convey tempo, dynamic, and character instructions in Italian.

4. Berlioz contemplated at least eighteen operas of which two were completed but abandoned or destroyed (*Estelle et Némorin* and *Les francs-juges*), and two were left unfinished. Ultimately, only three were staged. See chapter 5.

5. Hector Berlioz, *La belle voyageuse (The Fair Traveller)*, 1829, Paroles imitée de l'Anglais de Th. Moore par Gounet 2, no. 4 (London: Stanley Lucas, Weber, [1885]), n.p.

6. Hector Berlioz, *The Memoirs of Hector Berlioz*, trans. and ed. David Cairns (New York: Knopf, 2002), 71.

7. Berlioz, *Memoirs*, 72.

8. See appendix A, "Song Inventory."

9. Annegret Fauser, "The Songs," in *The Cambridge Companion to Berlioz*, ed. Peter Bloom, 108–24 (Cambridge: Cambridge University Press, 2000), 119–20.

10. Julian Rushton, "*Les Nuits d'été*: Cycle or Collection?" in *Berlioz Studies*, ed. Peter Bloom, 112–35 (Cambridge: Cambridge University Press, 1992), 134.

11. In French, the final "e," called a schwa and found here in Ophélie, is sounded when sung and reading poetry out loud but is silent in spoken French. Thus, here it has four syllables (rather than three), with the final schwa functioning as the lightest and shortest syllable and "li" the strongest. Going for a delicate, lingering effect, Berlioz brings out the schwa ever so gently by moving down from "li" by a half step.

12. See chapter 3 for discussion of the *idée fixe*.

13. Ernest Legouvé (1807–1903), author and playwright, was a good friend; Berlioz dedicated *Grande ouverture de Benvenuto Cellini* to him in 1838.

14. Berlioz, *Memoirs*, 36–37.

2. MUSIC FOR CHORUS

1. Katharine Ellis, *Interpreting the Musical Past: Early Music in Nineteenth-Century France* (New York: Oxford University Press, 2005), 224.

2. See Claire Rowden, "Choral Music and Music-Making in France," in *Nineteenth-Century Choral Music*, ed. Donna M. Di Grazia (New York: Routledge, 2013), 205–212.

3. Berlioz's ability to understand English improved substantially throughout his years of marriage to Harriet Smithson and reading Shakespeare's plays. See discussion of *Roméo et Juliette* in chapter 3.

4. Letter to his friend Ferrand in December 1830, in D. Kern Holoman, *Catalogue of the Works of Hector Berlioz* (Kassel, Germany: Bärenreiter, 1987), 71.

5. Music historians have used the term "lost" to describe missing scores that Berlioz inadvertently lost or, more likely, intentionally destroyed.

6. David Cairns, *Berlioz: The Making of an Artist* (Berkeley: University of California Press, 1989), 31.

7. D. Kern Holoman, *Berlioz* (Cambridge, MA: Harvard University Press, 1989), 274; English translation of Hector Berlioz, *Correspondance générale*, ed. Pierre Citron (Paris: Flammarion, 1972–2003), 739.

8. Berlioz, *Memoirs*, 376. Isaac Strauss, violinist, conductor at the Théâtre-Italien in Paris, and composer, was unrelated to the more famous Strausses of Vienna.

9. The printed full score later indicates there were 1,200 performers.

10. Rouget de Lisle wrote the original text and melody in 1792, and Berlioz arranged it for double chorus and orchestra in 1830. The melody and a revised text were officially adopted as the national anthem of France in 1879, but unfortunately Berlioz's arrangements of it are rarely heard.

11. Berlioz published *Collection de 32 mélodies* in 1863 but realized he had inadvertently omitted *Le cinq mai*, one of his most popular cantatas. Since the volume was selling well, his publisher agreed to add the work to a new printing under the title *33 mélodies*, which appeared the next year. In some library catalogs the phrase *à une ou plusieurs voix et choeur* (for one or more voices and chorus) is not clearly indicated, so the eleven works for chorus are easily overlooked. Often *mélodies* is erroneously interpreted to apply only to solo songs.

12. For the sake of clarity, the two separate edition titles, *Collection de 32 mélodies* and *Collection de 33 mélodies* published in 1863 and 1864, respectively, are merged into one title for the purposes of this discussion.

13. The listener could choose this earlier version with cello, which is not included in *32/33 mélodies*, or Berlioz's final version of 1848 with piano reduction from the orchestration made by Berlioz's friend, Stephen Heller.

14. In the double chorus version of *Hymne des Marseillais*, all five verses are sung by chorus in unison; only the brief refrain is for double chorus. Berlioz's instruction: "All with one voice, one heart and blood in its veins."

3. ORCHESTRAL MUSIC

1. Composed to share concerts with *Symphonie fantastique* as the second half, *Lélio* is a not a symphony but a melologue, which in this case is a drama with spoken and sung texts, chorus, and orchestra. At the time *mélologues* were quite in fashion.

2. Major works composition dates begin with *Messe solennelle* in 1824, the same year he completed his four years of medical school and was awarded the *Bachelier ès sciences physiques*, and his final opera, *Béatrice et Bénédict*,

1860–1862. Later he continued to arrange works, compile songs and choruses (*32/33 Mélodies*), and compose three sacred choruses for treble voices.

3. Beethoven's famous Ninth Symphony, completed in 1824, culminates in the fourth movement with vocal soloists and chorus, and other composers followed.

4. Titles characterizing Mozart and Haydn symphonies were given by publishers, reviewers, or performers well after composition. However, Beethoven, notably for his Third ("Eroica") and Sixth ("Pastorale") symphonies, assigned character titles to some symphonies and movements. Liszt, Schumann, and numerous other composers continued the approach.

5. On occasion *La fuite en Égypte* from *L'enfance du Christ* and the prologue to *Les Troyens à Carthage* are performed as overtures.

6. *Les francs-juges* is the one exception to Berlioz's custom of writing overtures based on famous literary sources. The libretto was by his friend Humbert Ferrand.

7. Holoman, *Berlioz*, 114.

8. Berlioz, *Memoirs*, 41–42.

9. Two music historians, Julien Tiersot and Nicholas Temperley, reconstructed the melody of *Je vais donc quitter pour jamais* (H.6) from its guitar accompaniment. Berlioz probably used it in his opera *Estelle et Némorin*, based on the pastoral play by Jean-Pierre Claris de Florian (1755–1794), but he burned the opera in 1827.

10. See chapter 1 for a detailed discussion of *Élégie en prose*.

11. English translation by Monir Tayeb and Michel Austin in "Berlioz Music Scores: Texts and Documents; *Symphonie fantastique*; The Symphony's Programme; Extracts from the Memoirs," Hector Berlioz Website, July 18, 1997, accessed July 6, 2017, http://www.hberlioz.com. The 1855 version of Berlioz's program is in appendix C.

12. Marches in *Les Troyens*, *La damnation de Faust*, and *Grande symphonie funèbre et triomphale* are resplendently memorable as well.

13. Berlioz uses a similar procedure in the cantata *Le cinq mai* discussed in chapter 2.

14. Berlioz previously contemplated composing a "Faust symphony" among his many projected projects, but in the meantime, in 1828, he wrote *Huit scènes de Faust* (Eight scenes from Faust; see chapter 4). He later fulfilled his vision by completing *La damnation de Faust* in 1846.

15. The *Dies irae* text from the Requiem Mass describes the day of judgment. On that day, according to Roman Catholic theology, the last trumpet summons souls before the throne of God, where the saved are delivered and the condemned cast into eternal flames. Since Berlioz already used the tradi-

tional *Dies irae* melody in *Symphonie fantastique*, he wrote a new melody for his *Requiem* composed seven years later.

16. Queen Mab, the seemingly whimsical fairy of dreams, is malevolent. She drives her miniature chariot into the noses and brains of her sleeping victims to compel them to experience dreams of wish fulfillment. Her intention, like those of the Verona establishment, is to obstruct the lovers.

17. Recordings identify each track by movement and either the section title or the first line of text.

18. Although for practical reasons both choruses must be onstage, Berlioz instructs only the Capulets (Juliette's family) to sing the funeral dirge.

19. Listen for Berlioz's similar use of fugatos for atmospheric effect that open *Harold en Italie* and parts 1 and 2 of *La damnation de Faust*.

20. Berlioz, *Memoirs*, 70–74.

21. Unfortunately, his father disapproved of Berlioz not continuing in medical school and marrying Harriet. He withdrew financial support and never came to Paris to hear his son's music or see him conduct.

22. Berlioz, *Correspondance générale*, 688.

4. EXTENDED CHORAL-ORCHESTRAL WORKS

1. *St-Louis* refers to King Louis XIV, who initiated building the chapel for war veterans in 1676.

2. See chapter 2 for more details about choral voicing.

3. Inspired by St. Peter's Basilica in Rome, Église du Dôme in turn inspired the United States Capitol.

4. Unlike the traditional Mass sung during regular and high feast services, Requiem Masses omit the Gloria, Credo, and Alleluia.

5. Berlioz's directions in the score regarding placement of the four brass choirs are explicit: they are to be positioned at the four corners of the performance forces, not the corners of the concert hall. In Verdi's later *Requiem*, by contrast, the trumpets are to be "from a distance" and are usually placed in the back of the hall. Berlioz needed close proximity between singers and brass choirs, who at times play quite softly in spare textures, for purposes of tuning and special effects of intermingling timbres. The brass choirs play not only in the famous *Dies irae* (mvt 2) but also in mvts 4 and 6. All twelve trombones from the choirs play again, quite softly, at the end of mvt 10.

6. Berlioz, *Memoirs*, 526.

7. A seventh chord generally has four pitches and includes an interval of a seventh from bottom to top. The first seventh chord outlined in *Requiem* is in

the bass voices: from the bottom up, the ascending pitches are E ♭ –G–B ♭ –D, which is an E ♭ major seventh chord.

8. Kristofer J. Sandchak, "The *Grande messe des morts*, op. 5 by Hector Berlioz: A Conductor's Guide to the Historical Background, Orchestration, Rhetorical/Drama-Liturgical Projection and Formal/Structural Analysis" (DM diss., Indiana University, 2015), 84. Berlioz's drawing is located in the Musée de lettres et de manuscrits in Paris.

9. The Delacroix images were made for Albert Stapfer's 1828 translation of Goethe's part 1.

10. Goethe in his *Faust* used the name Gretchen, which is the diminutive nickname in Germany for Margaret, or Marguerite in French.

11. Marguerite's single "fault" appears to be open to debate since there are several possibilities: (a) sleeping with Faust out of wedlock; (b) inadvertently poisoning her mother; or (c) not recognizing Méphistophélès as evil and in control of Faust.

12. Hugh Macdonald, *Berlioz*, new ed. (Oxford: Oxford University Press, 2000), 59; English translation of Hector Berlioz, *Correspondance générale*, ed. Pierre Citron, 8 vols. (Paris: Flammarion, 1972–2003), 4:1783.

5. OPERAS

1. This role was titled "Pope" in Weimar and "Cardinal" in Paris 1 and 2. For convenience, "Pope" will be used here.

2. Cairns, *Berlioz: Servitude and Greatness* (Berkeley: University of California Press, 1999), 151.

3. The school was directed by Alexandre-Étienne Choron, founder of a nationwide choral education and performance movement. The increase of not only professional artists but also amateur singing organizations and audiences was due in large part to Choron and also the Orphéon movement. See chapter 2.

4. A female composer of music, other than for solo voice, piano, or harp, was nearly unheard of. Berlioz's connection to Louise Bertin was through her father, the well-connected and influential publisher Louis-François Bertin, who was Berlioz's friend and employer at *Journal des débats*.

5. Each music phrase is assigned a letter, such as *a*; new phrases have new letters (*b, c, d*, etc.). An apostrophe indicates the music heard previously is now slightly varied (e.g., *b'* resembles *b*); multiple apostrophes indicate new variations (e.g., *b"* and *b'''*).

6. Theme/gesture letter assignments are inspired by Julian Rushton's detailed thematic and structural analysis of the *Overture to Benvenuto Cellini* in

The Musical Language of Berlioz (Cambridge: Cambridge University Press, 1983), p. 147 and 203–4.

7. Theme/gesture letter assignments are adapted from Rushton's analysis of the overture in Julian Rushton, *The Musical Language of Berlioz* (Cambridge: Cambridge University Press, 1983), 203–4, e.g., 101.

8. For those following the libretto, in Paris 1 the text is *ravissante promesse* (ravishing promise).

9. The following summary is thanks in large part to D. Kern Holoman's extensive discussion in his *Berlioz* (Cambridge, MA: Harvard University Press, 1989).

10. Fiona Cormack, "English Reviews of *Benvenuto Cellini*," in *The Musical Voyager: Berlioz in Europe*, ed. David Charlton and Katharine Ellis (Frankfurt am Main, Germany: Lang, 2007), 265–301. See also Sarah Hibberd, "Berlioz's Waterloo? *Benvenuto Cellini* London," in Charlton and Ellis, *Musical Voyager*, 66–79.

11. The translation of *Aeneid* by Robert Fagles contains an exemplary glossary.

APPENDIX C

1. *Vagues de passions*, translated here as "indefinable passion," is a phrase from *René*, a Chateaubriand play first published in 1802. It means emotional uncertainty and the aimlessness of passion typical of those in adolescence.

GLOSSARY

ad libitum. At the performer's discretion.

air or aria. A vocal solo from a choral-orchestral work such as a cantata, an oratorio, or an opera. Usually more technically demanding than a simple *romance*.

alto. Category of treble singer in a lower range, usually female.

arrangement. Setting of a preexisting work, whether by the composer or someone else, in a new format. Changes may include instrumentation, tempo, harmonies, dynamics, and so forth. An orchestra work may be arranged for piano, a piano work for orchestra, or a solo arranged for chorus.

articulation. The style of execution of music. Marks in a music score guide the performer to lengthen or shorten a note (tenuto and staccato), adjust weight and volume (accent, marcato, and sforzando), or smooth out movement from one note to another (slur and legato). Articulations may also be added by performers or understood as conventional for music from specific historical periods and regions.

augmentation. Subsequent presentation of a theme using longer note values than previously (opposite of diminution).

autograph score. A handwritten manuscript of the music written out by the composer; not a sketch or printed edition. A fair copy score is a neat and exact manuscript copy of an autograph score written out by either the composer or the designated copyist.

bar groups. A group of measures that comprise a phrase or a section as determined by theme contour and harmonic closure.

baritone. Lower male voice category, below tenor and above bass.

bass. Lowest male voice category.

bel canto. A style of singing emphasizing fluidity of line and evenness of tone.

broken chord or arpeggio. Notes of a chord played sequentially rather than all together.

cabaletta. A short and simple operatic aria.

cadence. A sequence of chords leading to a point of harmonic arrival.

cadenza. An expressive extension of a solo passage, whether vocal or solo instrumental, which usually displays virtuosity. Often the accompaniment ceases to give the soloist the spotlight.

cantabile. A flowing melodic style.

cantata. A genre of music composition for voice and instruments with multiple sections or movements including solo recitatives, arias, and often choruses.

caprice (also capriccio). A lively piece composed without adhering to the rules for any specific musical form.

cavatina. A simple short song or melody without a second section or repeat. In *Benvenuto Cellini*, Teresa sings no. 3b Cavatine, *Entre l'amour et le devoir*, and Pierrot sings no. 12, *Il plaît fort*.

chromatic. Notes out of the scale of a music passage written to add flavor (color); often signals a shift to another tonal center, whether momentary or long term.

coda. A final section of a work that brings a sense of culmination or simply closure.

collected works. Scholarly assemblage of all works by one composer and curated by preeminent musicologists. With discovery of new information and changes in editorial policies over time, publication of newly researched collected works is essential.

coloratura. Elaborate embellishments adding "color"; usually requires a light, agile voice or instrument.

consonance. Harmony and melody of calmness, resolution, and perhaps a sweetness.

contralto. Category of treble singer in the lowest range, usually female.

contrapuntal. Two or more melodies heard at the same time. Palestrina and J. S. Bach are considered among the finest contrapuntalists.

deceptive cadence. Arrival to a harmonic sonority that is unexpected and therefore particularly expressive; the sound may seem poignant, disruptive, or inquisitive.

diminuendo. Dynamic marking to gradually decrease volume; term used interchangeably with decrescendo.

diminution. Subsequent presentation of a theme in shorter note values than previously (opposite of augmentation).

dissonance. Harmony and melody of grist, crunchiness, and friction.

divisi. Instruments or voices within a section divided into multiple parts rather than only one, for example, four flutes in the Offertoire of *Requiem* or a four-part men's chorus of first and second tenors and first and second basses (TTBB).

double or doubling. Playing or singing the same notes at the same pitch level or at the octave. Bassoons double cellos or violas; oboes double violins.

falsetto. A male voice singing in the seemingly "false" register of alto and soprano voices. The sound, made by vocal folds vibrating only at their edges, is lighter and more fragile sounding.

fermata. A mark to hold a note, chord, or rest for an unspecified length of time *ad libitum*; meter and rhythm are momentarily abandoned.

feuilleton. A supplement to a newspaper usually in smaller type that carried gossip, fashion, criticism, reviews, epigrams, and charades, and fostered a culture of literary gamesmanship. Louis-François Bertin, Berlioz's employer at *Journal des débats*, is credited with creating it. Berlioz wrote feuilletons prolifically for *Journal des débats* and *Revue musicale* from the early 1830s to 1860s and compiled some of them in his other publications.

figured bass. Numerals written underneath music notation that indicate the intervals, quality (major or minor), and position (order of notes vertically) of chords. When notating a melody and bass line in a sketch, Berlioz often wrote in figured bass as shorthand for the harmony.

forte **and** *fortissimo.* Loud and loudest.

fugato. A free-style variety of a fugue in which conventional contrapuntal procedures are not necessarily present.

fugue. A contrapuntal strategy in which a melody (subject) is introduced and answered soon thereafter by another melody (countersubject); the two ideas are superimposed and spun out at different pitch levels, orders, and timing of entries. A standard fugue includes exposition, episodes and transitions, strettos, and a final restatement in the original key. Theme manipulation such as breaking up the subject and countersubject, diminution and augmentation, and moving into other key areas usually occurs. Fugues often signify inevitability or a sacred topic.

genre. A category characterized by similarities in form, style, instrumentation, or subject matter, for example, symphony, opera, oratorio (extended choral-orchestral work), cantata, and song. Each genre has subgenres.

gesture. A brief sequence of notes that recur and may imply an idea or feeling. The use of the interval of a minor sixth is a gesture possibly representing longing or love. Brief melodic-rhythmic or harmonic figures may "want to speak." A motive, only two or three notes generally, may be a gesture.

harmonic rhythm. Rate at which the chords change. Music written for large spaces or outdoors for hundreds of voices and instruments is likely to be written in a slow harmonic rhythm in which chords change infrequently.

harmonics. Overtones created by divisions of the length of a string or air column. First harmonic is an octave above the open string at a ratio of 1:2. Harps play harmonics in *Ballet des sylphes* of *La damnation de Faust*, and string sections play harmonics in the Queen Mab Scherzo of *Roméo et Juliette* and Sanctus of the *Requiem*.

harmony. Notes sounding simultaneously, as in chords.

homophonic. Multiple lines of pitches moving together in the same rhythm, as in a hymn.

idée fixe (fixed idea). A musical theme that recurs in different guises but is still recognizable. Changes may include different tempos, instrumentation, registers, augmentation (lengthening note durations), or diminution (shortening note durations). Generally intervallic relationships remain the same but may also be altered.

instrumentation. Study of instruments and their characteristics. *See* orchestration.

kapellmeister. In German, musical director and leader of performing organization, whether a church, town, or royal entity.

key. The note around which a music passage is centered, for example, the key of G. In general keys may be major or minor. *See* tonality, a term often used interchangeably with key.

libretto. Text of a cantata, an oratorio, or an opera usually written in styles suitable for recitatives (not rhymed) and arias (rhymed). From *La damnation de Faust* on, Berlioz wrote his own libretti for his extended works: *L'enfance du Christ*, *Les Troyens*, *Béatrice et Bénédict*.

lieder. In German, songs; *lied* is a song.

lithograph. A printing process whereby music staves and notation were etched by hand or stamped onto a surface of stone, usually limestone. Chemicals applied to the surface transferred the impressions from surface to paper. Lithography or metal plate engraving (copper, zinc, or pewter) was used for publishing music in the nineteenth century. Most of Berlioz's performing orchestra parts were hand-copied manuscripts, and his conducting scores were a fair manuscript copy of his autograph.

L'Opéra. Founded as the Académie royale de Musique in 1669 and now named l'Opéra national de Paris. Currently its ballets are given in the 1,970-seat Palais Garnier, which opened in 1875 after Berlioz's death; the operas are in the Opera-Bastille inaugurated in 1989. Berlioz attended l'Opéra productions in Salle le Pelletier, used from 1821 until it burned down in 1873.

lyric. Flowing melodies with notes seamlessly connected to one another.

measure (also bar). In music notation, the organization of pulses into a single group determined by meter and indicated by vertical lines. Phrases and sections of music are comprised of multiple measures, and musical form is thought of in groups of measures.

mélologue. A concert including spoken text and music. Berlioz composed one mélologue, *Le retour à la vie*, later called *Lélio*.

meter. Organization of pulses into groups of either two or three (duple or triple meter) or their multiples, such as compound duple (6/8) or compound triple (9/8).

metronome marking (MM = 120). Johann Maelzel invented the
   metronome, which mechanically measured the number of beats
   or pulses in a minute. MM = 60 indicates the pulse is a second
   long; MM = 120 indicates the pulse is twice as fast as a second.
   Berlioz usually added metronome markings to his printed scores
   after performing the music using manuscripts.

mezzo-soprano. Category of treble singer in a medium range between soprano and alto, usually female.

nocturne. Music inspired by or evocative of night, usually dreamy
   or pensive.

obbligato. A supporting melody in partnership with the primary
   melody.

opera. A genre in which a story is set to music for a staged performance; usually involves vocal soloists, instruments, chorus, dancers, costumes, props, sets, lighting, and so forth. Forms of music
   within an opera may include overture, intermezzo, recitative,
   aria, chorus, ballet, and so forth.

ophicleide. From the Greek word meaning "serpent" and invented
   in 1817, the instrument is lip-buzzed, coarse, and of questionable
   pitch accuracy. It has a conical bore and keys like a saxophone
   instead of pistons. It was commonly used in French military
   bands, nineteenth-century operas, and numerous Berlioz works.
   The modern tuba, which has a much more polished sound, is
   often substituted for an ophicleide.

orchestration. The art of combining sounds of instruments; deciding which instruments should play which notes in the melody and
   harmony of a composition.

pants role. The role of a young boy written for a female mezzo-
   soprano or alto to sing; Ascanio in *Benvenuto Cellini*.

pedal tone. A note held throughout a passage; it may or may not fit
   into the harmonies as the rest of the music changes around it.
   Pedal, as in foot pedals of an organ.

performance practices. Performance techniques specific to an era
   and region that were not notated by the composer due to being
   common knowledge at the time. In contrast, performance traditions are techniques also not notated by the composer that
   evolved down through generations of performers and teachers.
   Performers today may choose either approach.

piano (*p*). Soft dynamic. Additional *p* markings indicate softer, for example, *pppp* is extremely soft.

piano-vocal score (pv). The music score of a work for voice and piano. The piano part may have been written originally for piano or be a reduction of an instrument ensemble.

pizzicato. Pluck of a string by the player's index finger, producing a short "pop" sound.

Prix de Rome. Prize awarded annually in France by Académie des Beaux-Art to the composer writing the best cantata. Other areas of competition include architecture, literature, and painting. Benefits include a financial stipend and required residency in Rome for a one- to two-year period. Berlioz was elected to the institute awarding the prize in 1856.

pulse (or beat). Regularly recurring impetus in a tempo that moves the momentum forward. *See* metronome marking and tempo.

recitative. Music composed to sound as much spoken as sung. Usually the text is not in rhymed verse. Changes of tempo and mood, stops, starts, and gaps of silence are intended to impart context and information, whereas an aria is ongoing, more songlike. In accompanied recitatives, instruments frame the singer to set mood and introduce and respond to the story. Berlioz wrote recitative-style music to be sung and also for instruments alone.

refrain. A repeated phrase or section of music occurring between verses and sometimes at the beginning and end of a song.

register. Area of a voice or instrument, in low, medium, or high, which accordingly has different timbres.

retreat. A trumpet call that signals the end of the official day for soldiers.

rhythm. A pattern of sound measured by duration and accentuation.

rubato. A slowing and then quickening of notes in a phrase; may be instructed by the composer or is a liberty taken by the performer. Berlioz meticulously indicated where he desired flexibility in a tempo and asked performers not to take liberties.

saltarello. From the Latin "to jump"; a lively Italian dance in 3/4 or 6/8 meter characterized by a hop or step beginning each measure.

saxhorn. Family of brass valved instruments, from soprano to contrebasse, patented by Adolphe Sax in Paris in 1845. All are in the shape of a tuba but with a less wide bore and less fullness of sound. Berlioz wrote for offstage saxhorns and a solo tenor saxhorn in the *Les Troyens* Royal Hunt and Storm scene beginning act 4. French horn is substituted today.

soirée. An evening gathering for entertainment and learning usually held by invitation in an aristocratic or wealthy person's residence. Berlioz's songs, choruses, and arias excerpted from extended works were frequently performed in Parisian soirées.

soprano. Category of treble singer in the highest range, usually female.

staccato. In music notation, a dot above or below a note indicating the pitch is to be played short and possibly more lightly.

stage right, stage left. Location onstage from the performer's perspective while facing the audience.

stretto. A passage often in a fugue in which entries of thematic material happen in closer succession and consequently increase the sense of excitement.

strophic. A form of music, usually vocal, in which the same music recurs for each new verse (stanza). There may be an instrumental introduction, transitions between verses, and a refrain. *Romances* are usually in strophic form.

supernumeraries. A performer who appears in a dramatic production without speaking any lines; an "extra."

tattoo. A distinctive rhythmic pattern played repeatedly by percussion to signal the next event in a battle or procession; played in military and marching bands.

tempo. Rate of the regular pulse, from fast to slow. Berlioz used standard Italian terms to indicate tempo, plus a phrase to characterize the music and a metronome marking, for example, pulse = 60. *See* metronome marking and pulse.

tenor. Category of male singer in the highest range.

tenore di forza. A tenor who sings forcefully with chest resonance in his high register. The sound is rich and brilliant.

tessitura. General pitch area (high, medium, and low) in the range of a voice or instrument.

texture. The density and spacing of voices or instruments and their relationships. Types of textures include monophony (one line), polyphonic (contrapuntal), and homophony (hymn style). Textures may be described as rich or thin.

theme. A musical idea comprised of melody, harmony, and rhythm; similar to a topic sentence in a paragraph.

through-composed. Form of music that has no repeating sections. In a through-composed song, each verse of text is set to different music.

tonality. The sense of melodies and harmonies moving away from and toward a fundamental pitch center, "home." Tonalities may be major or minor and are based on a variety of scales.

transpose. Resetting a music selection or passage to a higher or lower key, such as raising the music from F major to G major. Transposition of songs to better suit the performer's range is common.

tremolo or tremolando. A fast, agitated, and repetitive alternation between at least two notes to create tension, excitement, or shimmer.

tutti. From the Italian for "all" used to indicate all instruments or voices are to play a passage together.

vagues des passions. Emotional uncertainty, aimlessness of passion typical of adolescents. The expression, coined by Chateaubriand, is used frequently with reference to *Symphonie fantastique*.

voicing. Voice categories chosen for a song or chorus. Voicing for Berlioz's mixed choruses can be STB (soprano, tenor, and bass) or divisi STB (soprano, tenor, and bass divided into higher and lower categories within each section; SSTTBB), SATB (soprano, alto, tenor, and bass), or SSATTBB.

SELECTED READING AND BIBLIOGRAPHY

Items with an asterisk are recommended to the general reader as a complement to this book.

Albright, Daniel. *Berlioz's Semi-Operas: Roméo et Juliette and La damnation de Faust.* Rochester, NY: University of Rochester Press, 2001.

Berlioz, Hector. *Correspondance générale.* Edited by Pierre Citron. 8 vols. Paris: Flammarion, 1972–2003.

°———. *The Memoirs of Hector Berlioz.* Translated and edited by David Cairns. 1969. New York: Knopf, 2002.

———. *Hector Berlioz: New Edition of the Complete Works (NBE).* Edited by Hugh Macdonald. 26 vols. Kassel, Germany: Bärenreiter, 1967–2006. See Holoman, *Catalogue* (vol. 25) and Braam, *Portraits* (vol. 26).

———. *La belle voyageuse (The Fair Traveller).* 1829. Paroles imitée de l'Anglais de Th. Moore par Gounet 2, no. 4. London: Stanley Lucas, Weber, [1885].

———. *La damnation de Faust: Werke.* Edited by Charles Malherbe and Felix Weingartner. Translated by John Bernhoff. Series 5, band 11–12, Leipzig, Germany: Breitkopf & Härtel, 1901.

Berlioz, Hector, Monir Tayeb, and Michel Austin. "Berlioz Music Scores: Texts and Documents; *Symphonie fantastique*; The Symphony's Programme; Extracts from the Memoirs." Hector Berlioz Website, July 18, 1997. Accessed July 6, 2017. http://www.hberlioz.com.

°Berlioz, Hector, and Alastair Bruce. *The Musical Madhouse: Les grotesques de la musique.* Rochester, NY: University of Rochester Press, 2003.

°Berlioz, Hector, Katherine Kolb, and Samuel N. Rosenberg. *Berlioz on Music: Selected Criticism, 1824–1837.* Oxford: Oxford University Press, 2015.

°Berlioz, Hector, and Hugh Macdonald. *Berlioz's Orchestration Treatise: A Translation and Commentary.* Cambridge: Cambridge University Press, 2002.

°Berlioz, Hector, Hugh Macdonald, and Roger Nichols. *Selected Letters of Berlioz.* 1st American ed. New York: Norton, 1997.

Berlioz, Hector, Robert Schumann, and Edward T. Cone. *Fantastic Symphony: An Authoritative Score; Historical Background; Analysis; Views and Comments.* New York: Norton, 1971.

Berlioz, Hector, and Humphrey Searle. *Hector Berlioz: A Selection from His Letters.* New York: Vienna House, 1973.

Bernac, Pierre. *The Interpretation of French Song.* New York: Norton, 1978.

Bloom, Peter. *Berlioz: Past, Present, Future; Bicentenary Essays*. Rochester, NY: University of Rochester Press, 2003.

———. *Berlioz: Scenes from the Life and Work*. Rochester, NY: University of Rochester Press, 2008.

———. "Berlioz's First Nights." In *City, Chant, and the Topography of Early Music*, edited by Michael S. Cuthbert, Sean Gallagher, and Christoph Wolff, 53–69. Cambridge, MA: Harvard University Department of Music, 2013.

———. *The Cambridge Companion to Berlioz*. Cambridge: Cambridge University Press, 2000.

———. "Hector Berlioz's 'To Be or Not to Be.'" *Hudson Review* (Summer 2014). Accessed October 10, 2014. http://hudsonreview.com.

———, ed. *Music in Paris in the Eighteen-Thirties: La musique à Paris dans les années mil huit cent trente*. Stuyvesant, NY: Pendragon, 1987.

Boldrey, Richard. *Guide to Operatic Roles and Arias*. Dallas: Pst, 1994.

Bonds, Mark Evan. *After Beethoven: Imperatives of Originality in the Symphony*. Cambridge, MA: Harvard University Press, 1996.

°Braam, Gunther, et al. *The Portraits of Hector Berlioz*. In *Berlioz NBE*, vol. 26. Kassel, Germany: Bärenreiter, 2003.

°Cairns, David. *Berlioz: The Making of an Artist*. Berkeley: University of California Press, 1989.

° ———. *Berlioz: Servitude and Greatness*. Berkeley: University of California Press, 1999.

Caswell, Austin B. "Loïsa Puget and the French Chanson." In *Music in Paris in the Eighteen-Thirties: La musique à Paris dans les années mil huit cent trente*, edited by Peter Bloom, 97–115. Stuyvesant, NY: Pendragon, 1987.

Charlton, David, and Katharine Ellis. *The Musical Voyager: Berlioz in Europe*. Frankfurt am Main, Germany: Lang, 2007.

Cone, Edward. "The Historical Background." In *Fantastic Symphony: An Authoritative Score; Historical Background; Analysis; Views and Comments*, edited by Edward Cone, 3–46. [1st ed.] New York: Norton, 1971.

Cormack, Fiona. "English Reviews of *Benvenuto Cellini*." In *The Musical Voyager: Berlioz in Europe*, edited by David Charlton and Katharine Ellis, 265–301. Frankfurt am Main, Germany: Lang, 2007.

Del Mar, Norman. *Conducting Berlioz*. Oxford, UK: Clarendon, 1997.

°Di Grazia, Donna M. "Hector Berlioz." In *Nineteenth-Century Choral Music*, edited by Donna Di Grazia, 231–65. New York: Routledge, 2013.

Durst, Dennis. "Nineteenth-Century French Anti-Semitism." *Nomocracy Blog*, Nomocracy in Politics, February 26, 2015. Accessed April 3, 2015. https://thenomocracyproject.wordpress.com.

Ellis, Katharine. *Interpreting the Musical Past: Early Music in Nineteenth-Century France*. New York: Oxford University Press, 2005.

Fauser, Annegret. "The Songs." In *The Cambridge Companion to Berlioz*, edited by Peter Bloom, 108–24. Cambridge: Cambridge University Press, 2000.

Goethe, Johann Wolfgang von, Walter Arndt, and Cyrus Hamlin. *Faust: A Tragedy; Interpretive Notes, Contexts, Modern Criticism*. 2nd ed. New York: Norton, 2001.

Hadlock, Heather. "Berlioz, Ophelia, and Feminist Hermeneutics." In *Berlioz Present, Past, Future*, edited by Peter Bloom, 123–33. Rochester, NY: University of Rochester Press, 2003.

Hibberd, Sarah. "Berlioz's Waterloo? *Benvenuto Cellini* London." In *The Musical Voyager: Berlioz in Europe*, edited by David Charlton and Katharine Ellis, 66–79. Frankfurt am Main, Germany: Lang, 2007.

Holoman, D. Kern. *Berlioz*. Cambridge, MA: Harvard University Press, 1989.

———. *Catalogue of the Works of Hector Berlioz*. In *Berlioz NBE*, vol. 25. Kassel, Germany: Bärenreiter, 1987.

———. *The Nineteenth-Century Symphony*. New York: Schirmer, 1997.

———. "Selected Masterworks from the Choral-Orchestral Repertoire." In *Nineteenth-Century Choral Music*, edited by Donna Di Grazia, 39–109. New York: Routledge, 2013.

Jones, Nick. Program notes for *Grande messe des morts* by Hector Berlioz. Manchester, NH: New Hampshire Symphony Orchestra and Chorus, St. Marie Church, March 29, 1987.

°Kelly, Thomas Forrest. *First Nights at the Opera*. New Haven, CT: Yale University Press, 2004.

°———. "Hector Berlioz: *Symphonie fantastique*." In *First Nights: Five Musical Premieres*, 180–255. New Haven, CT: Yale University Press, 2000.

Kemp, Ian. *Hector Berlioz, Les Troyens*. Edited by Ian Kemp. Cambridge: Cambridge University Press, 1988.

Lang, Paul Henry. *The Experience of Opera*. London: Faber, 1973.

Laudon, Robert T. *The Dramatic Symphony: Issues and Explorations from Berlioz to Liszt*. Hillsdale, NY: Pendragon, 2011.

Lawson, Colin, and Robin Stowell. *The Cambridge History of Musical Performance*. Cambridge: Cambridge University Press, 2012.

Locke, Ralph P. "Paris: Centre of Intellectual Ferment." In *The Early Romantic Era: Between Revolutions, 1789 and 1848*, edited by Alexander L. Ringer, 32–83. Englewood Cliffs, NJ: Prentice Hall, 1991.

Mabillard, Amanda. "Introduction to Ophelia in *Hamlet*." Shakespeare Online, August 20, 2000. Accessed September 24, 2014. http://www.shakespeare-online.com.

Macdonald, Hugh. *Berlioz*. London: Dent, 1982.

°———. *Berlioz*. New ed. Oxford: Oxford University Press, 2000.

°———. *Music in 1853: The Biography of a Year*. Woodbridge, UK: Boydell, 2012.

Macdonald, Hugh, and David Cairns. Liner notes to *Benvenuto Cellini*, Hector Berlioz et al. Paris: Erato, 2004.

O'Neal, Melinda. "Coming to Terms with Historical Performance Practices." In *Up Front! Becoming the Complete Choral Conductor*, edited by Guy B. Webb and Ray Robinson, 71–94. Boston: ECS Publishing, 1993.

°Price, Roger. *A Concise History of France*. 2nd ed. Cambridge: Cambridge University Press, 2005.

Rodgers, Stephen. *Form, Program, and Metaphor in the Music of Berlioz*. Cambridge: Cambridge University Press, 2009.

———. "Miniatures of a Monumentalist: Berlioz's *Romances*, 1842–1850." *Nineteenth-Century Music Review* 10 (2013): 119–49.

Rosen, Charles. *The Romantic Generation*. Cambridge, MA: Harvard University Press, 1995.

Rowden, Claire. "Choral Music and Music-Making in France." In *Nineteenth-Century Choral Music*, edited by Donna Di Grazia, 205–12. New York: Routledge, 2013.

Rushton, Julian. "Berlioz Nationalist, Berlioz Internationalist?" In *Hector Berlioz: Miscellaneous Studies*, edited by Fulvia Morabito and Michela Niccolai, xvii–xxvi. Bologna, Italy: Ut Orpheus, 2005.

———. "*Les nuits d'été*: Cycle or Collection?" In *Berlioz Studies*, edited by Peter Bloom, 112–35. Cambridge: Cambridge University Press, 1992.

———. *The Musical Language of Berlioz*. Cambridge: Cambridge University Press, 1983.

———. *The Music of Berlioz*. Oxford: Oxford University Press, 2001.

Sandchak, Kristofer J. "The *Grande messe des morts*, Op. 5 by Hector Berlioz: A Conductor's Guide to the Historical Background, Orchestration, Rhetorical/Drama-Liturgical Projection and Formal/Structural Analysis." DM diss., Indiana University, 2015.

Spitzer, John, and Neal Zaslaw. *The Birth of the Orchestra: History of an Institution, 1650–1815*. Oxford: Oxford University Press, 2004.

Taruskin, Richard. *Music in the Nineteenth Century*. Oxford: Oxford University Press, 2010.

Virgil. *The Aeneid*. Translated by Robert Fagles. New York: Viking, 2006.

Wasselin, Christian. "Benvenuto Cellini." Hector Berlioz Website, 2004. Accessed June 15, 2016. http://www.hberlioz.com.This article was written for the concert performances of *Benvenuto Cellini* on December 8 and 11, 2003, at Maison de Radio France (salle Olivier Messiaen), Paris, conducted by John Nelson.

WEBSITES OF NOTE

Association nationale Hector Berlioz, http://berlioz-anhb.com
Berlioz Society, http://www.berlioz.org.uk
Berlioz 2003 Bicentennial Celebration, UC Davis, http://hec-
    tor.ucdavis.edu/Berlioz.html
Festival Berlioz, http://www.festivalberlioz.com/English
Hector Berlioz Website, http://www.hberlioz.com
Musée Hector Berlioz, http://www.musee-hector-berlioz.fr

SELECTED LISTENING

SONGS

Alagna, Roberto, et al. *Berlioz*. London: EMI Classics, 2003. CD.

Bartoli, Cecilia, et al. *Chant d'amour: Mélodies Françaises*. London: Decca Music Group, 1996. CD.

Berlioz, Hector. *Anne Sofie von Otter Sings Berlioz*. Anne Sofie von Otter, James Levine, et al. Hamburg, Germany: Deutsche Grammophon, 1995. CD.

———. *Les nuits d'été*. Colin Davis et al. London: Philips, 1969, 1980. CD.

———. *Les nuits d'été: Arias*. Susan Graham, John Nelson, et al. New York: Sony Classical, 1997. CD.

———. *Mélodies*. Isabelle Vernet. Bellerive-sur-Allier, France: Ligia Digital, 1995. CD.

———. *Mélodies and duos*. Gilles Ragon et al. Marly le Roi, France: Maguelone, 2005. CD.

———. *Mélodies: Songs = Lieder*. Anne Sofie von Otter et al. Hamburg, Germany: Deutsche Grammophon, 1994. CD.

CHORAL WORKS

Berlioz, Hector. *Choral Works: La mort d'Ophélia*. Bernard Tetu et al. Arles: Harmonia Mundi France, 1993. CD.

———. *Grande messe des morts: 1837*. Robert Murray, Paul McCreesh, et al. Perival, UK: Signum Classics, 2011. CD.

———. *La damnation de Faust*. Günter Neuhold et al. Bietigheim-Bissingen, Germany: Bayer Records, 1995. CD.

———. *La damnation de Faust: Légende dramatique*. Sylvain Cambreling et al. Halle, Germany: Arthaus Musik, 2000. DVD.

———. *La damnation de Faust: Légende dramatique*. Georg Solti et al. Leipzig, Germany: Arthaus Musik, 1989. DVD.

———. *La mort d'Orphée: Scène héroïque; Le Cinq mai: Op. 6; L'Impériale: Op. 26*. Jean Fournet et al. Tokyo: Denon, 1988. CD.

———. *L'enfance du Christ*. Colin Davis et al. London: Decca, 1994. CD.

———. *L'enfance du Christ*. John Eliot Gardiner et al. Paris: Erato, 1988. CD.

———. *La Révolution Grecque: Grandes œuvres chorales*. Michel Plasson et al. London: EMI Classics, 2003. CD.

————. *Messe solennelle*. John Eliot Gardiner et al. Amsterdam: Philips, 1994. CD.
————. *Vocal Works with Orchestra*. Syvain Cambreling et al. Stuttgart, Germany: Haenssler Classics, 2008. CD.
Entremont, Phillippe, et al. *Vive la liberté*. Roswell, GA: Pro Arte Audio Intersound, 1988. CD.
Plasson, Michel, et al. *Révolution Française*. Boulogne-Billancourt, France: Pathé Marconi EMI, 1988. CD.

SYMPHONIES AND OVERTURES

Berlioz, Hector. *Grande symphonie funèbre et triomphale*. John Wallace et al. Monmouth, UK: Nimbus, 1992. CD.
————. *Harold en Italie*. Tabea Zimmermann, Colin Davis, et al. London: LSO Live, 2003. CD.
————. *Harold en Italie; Tristia*. John E. Gardiner et al. London: Philips, 1996.
————. *Roméo et Juliette*. Colin Davis et al. London: LSO Live, 2002. CD.
————. *Roméo et Juliette*. Eliahu Inbal et al. Tokyo: Denon, 1990. CD.
————. *Symphonie fantastique: Op. 14*. John Eliot Gardiner et al. Eindhoven, Netherlands: Philips, 1993. CD.
Norrington, Roger, et al. *Early Romantic Overtures*. Hayes, UK: EMI, 1990. CD.

OPERAS

Berlioz, Hector. *Béatrice et Bénédict*. Colin Davis et al. London: LSO Live, 2002. CD.
————. *Béatrice et Bénédict*. John Nelson et al. l'Opera de Lyon, France: Warner Classics International, 2011. CD.
————. *Benvenuto Cellini*. Colin Davis et al. London: Philips, 2003. CD.
————. *Benvenuto Cellini*. John Nelson, et al. London: Virgin Classics, 2004. CD.
Berlioz, Hector, et al. *Les Troyens: Opera in Five Acts*. Colin Davis et al. London: LSO Live, 2001. CD.
————. *Les Troyens: Opera in Five Acts*. John Eliot Gardiner et al. London: Opus Arte, 2004. DVD.
————. *Les Troyens: Opera in Five Acts*. Antonio Pappano et al. London: Opus Arte, 2013. DVD.
————. *Les Troyens: Opera in Five Acts*. John Nelson et al. Erato 2017. CD.

COLLECTION

Berlioz, Hector. *Berlioz Masterworks*. Charles Dutoit et al. London: Decca Music Group Limited, 2013. CD.

REVIEWS

For locating reviews, search by composer and title in the following suggested sites. All offer recent and archival reviews.

www.naxos.com
www.allmusic.com
www.gramophone.co.uk
www.classical-music.com
www.query.nytimes.com
www.newyorker.com

INDEX

Algeria, 186
Amsterdam, 160
Antwerp, 101, 103, 160
Athens, 38; Acropolis, 38; Ilyssus, 38
Auber, Daniel-François-Esprit, 50, 151, 158–159, 160, 176
Augustus, Caesar, 193
Austerlitz, 44

Baden-Baden, 39, 41, 149, 194
Bandinelli, Bartolommeo (*Hercules and Cacus*), 154
Beethoven, Ludwig van, xxi, xxiii, 6, 13, 50, 77, 87, 93, 151, 171, 173, 226n4; Symphony no. 1, 93; Symphony no. 3, 93, 226n4; Symphony no. 5, 93, 172; Symphony no. 6, 226n4; Symphony no. 9, 226n3
Bellini, Vincenzo, 78, 151, 158
Belloc, Louise, 11
Béranger, Pierre-Jean de, 48–49
Berlioz, Adèle-Eugénie, 45, 139
Berlioz, Louis (son), 18, 63
Berlioz, Louis-Hector, career: concert touring, xx, xxvi, xxxi–xxxiv, 10, 26, 45, 65, 118, 125, 137, 139; conductor, xx, xxv–xxvi, 26, 45, 75, 77, 93–94, 95, 117, 177, 179–180, 194; editor of his own scores, 1, 10, 54, 57, 77, 118, 225n12; international music scene and reception of his works, 65, 75, 118–119, 137, 139, 149, 153, 179–180, 194–195, 200; musicians, relationship with, 26, 75, 78–79, 93, 102–103, 117–118, 122–123, 177, 178, 179; Paris, music scene, 5–7, 13–14, 29–32, 75, 76–77, 78–79, 117, 125–126, 151–152, 153, 155, 176–179; Paris, reception of his works, 7, 26, 39, 58, 102–103, 118–119, 125–126, 139–140, 149, 152–153, 162, 178–179, 200; patriotic music. *See* Berlioz, Louis-Hector, career, political upheaval, influence on career and compositions; performance of his works during his lifetime, 48, 49–51, 75, 93–95, 102–103, 117–118, 157–161, 177–180, 181–182; political upheaval, influence on career and compositions, 34–35, 45–46, 49, 52–53, 106, 117, 215–216; producer of his own concerts, 49–50, 93, 103, 117, 125–126; rehearsal techniques, xxv–xxvi, 42–44, 48, 50, 93–94, 117, 118, 199; reinventor of prior compositions, xxvi, 3–4, 10–11, 32, 39–40, 52, 198, 200; reinventor of prior compositions, cross references. *See* Berlioz, Louis-Hector, compositional traits, self-borrowings; Berlioz, Louis-Hector, works (general), versions, multiples of same title

ABOUT THE AUTHOR

Melinda P. O'Neal is a choral-orchestral conductor, professor of music at Dartmouth College where she conducted Chamber Singers and Handel Society for many years, and artistic director and conductor *emerita* of Handel Choir of Baltimore. Her fascination the music of Berlioz began when rehearsing the final mystical chorus of *L'enfance du Christ* in graduate school. Berlioz's music has been an ever-recurring subject in her teaching and writing, and she has prepared choruses and conducted in performance most of his vocal-orchestral works.